D1060725

CENTENNIAL ESSAYS FOR PUSHKIN

LONDON : HUMPHREY MILFORD

OXFORD UNIVERSITY PRESS

CENTENNIAL ESSAYS
FOR PUSHKIN

EDITED BY

SAMUEL H. CROSS

ERNEST J. SIMMONS

NEW YORK / RUSSELL & RUSSELL

FOREWORD

The present volume, embodying essays by a number of scholars professionally engaged in the study of Russian history and Russian literature throughout the United States, is intended as a modest contribution to the world-wide celebration of Pushkin's centenary. While Pushkin's individuality is so intensely national that his artistic creations have seldom been appraised at their full value except by persons able to read Russian, his significance as the founder of modern Russian literature passes the frontiers of nationality and language. It is therefore hoped that these essays may in some degree aid toward a more general comprehension of his role in the intellectual and social progress of Russia and of the veneration which his compatriots cherish for his memory.

To the scholars who, in the midst of manifold academic duties, found time to prepare studies for this book, the Editors extend their cordial thanks.*

SAMUEL H. CROSS
ERNEST J. SIMMONS

Cambridge, February 9, 1937

* Throughout the present volume, all references to Pushkin's works have been adapted to the *Full Collection of Works in Six Volumes* (*Polnoe Sobranie Sochineni v Shesti Tomakh*), 2nd ed., Moscow: Gosudarstvennoe Izdatelstvo Khudozhestvennoi Literatury, 1934. All references to Pushkin's correspondence likewise apply to the *Perepiska Pushkina*, ed. V. I. Saitov, 3 vols., St. Petersburg: 1906-1911.

CONTENTS

PUSHKIN

A Monument

This monument, not raised by human hand,
Will lead the pilgrims of my fatherland
More loftily than the great column built
To Alexander's glory, and his guilt.

No, I shall never die; the sacred lyre
Outlives the dust. Its echoes shall inspire
The final poet, who in silence hears
My voice unchanged through all the changing years.

All Russia shall pay homage to my fame,
And all its peoples shall evoke my name.
The noble Slav, the Finn, — though language vary, —
The Tungus and the Kalmuck of the prairie.

Remember me, my fatherland, as long
As noble strings sound with their noblest song:
Amid dark years, freedom that glorifies,
And mercy that bids fallen men arise.

Before the voice of God, O Muse, bow down;
Accept no insult and demand no crown;
Aloof from blame, to adulation cool,
And silent in the presence of a fool.

Translated by Robert Hillyer

A BIOGRAPHICAL STUDY OF PUSHKIN *

By Ernest J. Simmons

I

A cultured Russian would be ashamed to admit that he had not read Shakespeare. But an American who has read Pushkin is either a specialist in Russian literature or a person of considerable intellectual curiosity. Yet Pushkin is Russia's Shakespeare in the sense that he is her greatest poet. There his fame is not eclipsed, as it is outside of Russia, by the popularity of the renowned novelists. As a boy Dostoevski wept over his tragic death, and more than forty years later, in a remarkable speech, he glorified Pushkin as the incarnation of the Russian spirit. Turgenev was his pupil, and many of the splendid heroines of his novels were drawn in the image of Pushkin's immortal Tatyana; and in a like manner the "superfluous heroes" of Turgenev are cast in the mold of the world-weary, ineffectual Eugene Onegin. Even the independent Tolstoi admired Pushkin's genius and learned his poetry by heart. Natives have always felt an everlasting charm in Pushkin's verse, and in Soviet Russia today his works are perhaps more popular than they were in his own lifetime.

It is not difficult to understand why Pushkin is so little known to peoples outside of Russia. The chief obstacle, of course, is translation. In most cases the substance of the poems may be easily rendered into a foreign language, and a skillful translator may catch something of the loose dress and ornament. But the style, "Pushkin's language," defies duplication. A classicist in style, his final product gives the impression of the utmost economy of effort. But in reality his striking effects are achieved by the most

* The material for this study is drawn largely from my biography of the poet (*Pushkin*, Harvard University Press, 1937).

subtle arrangements of words and metrical patterns. The connotative or suggestive element is difficult to capture within the prescribed limits of the form without violating the sense. Very few of the fairly numerous translations of Pushkin into English have caught anything of this characteristic flavor of the original. Certainly, from these translations the English reader could hardly be blamed for failing to accept the fact that Pushkin ranks among the great poets of Europe in the first forty years of the nineteenth century. And it is no exaggeration to say that none of these poets ever equalled him in perfection of form, the quality that is well-nigh impossible to duplicate in translation.

Perhaps the versions of Pushkin in English are harder for the reader to accept because they seem quite foreign to his conception of the substance and tone of Russian literature. It is perfectly true that his poetry has little in common with the dark and tortured side of Russian life made familiar to the foreigner by the widely-known and popular works of the great novelists. There is truth in this somber picture of human suffering. But it is only part of the truth. And in Pushkin's poetry we come closer to the whole truth. He pleads no causes, preaches no philosophy, and offers no dogmatic panaceas for the burden and misery of Russian life. His poetry reveals the expansive soul and genius of his race in all their variability. Here are found tragedy and sadness, but also love and lightness, gaiety and humor, nature's beauties and man's joy in existence. Every mood of the poet is reflected and all is expressed in the harmonious strains of pure, unadulterated art. As Dryden said of Chaucer, so one might say of Pushkin: "Here is God's plenty."

II

On both sides of his family Pushkin could claim noble descent, and he was excessively proud of this nobility of six hundred years. On his mother's side the family line came into Russia, so to speak, by the back door. Pushkin's maternal great-grandfather, Abram

Petrovich Hannibal, was an Abyssinian whom Peter the Great procured from a Turkish seraglio at the age of eight. The allegation of a literary enemy that the boy was bought for a bottle of rum was hotly denied by Pushkin. It has been good-naturedly argued that the name of Hannibal indicated descent from the great Carthaginian general. In reality, Abram was the son of an Abyssinian prince and had been sent to Constantinople as a hostage. He prospered in Russia, gained high honors, and founded a numerous family. Pushkin liked to think of his great-grandfather as a Negro, and he gaily wrote of himself:

> But I, a rake on pleasure bent,
> Ugly offspring of negro descent . . .[1]

It would be difficult to say, however, how much, if any, negro blood ran in the veins of Abram Petrovich.

On his father's side the Pushkins came from an ancient and honored family of Russian boyars, many of whom occupied positions high in the government and close to the throne. But by the end of the eighteenth century both branches of the family had lost their distinguished position along with much of their wealth. As in the case of many other ancient Russian families of this time, the Pushkins had gradually slipped into a respected but undistinguished class of middle nobility.

Pushkin's father, Sergei Lvovich, married Nadezhda Osipovna Hannibal in 1796 in St. Petersburg, and two years later he retired from the army with the rank of major. The young couple moved to Moscow, where Pushkin was born on May 26, 1799. It was Holy Thursday and the church bells rang all day. They christened the infant Alexander, no doubt in honor of his great-grandfather Alexander Petrovich Pushkin — perhaps not a hopeful augury, for this noble ancestor had murdered his wife.

The father and mother were ideally mated, for they shared the same weaknesses and each was an effective counter-irritant to the other. Sergei Lvovich had illusions of grandeur, was forever falling into debt, and everlastingly evading the cold realities of life. Yet there was an attractive side to his nature. He was formed for the *salon* and spent most of his time there. Given an occasion, he shone as a clever conversationalist and accomplished versifier. But he was oblivious to the needs of his household and utterly incapable of understanding his talented son, with consequences unhappy for both.

All the business of the household Sergei Lvovich left to his wife, who was as poorly fitted for the task as her husband. Nadezhda Osipovna also loved society, and she treated her children (there was a daughter, Olga, and a younger son, Lev) with conspicuous neglect. She was highly emotional, capricious in her affections, and capable of sulking for days over some petty grievance or other. The Pushkins' door was never closed to visitors, and the house was in a continual state of chaos.

Little Sasha (Alexander) became the ugly duckling in this household. Unattractive and awkward in his movements, his dark, coarse features betrayed the Abyssinian blood in him. Unsociable and rebellious, Sasha was always getting into difficulties, and punishments were frequent. His society-loving mother had more interesting things to do than bother with a moody, recalcitrant child. Her indifference eventually turned to coldness, and when the maternal spirit moved Nadezhda Osipovna, she lavished her affection on the other two children who always remained the favorites. An unloved child, Sasha was soon left to himself, a position which he seemed to prefer.

There were comforts in this unloved existence. His grandmother, Marya Alekseevna, understood the intractable ugly duckling and gave him secret consolation in his childish unhappiness. And clumsy little Sasha was the favorite of his kind and wise old nurse, Arina Rodionovna. Eagerly he anticipated those "golden moments" when Arina stole into his room at night and in a tense whisper told him tales of Bova Korolevich and of fairy princesses transformed into pure white swans. The boy never for-

got those breathless nights or the enchanting tales. Arina Rodionovna awoke and fostered in him a love for the folklore of his
native land which was to inspire some of his greatest poems. He
always treasured her memory, and as Tatyana's nurse in *Eugene
Onegin* he preserved her image for posterity.

Sasha's formal education at this time was a thing of shreds and
patches. Like most noble families, the Pushkins hired French
tutors. They were not always well-equipped for their task, and
Sasha was hardly an attentive scholar. Often he worried these
tutors by the various devices with which small boys make their
teachers acutely unhappy. The four rules of arithmetic vexed him
to tears, and his tutors, like his parents, were inclined to leave
him in peace.

Of more importance than this hit-and-miss formal education
was Sasha's independent reading. His father's fine library was
stocked with works of the great eighteenth-century French authors
and translations of the classics. The boy early developed a fond-
ness for this mature literature, and his neglectful parents allowed
him to spend sleepless nights in the library, poring over the works
of Voltaire, Molière, Racine, and La Fontaine. Like the young
Browning, he devoured these and many other authors, and the
experience of books took the place of the normal experiences of
childhood.

The Pushkin household was a favorite resort for well-known
authors. Sergei Lvovich was adept at versifying, and his brother,
Vasili Pushkin, had won considerable fame as a poet. Little Sasha
sat quietly on the divan in his father's study and heard the brilliant conversation of such men as Karamzin, Zhukovski, and
Dmitriev. With his extraordinary memory he forgot nothing of
what was said. Poetry was in the air and he eagerly drank it in. It
seemed as though he were born to poetry, for it came to him as
naturally as leaves to the trees. He acquired a command of literary
French before he learned to write his native tongue, and at the
age of eight he began imitating the French poets he read in his

father's library. Nothing but an epic attempt would satisfy the youthful bard. He planned a grandiose parody in six cantos of Voltaire's *Henriade*, which he entitled the *Tolyade*. The ridicule of his tutor caused the enraged poet to consign his unfinished epic to the flames. He next attempted to write a comedy in the manner of Voltaire, but the audience, composed entirely of his sister, hissed his attempt off the boards.

Thus Sasha grew up in his father's house to the age of twelve, reading quantities of books, scribbling French verses, and living pretty much in a world of his own creating. His carefree parents finally decided that it was time for the youngster to be shipped off to school. They had failed to turn him into a good little boy like all the other good little boys, and the budding seeds of genius in their strange son went entirely unnoticed. But he had reached an age when it was conventional to send a boy to school, and the parents were nothing if not conventional. A friend had learned that the emperor Alexander I was about to open a Lyceum for the sons of noble families, and the fact that they would have to pay no stipend settled the question in the minds of the parents. In the summer of 1811 Sasha set out for St. Petersburg, accompanied by his jolly uncle Vasili, to take the examinations which would prove his fitness to enter the tsar's new Lyceum. His kind grandmother had given him a parting present of a hundred rubles, which uncle Vasili borrowed on the road and then forgot to repay. Sasha left the home of his parents without any regrets. Perhaps in the whole chaotic Pushkin household his old nurse was the only one to weep sincere tears over the departure of her nursling.

III

Alexander I intended his new Lyceum of Tsarskoe Selo to prepare the sons of noble families for civil and military service. Ironically enough, its most illustrious graduate was not a famous general or diplomat, but Russia's greatest poet. A fine excess of idealism lay behind the founding of this school, for the educational scheme was to be humanized and liberalized. The director was responsible to the emperor alone, the teachers were to be the best in the country, and the building was a wing of the summer palace where the students would have access to the tsar's beautiful and expansive gardens. Little wonder that the Pushkins were eager to avail themselves of this splendid opportunity to further the education of their son.

Young Sasha passed the examinations, which were not difficult, and was listed fourteenth in a group of thirty successful candidates. On October 19, 1811, the Lyceum opened with much pomp and ceremony. The royal family and many high officials attended the formal inauguration, and the hopeful students in resplendent uniforms were adjured by the orator of the day to grow and increase in knowledge. They were destined to spend six years within the walls of the Lyceum, and their comparative isolation molded them into a compact student family.

The ties denied the twelve-year-old Pushkin at home were quickly formed in the Lyceum, and he cherished them all his life. He gained there a rich experience, and his schooldays stimulated a sentiment and devotion which never faded from his memory and found expression in some of his sincerest poetry. His sprouting individualism often made it difficult for him to get along with his companions and teachers, but his standoffish behavior was the result of timidity rather than any youthful desire to pose. On other occasions, however, he would become all life and action, a leader in boyish escapades. But he was not adaptable and often suffered the usual penalty for strangeness in a conventional schoolboy society. Thoughtless jokes and caustic remarks placed him in difficult situations, and he began to show that lack of tact which later, in more important social contacts, caused him no little misery. A few discerning companions, however, found another side to Pushkin's nature — an unusually strong sense of honor and a passionate loyalty. A little band of devoted friends gathered around him — I. Pushchin, Malinovski, Kiukhelbeker, and the poet Delvig. These were not passing schoolboy friendships. They deepened with the years, and in Pushkin's life no warmer ties were ever formed.

The fine educational ideals of the tsar disintegrated under the fire of practical application. For a time, largely owing to the sudden death of the first director, a mild chaos existed in the Lyceum. The professors hardly lived up to their advance reputations, and their familiarity with the students only served to breed contempt. The boys were not overworked, and whoever wished to avoid classes could do so with some impunity, for corporal punishment was forbidden. This free life left them much time to follow their own inclinations. Pushkin learned with an ease that discouraged his comrades who marvelled at his phenomenal memory. However, he was a lazy scholar in prescribed studies, and the rather uniform testimony of his teachers described him as a brilliant boy who lacked the habit of persistent application. In those subjects he liked, such as French literature (his comrades nicknamed him "Frenchman"), he was outstanding. Despite the apparent failure to apply himself to formal studies, Pushkin was rarely idle in the Lyceum. When he was not up to some deviltry, the time he stole from classes he spent in writing poetry or in feverish reading. With a sure instinct, most of what he did seemed designed to feed the flame of his genius.

When E. A. Engelhardt became director in 1816, he set out to remedy the growing reputation of the students for bad behavior. His chief aim was to give the boys more opportunity for social contacts, and he allowed them to visit families in Tsarskoe Selo. Pushkin took advantage of these new liberties and soon fell afoul of the director. There were many stories told of his escapades. The tsar complained that Pushkin kissed one of the maids of honor in a dark corridor of the palace (he had mistaken her for a pretty serving girl, Natasha). He roamed the town, ogling girls, falling in love with an actress in the domestic troupe of one of the prominent citizens, and visiting the quarters of the gay

Hussars. The officers placed him on a comradely basis, and he indulged in valorous wassailing with them far into the night. It was always easy to bribe the porter of the Lyceum to let him in after hours. But many of these young officers, fresh from the Russian occupation in France, were filled with liberal idealism and a burning desire to reform the social and political abuses of their country. Pushkin had many warm discussions with them and imbibed dangerous liberal ideas. At these gatherings he met the brilliant young officer P. Chaadaev who became a close friend and an influence in his free-thinking.

The teachers encouraged literary efforts among the students and here Pushkin played the leading role. He was the poet laureate of the school and no one questioned his supremacy. "Our poet," wrote one of his comrades, "withdrawing to a deserted hall of the Lyceum or to the shady walks of the garden, would stormily knit his brows, pout, and bite his pen from vexation as he wrestled mightily with the capricious, coquettish muse; but nevertheless we all saw and heard how his light verses flew forth like a 'puff from the mouth of Æolus.'" [2] Pushkin was the leading spirit in the school papers, wrote solicited odes, and at a public examination won a great triumph with his best Lyceum poem, *Reminiscences in Tsarskoe Selo*,[3] which was highly praised by the patriarch of Russian poetry, Derzhavin, who was present on this occasion.

In the eyes of his comrades Pushkin's literary glory was immeasurably enhanced by his contacts with great Russian authors, many of whom he had met at his father's house or through his uncle Vasili. He not only wrote letters to such celebrities as Karamzin, Zhukovski, Batiushkov, and his uncle, but they answered him and discussed his literary plans. They expected much from him, and before he graduated they elected him to their literary society, the Arzamas, a great honor for a mere youth.

In the Lyceum Pushkin wrote over a hundred poems on an extraordinary variety of subjects. They range all the way from precise lyrics on the joys and sorrows of Venus and Bacchus to imitations of Ossian, formal odes, epigrams, and verse epistles. His models were largely the sensual eighteenth-century French poets. But despite the lack of originality in content, he achieved in these youthful efforts a remarkable clarity of diction and pervasive beauty of style. A few of these poems were published before he graduated.

Towards the end of the Lyceum course Pushkin grew impatient with schoolboy life and yearned for the wider experience of the great world. In the matter of prescribed studies he had not learned very much in the Lyceum, and for years he was to curse his "damnable education" and the necessity he always felt of supplementing it. His was the usual case of the misfit genius brought into contact with educational conventions and intellectual mediocrity. And among his instructors and schoolmates he had gained the reputation of a giddy, irritable, and cynical youth, who was fond of escapades and proud of his ability to turn out scurrilous epigrams. In the minds of many of his contemporaries this reputation clung to him for the rest of his life. But a few close school friends recognized the likeable qualities of his nature as well as his unquestioned talent. In the Lyceum his imagination grew and his responsiveness to various impressions of life quickened. There fame came to him easily as to one destined to it, and some notion of the divine mission of the poet was already beginning to dawn in his soul.

Graduation at last arrived on June 9, 1817. At the public examination the best Pushkin could do was to finish nineteenth on the list. For Russian literature he composed a cold, didactic poem, *Disbelief*,[4] a theme which might have been suggested by the director as a penance for his erring pupil. With other students of his rating he was given a rank of the tenth class (collegiate secretary) and a minor position in the Foreign Office. Alexander I offered the graduates some fatherly advice, and after the school hymn had been sung and albums filled with the verses of comrades, the boys went their separate ways. Pushkin was sad at leaving the school that had been his home for six years, but he soon forgot his sadness in the thought that at last he was free to enter the great world.

IV

Young Pushkin found the great world of St. Petersburg more equal to his capacity for pleasure than the Lyceum. He was now eighteen years old and the essential traits of his nature, while still to develop, had attained well-defined characteristics. His short frame was muscular and he was much given to vigorous exercises. His features, however, were anything but attractive — a shock of dark, curly hair, flat nose, thick lips, and a swarthy complexion. Two rows of large glistening teeth were revealed by his smile, and he affected extremely long fingernails of which he was inordinately proud. But his face was unusually expressive, animated by brilliant eyes that suggested a world of contemplation and poetic beauty. Vivacity was his most distinctive personal trait. Friends in the literary circle of the Arzamas called him the "Cricket," a nickname fairly descriptive of his restless, ebullient nature.

Pushkin's parents had moved to St. Petersburg and he lived with them. While he had been at school the long separation of six years had done little to remedy the coolness between them. In fact, constant bickering over money matters provoked further estrangement. He never entirely lost a sense of filial duty to his mother and father, but they did nothing to stimulate in him any real affection. This unhappy family life was partly responsible for the compensating and furious existence he sought in the pleasures of the capital. It was a period for sowing wild oats. Since his position in the Foreign Office was purely nominal, he had plenty of leisure. And for a time the Cricket chirped very gaily in St. Petersburg.

Pushkin soon revolved in a glittering circle of worldly and rich young men, many of whom belonged to the aristocratic Guards regiments. Debauchery and dangerous adventures were orders of merit among these youths. He also belonged to the Society of the Green Lamp, and the exaggerated gossip of the scandalous orgies of its members recalls the stories about the unholy mysteries of Abbot-Byron, his monk-companions, and the Paphian girls in the vaults of Newstead Abbey. For a time the Cricket's days and nights were occupied with the theater and pretty actresses, carefree bottle-companions, disreputable pothouses, gambling, and duels. He fully subscribed to the philosophy of his jingle:

> Love and wine
> We need together;
> Without them man
> Would yawn forever.[5]

An enormous store of vital energy and a passionate desire for experience drove him to excesses. Affairs with women were many. Older literary friends began to worry about his health, and the inevitable finally happened. A. I. Turgenev wrote to Vyazemski: "Venus has nailed Pushkin to his bed." [6] Yet he had scarcely recovered when a serious attack of typhoid fever almost proved fatal. He was obliged to take a rest in the country, but friends soon saw the Cricket once again hopping along the boulevards of the capital. It is easy to exaggerate these youthful dissipations. But such behavior was regarded as the hallmark of the gentleman in the fashionable society in which he moved.

Apart from his revelling companions, Pushkin was a welcome guest in most of the brilliant *salons* of St. Petersburg. Here his growing talents as a conversationalist and a wit shone to good advantage. Many admired his cleverness and feared the satire of his sharp epigrams. One evening, at an intellectual gathering at the Olenins', he first met beautiful Anna Kern. Several years later he fell passionately in love with her.

In the midst of dissipations and the pleasures of fashionable *salons* and balls the Cricket did not forget his muse. Some inner compulsion forced him to continue to pour out verses, and especially among the younger set he soon became a literary idol. His older literary friends watched over his genius and regarded with dismay his pleasure-seeking existence. Zhukovski called his talent miraculous; Batiushkov, a great poet in his own right, crumpled up the paper on which were written the verses Pushkin had sent him, and exclaimed enviously: "O, how this rascal has learned to write!" [7]

Despite his laziness and ceaseless carousing, the Cricket had learned to write, for by constant application he had almost reached the maturity of his style. Ease and elegance showed in the erotic elegies and polished epigrams that he poured out indiscriminately. Only the fullness and mellowness of his later poetry are lacking. But literary friends were demanding something more than perfect little anthology pieces. They wanted something "great," a work that would fully test his abilities. Pushkin was not deaf to their appeals. In the Lyceum he had already begun a long poem on a folk-tale subject. Feverishly he continued to work upon it in St. Petersburg, usually during the mornings after nights of debauchery. Friends were jubilant over the fragments he read them and they prodded him on. Finally, in March 1820, *Ruslan and Liudmila*, a poem in six cantos of over three thousand lines, was finished. Towards the end he had become bored with it, but the composition had cost him infinite labor. *Ruslan and Liudmila,* a sophisticated retelling of a folk tale, is a charming poetic pageant of delicate filigree work, sly humor, and fantastic adventures. The hopes of young Pushkin's literary friends were amply fulfilled — *Ruslan and Liudmila* heralded the advent of Russia's greatest poet. Before its publication, however, Pushkin was forced to leave St. Petersburg.

At this time (1819-1820) a conspiracy was under way in the capital which aimed at the overthrow of the Russian government. The hopeful liberalism at the beginning of Alexander I's reign had by now degenerated into a benighted reactionary rule. The tsar had fallen under the baleful influence of narrow-minded favorites and female mystics. Dreams of constitutional and social reforms among many young intellectuals and officers, who had observed the democratic conditions of Western Europe, were rudely dissipated by the returning reality of Russian despotism. Their reforming zeal was driven underground, and a vast revolutionary movement was spreading over the entire country.

Pushkin was attracted by this movement in which many of his young friends were active figures. A secret political society had been formed, and though Pushkin did not join, he was much influenced by certain of its members. He had imbibed a good deal of the liberalism of the Hussar officers at Tsarskoe Selo, and his experiences in St. Petersburg served to encourage his reforming zeal. To be sure, he was a poet and not a revolutionist, and it was largely as a poet that he aided the revolutionary cause. He committed certain public acts of youthful bravado which terrified even his conspiratorial friends, but his worst offenses in the eyes of the government were his poems directed against social and political abuses.

Pushkin levelled epigrams dripping with sarcasm against reactionary government officials and prominent obscurantists. The tsar himself did not escape. And serious political poems, in which he laid bare the stupid existence of the peasantry and warned tyrants to beware of a bloody fate, rejoiced his reforming comrades and horrified the police. These efforts circulated widely in manuscript and were on everybody's lips. The alarmed government soon took action.

Pushkin was called before the governor-general of Petersburg and asked to explain his behavior. Meanwhile, the matter had come to the attention of the tsar. The poet was in grave danger of exile to Siberia. Anxious and powerful friends interceded in his behalf. The impending danger somewhat chilled his liberal zeal and chastened his conduct. Alexander I refused to pardon him, but the pleas of friends mitigated Pushkin's punishment. It was decided to send him to the south of Russia while still allowing him to remain in the service.

The enforced departure from St. Petersburg, however, did not entirely displease Pushkin. He had grown weary of his two years of dissipation in the capital and wished for a change. Rumors had placed him in a humiliating position in society. And there is good reason to suppose that an unrequited love at this time filled him with the desire for new scenes. Then he firmly believed that he would be allowed to return to the capital within a few months.

On May 6, 1830, Pushkin set out for Ekaterinoslav with a letter of explanation from the Ministry of Foreign Affairs to his new superior, General Inzov. His unhappy frame of mind was somewhat alleviated by the knowledge that his first long poem would soon appear in print. Zhukovski, his teacher in poetry, had sent him his portrait, bearing the inscription: "To the victorious pupil from the conquered master, on this most solemn day on which he has finished his poem, *Ruslan and Liudmila*." [8]

V

Pushkin reached Ekaterinoslav, about a thousand miles from Petersburg, in the middle of May. His official guardian, General Inzov, Chief of the Board of Protection of Foreign Colonists in Southern Russia, was a kindly old bachelor, admirably suited to appreciate Pushkin's intellectual powers and poetic talents; and in turn the poet benefited much from his earthy wisdom.

A severe attack of fever and the timely arrival of the Raevski family, which Pushkin had got to know in St. Petersburg, quickly terminated his stay in Ekaterinoslav. For General Raevski offered to take him on a vacation tour of the Caucasus. Inzov gave his permission and they set out for the mountains. After several weeks in the Caucasus, where Pushkin enjoyed the magnificent scenery and the mineral baths, the party proceeded to the Tatar village of Gurzuf on the southern shore of the Crimea. They remained there about two weeks.

In this beautiful spot Pushkin spent one of the happiest periods of his life. The Raevski family, consisting of two sons and four daughters, was unusually cultured, and Pushkin found among them the understanding, affection, and domestic care which were so conspicuously lacking in his own family. He enjoyed the outdoor life, flirted with the daughters, and perhaps fell in love with Mariya Raevskaya. The intellectual stimulus provided by this family, especially by young Nikolai Raevski, and the inspiration of the magnificent scenery of the Caucasus, helped him to forget the pain of his departure from St. Petersburg and encouraged him to return to poetry. At this time the excellent epilogue to *Ruslan and Liudmila* was written, and the *Prisoner of the Caucasus* begun.

But the vacation had to end. Pushkin was obliged to return to General Inzov, who in the meantime had been ordered to Kishinev in Bessarabia. He traveled across the Crimean mountains to Bakhchisarai, parted with the Raevskis, and set out for Kishinev by way of Odessa.

Pushkin arrived in Kishinev at the end of September 1820, and found this little town more Asiatic than European. It had the ethnographical interest of an international bazar, for the population was made up of a bewildering variety of racial types dressed in native costumes; and the unnatural gaiety and moral looseness of a frontier town prevailed. He liked to compare it with Sodom, but he maintained that Kishinev had all the vices and none of the virtues of the Biblical city.

Except for two trips to Kamenka, near Kiev, where he spent some time again with the Raevskis, and visits to Odessa and outlying districts, Pushkin remained in Kishinev for over two years. It was an eventful and disillusioning period. In a society of adventurous men and exotic women he led a life of gambling, love intrigue, hard drinking, and duelling. With the instinct of a reporter of life, he quickly made friends and enemies. Inzov, with whom he lived, tried to act as a restraining influence, but Pushkin's deeds and sayings grew to the proportions of a lengthy and unsavory saga before he left Bessarabia. Dangerous duels with Russian officers, many love affairs, and violent quarrels with natives seemed to be prompted by something more than mere youth or a proud insistence upon his own individuality. There was a certain purposefulness behind his actions and words, and his dissipation appeared to be born of a spirit of despair. The carefree attitude that had characterized his behavior in St. Petersburg had now changed to the attitude of the fatalist. Friends observed his remarkable courage at the barrier. One of them wrote: "It seemed that he was smiling satirically while looking into the muzzle, as though he were thinking up an evil epigram on the shooter or on a miss." [9] Eagerly he plunged into the excitement of the Greek revolt against the Turks, which had raised the whole region, and for a time he wished to get into the fighting. And once again he narrowly missed the engulfing danger of the Russian political conspiracy. The secret reform movement, radiating from St. Petersburg, had already penetrated the south and was rapidly gaining adherents. On one of his visits to the Raevskis at Kamenka he met a number of prominent conspirators, and at Kishinev he came in contact with Pestel, a leader in the movement. Fortuitous circumstances, and no doubt the hesitancy of the conspirators themselves, saved Pushkin. It seems clear that he would have joined the secret political society if he had been asked, but the members distrusted his frank, open nature, and then some of them were wise enough to feel that his great talent should not be risked in such a cause.

The "Sodom" of Bessarabia exhausted the senses. Pushkin was not a rake by temperament, and a diet of the flesh never sustained him for long. He dissipated in Kishinev partly because it was the fashion among his set and partly to escape the material and spiritual oppression of adverse circumstances. Poetry comforted him in his black hour of despair, and despite the distractions of the town and the fevered restlessness of his state of mind, he experienced a considerable intellectual and poetic activity during this period. He plunged into varied reading, studied the languages of the natives, and wrote much.

The dominating influence in Pushkin's poetry in the south was Byron. In the Caucasus he had already been attracted by the Byronic protest against society and by the strong personality of Childe Harold in exile. The hero of *The Prisoner of the Caucasus* [10] had reflected the melancholy of isolation and the Byronic disdain of people and worldly culture. In the summer of 1822 he began *The Bakhchisarai Fountain*, [11] a poem even more Byronic than *The Prisoner of the Caucasus*. These poetic tales, along with the fragment, *The Robber-Brothers*, [12] were clearly inspired by Byron's popular Eastern verse tales. There were also many lyrics written at this time, and the amusing but thoroughly blasphemous *Gavriliada*, [13] which later caused him considerable trouble with the authorities.

Pushkin was a truly cosmopolitan poet, and this fact should not be ignored in considering the Byronic influence on him at this stage in his career. The literatures of Western Europe were his natural birthright. He borrowed where he pleased, but like any great author he thoroughly assimilated what he borrowed, and the final results were not mere imitations but original productions. All Europe was at the feet of Byron, and in a sense Pushkin was simply following a fashion. Byron broadened his literary horizon and encouraged to a remarkable degree his budding romanticism, and it was under this stimulus that he began in Kishinev, on May 9, 1823, his great masterpiece, *Eugene Onegin*.

There were psychological reasons behind the literary influence of Byron, for during his exile in the south Pushkin tended to identify himself with the positive personality of the English poet. There was a passing similarity in their fates. Upon his enforced departure from St. Petersburg, he had firmly believed that he would soon be allowed to return. As the months lengthened into years and all his efforts to obtain a recall were denied by the government, he began to grow bitter. He felt deserted, for-gotten, an ostracized person, and the conviction grew on him that his exile was real and permanent. Loneliness and burning resentment run through the letters that he sent to his friends. (These letters from Kishinev mark the beginning of a large correspondence which is one of the glories of Russian prose). Under such circumstances it was easy for Pushkin to slip into a Byronic pose, for there was much in the real and legendary Byron that strongly appealed to him.

On the other hand, pessimism and cynicism came hard to Pushkin. He laughed too loud and enjoyed living too much to make his Byronic pose anything other than a pose which could be shuffled off at the proper time just as easily as he had assumed it. He was altogether too powerful a genius to be a mere imitator or follower of anyone. With changed circumstances and the addi-tion of a couple of years to his swiftly-maturing mind, he threw off Childe Harold's mantle.

By 1823 influential friends in St. Petersburg grew thoroughly alarmed over Pushkin's behavior in Kishinev. They interceded successfully in his behalf, and by the end of July 1823 he left the "Sodom" of Bessarabia for Odessa. The fabric of his moral nature had been stretched to the breaking point. But his experiences had not been unfruitful. Kishinev was a furnace in which his fine quality had been tempered rather than consumed. The town brought him into contact with a new world of social relations and revealed to him hidden factors in human nature. All this was fresh material for his pen.

Odessa was a European city compared to semi-Asiatic Kishinev, and for a time Pushkin was delighted with the change. As though determined to reform his previous manner of existence, he settled down to a quiet life and renewed application to litera-ture. A mature awareness of his importance to Russian letters was dawning on him, and he was also beginning to realize the commercial possibilities of his poetry. The need for money be-

came the burden of his letters, and he was to chant it with despair-
ing monotony for the rest of his life. Up to date he had received
precious little for his work, but with the publication of *The Baḳh-
chisarai Fountạin* he was paid three thousand rubles, a splendid
price. To his friend Vyazemski he defended this commercial attitude, a unique position for a Russian poet at that time: "Since
I do not belong to the authors of the 18th century, I write for
myself and print for money, but not at all for the smiles of the
fair sex." [14] In reality, his poems were creating a sensation, and
the younger critics were hailing him as a new and great force in
Russian literature. He worked feverishly on *Eugene Onegin* and
completed a draft of the *Gypsies*. In his conception of Aleko, the
hero of the *Gypsies,* he clearly indicated that he was moving away
from the powerful influence of Byron.

Always a social animal, however, Pushkin soon began to take a
prominent place in the gay life of Odessa. With Amaliya Riznich, the fascinating wife of one of his friends, he fell passionately
in love. It is not known how intimate were their relations, but
the scandal resulted in the husband's sending his wife abroad,
where she soon died. The memory of this affair long remained
with Pushkin, and he dedicated several beautiful elegies to
Amaliya Riznich.

In the government social circle of Odessa, headed by Count
M. S. Vorontsov, the governor-general of the region, and his
attractive wife, Pushkin felt ill at ease. Nominally he was still in
the government service, and Vorontsov, to whom he had been
recommended, was his superior. An aristocrat, careerist, and
pronounced Anglophile, Vorontsov was the sort of individual
who would especially resent a man of Pushkin's temperament.
Although he possessed fine qualities as an administrator, he was
cold, excessively proud of his lineage, and irritating in his con-
descension to subordinates. Pushkin soon sensed the hostility of
his chief, and he immeasurably aggravated the situation by falling
in love with his wife. Little is known of this affair, but there is

some reason to suppose that Pushkin was not very successful with the pretty Countess Vorontsova.

Count Vorontsov finally decided that his subordinate must leave Odessa. He resented Pushkin's proud and independent attitude, and then scurrilous epigrams on himself, attributed to the poet, came to his attention. But no doubt the decisive reason for Vorontsov's action was Pushkin's pursuit of his wife, which seemed all the more offensive to the count because of the poet's inferior rank. Vorontsov wrote to the authorities in St. Petersburg requesting that Pushkin be sent elsewhere, and in his report he represented him in a very unfavorable light. Meanwhile, Pushkin inadvertently compromised his position in the eyes of the government. In a letter to a Moscow friend he lightly mentioned that he was taking lessons in "pure atheism." This casual remark came to the attention of the authorities and weighed heavily against him, for it was a time of religious obscurantism. Since the government delayed its reply, Vorontsov took matters into his own hands. He sent Pushkin off on an expedition to stamp out a locust plague. Such a menial task, and the motives behind it, deeply offended Pushkin, and upon his return he handed in his resignation, which Vorontsov quickly forwarded to St. Petersburg. The government's answer finally arrived, and the position it took was extreme. The emperor had been angered by the "atheism" letter. Pushkin was discharged from the service and ordered to proceed at once to his mother's village of Mikhailovskoe, where he was to remain under surveillance.

On July 30, 1824, Pushkin left Odessa for his long trip north. His southern exile had come to an end and a new one was to begin. In the four years in the south of Russia he had seen much, thought much, and experienced and felt a good deal more. It had been a period of scepticism, of tortuous doubts in himself and in everything. But his wanderings had been a fruitful school of life for him. Furthermore, he had written and published much poetry during these four years. In the south he had come of age as a man and as Russia's greatest poet. To be sure, the future did not look very promising. Instead of leaving the south a free man, he was traveling to a village where his personal liberty would be even more restricted. Yet at the moment it was a comfort to place distance between him and the thoroughly-disliked Count Vorontsov.

VI

On the long road back north Pushkin bewildered the village yokels with his exotic Kishinev costume — wide, varicolored Turkish trousers, a Moldavian cloak, and a fez with a long tassel. His thick curly hair fell to his shoulders and he twirled his iron cane like a drum-major. The faithful valet Nikita, dressed as a Tatar, trailed after him. Pushkin arrived in Mikhailovskoe, in the province of Pskov, on August 8, and was accorded a warm greeting by his surprised parents and brother and sister. They had not seen him for four years, and in the meantime they had become fully conscious of the fact that he was now a famous writer. His mother and father did not grow old gracefully. Little remained of their former social brilliance, except an empty pride and invincible egoism. And they were forever fault-finding.

Pushkin's literary glory fell away from him like a discarded cloak the moment his parents learned of his new exile and the reasons for it. They feared that they too would become involved with the authorities. The son soon found himself in the position of a criminal in his own family, an "atheist" whose contagious influence was dreaded by his parents. The officials of the district were ordered to keep him under surveillance, and in a weak moment his father accepted their offer to spy on his son. There were continual quarrels. The father charged him with teaching atheism to his brother Lev. In one disgraceful scene the father shouted through the house that his son tried to beat him. In deep despair Pushkin wrote to Zhukovski at St. Petersburg to come to his aid. Fortunately the situation soon cleared up, for in November the

Pushkin family took itself off to the capital, and the harassed son was left alone at Mikhailovskoe with the company of his good old nurse, Arina Rodionovna. The calm that ensued after three months of family wrangling was a welcome relief.

For over two years Pushkin was obliged to remain at Mikhailovskoe, and his country existence was very much the same as that of his hero in *Eugene Onegin*. It was pretty much the life of a recluse. Although he avoided the local gentry, he made an exception in the case of Praskovya Osipova and her large family in the neighboring estate of Trigorskoe. Madame Osipova was devoted to him, and at Trigorskoe there were girls without end — the daughters and nieces of the mistress of this large manor house. Romance hid in every corner, for all these young ladies coquetted with Pushkin, and some fell seriously in love with him. And he, as was his custom, fell a little in love with all of them.

It was at Trigorskoe that he met once again the beautiful Anna Kern whom he had seen five years before in St. Petersburg. Unhappily married to a crusty old general, she was at this time paying a visit to her relative, Praskovya Osipova. He now fell passionately in love with Anna Kern, and when she departed, shortly after this meeting, he presented to her the following lines, one of his best-known lyrics:

> Oh, I remember our brief meeting;
> Thou didst appear, all tenderness,
> Like some fair vision past me fleeting,
> Some genius of pure loveliness.
>
> By pain of hopeless grief surrounded,
> Amid the fears of noisy care,
> Thy tender voice to me long sounded,
> And I recalled thy features fair.
>
> Years passed. The rebel blast, still stronger,
> Scattered my former dreams to air;
> I heard thy tender voice no longer,
> Remembered not thy features fair.

Far off in exile's desolation
Slowly my days dragged on in strife,
Without God, without inspiration,
Without tears, without love or life.

Then something in my heart came beating;
I saw thee now, all tenderness,
Like some fair vision past me fleeting,
Some genius of pure loveliness.

My heart now beats in exaltation;
There steals into it from above
Both Deity and inspiration,
And life, and tears, and holy love.[15]

For a short time Pushkin maintained an extraordinary correspondence with Anna Kern, and his letters eloquently reflect the emotional fury she inspired in him. Sometime later, in St. Petersburg, he met her again and consummated his passion. But she soon ceased to be his "genius of pure loveliness."

There was some male companionship, however, in this welter of female society at Trigorskoe. Aleksei Vulf, the son of Praskovya Osipova, spent his holidays from school in the country. He was Pushkin's pupil in the "science of the tender passions," and on one occasion he brought with him the young poet Yazykov. In January 1825, Pushkin's old school friend Pushchin paid a memorable visit to Mikhailovskoe. (Scarcely a year later the idealistic Pushchin was on his way to Siberia for the part he played in the Decembrist Revolt.) In April, 1825, another Lyceum comrade, Delvig, cheered Pushkin's loneliness by a visit.

The chief happiness of Pushkin in his village exile was work. He had plenty of leisure, and the country life and constant correspondence with literary friends provided him with inspiration. Now thoroughly aware of his leading position in Russian literature, he placed behind him the romantic themes of his youth and turned to subjects more directly connected with his country's past and present. At Mikhailovskoe his lyrical production was not extensive, but the short poems he wrote there are among his best. His main concern, however, was with longer poems. He finished the first six chapters of *Eugene Onegin*, and though it was not clear to the critics at the time, these chapters represent the most original and most Russian poetry he ever wrote. In this brilliant psychological novel in verse there is much lyricism, some conscious romanticism, and a good deal of sheer subjectivity in treatment. But the real direction he pursues in *Eugene Onegin* is that of objective realism. And this same direction is manifested in *Boris Godunov*. For with Shakespeare as his model, he also wrote at this time a chronicle play on Russian history, which was designed to liberate the drama from th⁻ confining rules of neoclassicism.

It must not be thought, however, that Pushkin was happy in his detention camp of Mikhailovskoe. Freedom of movement and freedom of expression were vital conditions of existence for him, and he never possessed either in an unqualified degree. In the village he was continually under surveillance, and he longed for the city life and intellectual companionship which he loved. His resentment against the government grew intense, and he finally planned to escape from his detention camp. At first he endeavored to get permission to go abroad on the plea that he required medical assistance for a severe case of aneurysm. But the authorities would not trust him out of their control. He next devised an elaborate scheme for escaping across the border, yet this also came to nothing. Mournfully he wrote to Zhukovski: "It is all the same, to die from boredom or aneurysm; but the first is more infallible than the other." [16]

Pushkin became convinced that as long as Alexander I lived his exiled position would never be remedied. Consequently, the death of this monarch in 1825 gave him new hope. But this hope was dashed by the ill-fated Decembrist Revolt which ushered in the reign of Nicholas I. Pushkin had barely escaped taking part

in the outbreak, for he had planned a secret trip to St. Petersburg
on the eve of the uprising. Now his friends were being arrested
on every hand. He had known many of the conspirators personally, and although he had not belonged to any secret political
societies, his reputation for liberalism and his connection with the
Decembrists gave him plenty of cause for anxiety.

Influential friends cautioned Pushkin to remain quietly at Mikhailovskoe. But as the news of arrest after arrest reached him,
his fears grew. Many of the conspirators testified that his youthful
political verse had fired their liberal idealism. Boldly, however,
he sent a personal request to the new tsar, asking for a recall.
Meanwhile, the authorities had been thoroughly investigating his
case. A special agent was even sent into the region to ascertain
what had been his relations with the peasants. Fortunately he
received a clean bill of health. Late on the evening of September
3, 1826, an imperial courier arrived at Mikhailovskoe. Pushkin
was handed a message. The tsar ordered him to set out for Moscow at once, where he was to present himself to the general of
the day for instructions. The order obliged him to travel under
the escort of the imperial courier, but "not in the position of a
prisoner." In a sense, this was to be Pushkin's status for the re-
mainder of his life. Altogether uncertain of what the immediate
future held in store for him, he left Mikhailovskoe with the feeling that he would regain his freedom or be sent to Siberia.

VII

On September 8 Pushkin arrived in Moscow, and still in his
dirty travelling clothes he was taken to the Kremlin and presented
to the Tsar of all the Russias. We know little of what took place
at this famous interview. Pushkin was a political suspect and
hence in a dangerous position. His liberalism was well known,
and until the day of his death he remained a liberal. However,
despite his natural alliance with the reforming element in Russia,
it must be admitted that he had no special talent for revolutionary

activity, nor had he any deeply-rooted inclination to espouse the Decembrist cause other than through his poetry. His main business, his whole life was poetry. Like many a liberal, he wished for reform, but he preferred to see it brought about by intelligent development rather than by bloody revolution.

In the interview Nicholas I is credited with asking Pushkin if he were not a friend of many of the conspirators who had been sent to Siberia. He replied: "It is true, Sire, I loved and esteemed many of them, and I continue to nourish the same feeling for them." [17] And when the tsar asked him what he would have done if he had been in St. Petersburg on the fourteenth of December, Pushkin frankly answered: "I would have been in the ranks of the rebels." [18] Nicholas I seemed to have been much impressed by the poet, and later he told a friend that he had talked with the most intelligent man in Russia. He gave Pushkin his freedom and told him that in the future he himself would be the censor of all his works. The poet left the palace with tears in his eyes. His long exile was ended. Yet he was soon made to realize that he was a "free" man only when and as the tsar wished.

The pardoned poet became the darling of the hour, and this occasion marks the high point in Pushkin's popularity. Moscow made a national hero of him and his name was on everybody's lips. In society all eyes were directed on him, and when he entered the theatre the audience ceased to be interested in the performance. After his prolonged exile, this hymn of praise was sweet music to his ears. In the literary circles of Moscow he read *Boris Godunov*, and the drama was everywhere listened to with rapture.

Although Pushkin loved fame, he was easily surfeited. Soon the intensive social life he had plunged into began to pall, and he also felt a strong desire to get back to writing poetry. He had hardly been more than two months in Moscow when he suddenly decided to return to Mikhailovskoe for a visit. The rejection of a hasty marriage proposal which he had made to a distant kinswoman, Sofya Pushkina, no doubt had something to do with his decision to leave the city.

Once in his village Pushkin set to work to compose an article on national education which Nicholas I had suggested. He was already beginning to feel the burden of being the favored poet of an emperor. And he also began to understand a little more clearly what his "freedom" meant and what a mixed blessing it was to have a tsar for censor. Pushkin regarded Nicholas through the prism of the generosity he had displayed at the famous interview. What he did not sense at once was the tsar's deliberate intention to place him under a special moral obligation to behave and do what he was told in return for his majesty's kindness. This moral obligation, which he was never allowed to forget, weighed on his conscience and ultimately stung and tortured his sense of pride. For freedom of movement (which at best was hardly real) he had sacrificed his moral freedom. Nicholas I never for a moment ceased to suspect Pushkin, and every move he made was observed and reported by the police.

While at Mikhailovskoe Pushkin received a letter from Benkendorf, chief of the tsar's secret police, in which he was reprimanded for reading *Boris Godunov* to Moscow audiences before he had sent the play to the tsar for his majesty's approval. The drama was immediately forwarded to Nicholas and permission requested to print it. The request was denied. Nicholas confessed to enjoying *Boris Godunov*, although it is pretty certain he did not read it, and suggested that it be turned into an historical romance after the manner of Walter Scott. Pushkin scorned this advice. And his essay on national education, which was soon finished, also received a snub from the royal censor. The tsar refused permission to print it because he felt that Pushkin had failed to emphasize sufficiently such necessary virtues in Russian education as discipline and morality. The worried poet began to wonder how it would be possible to make a living at literature if his royal censor continued to be so difficult to please.

Pushkin returned to Moscow in December only to be called to account by the police for a poem which had received wide manuscript circulation. He was charged with having written these verses on the revolt of the fourteenth of December, and he had much difficulty in proving that the poem really concerned the French revolutionary writer André Chénier. Dejected and discontented with his life in Moscow, he received permission to go to St. Petersburg in April.

Pushkin had now grown introspective. His past was not a happy memory and the future stretched out before him like an infinity of pain. Shortly after his arrival in St. Petersburg he wrote the beautiful poem *Remembrance*, recalling the memories that ran through his mind in the quiet of a sleepless night:

> And with disgust I read the lengthy scroll of years,
> I shudder, and I curse too late,
> I bitterly complain and shed my bitter tears,
> But can't erase the lines of fate.[19]

Only a radical change in his life could cure this spiritual illness.

From the end of 1827 to the first half of the next year, Pushkin led one of the stormiest and most restless periods of his existence. He seemed bent on forgetting his distraught state of mind in one last desperate fling at bachelor life. Now he plunged into the dissipations of the capital with all the ardor of that period of eight years before when he had graduated from the Lyceum. There were many affairs of the heart, furious gambling, and wild escapades. Although his fame as a poet gave him access to the best society, the uncultured bureaucrats, who had come into power with the reign of Nicholas I, soon made him realize that they tolerated him as an artist, as a kind of uninvited guest from a sphere of society alien to theirs and infinitely below them. This snobbism cut deeply and set up an antagonism that did much to corrode his natural quality of friendliness.

The persistent spying of the police and the obvious suspicions of the government contributed greatly to his disturbed state of mind. He could not understand the hostile attitude of the tsar, whom he sincerely liked, and the repeated refusals of Nicholas to allow him to travel abroad convinced him that he was still as much of a prisoner as he had been during his exile at Mikhailov-skoe. His detention camp was simply larger. At every turn the government pulled him up, and on one occasion he got into very serious difficulties when his blasphemous poem *Gavriliada* came to the attention of the police. In 1828 he wrote the following well-known verses which clearly reflect the bitter spiritual misery under which he labored:

> Gift in vain and gift of chance,
> Life, why wert thou given me?
> Why have I been thus condemned
> To a secret fate by thee?
>
> Who with some strange hostile power,
> Summoned me from nothingness,
> And disturbed my mind with doubt,
> Filled my soul with passion's stress?
>
> Goal there's none before me now:
> Empty heart and idle brain,
> Life's monotonous roaring sound
> Burdens me with endless pain.[20]

There was poetry, of course, to retreat to, but in his disturbed state of mind Pushkin found inspiration only by fits and starts. By the end of February 1828, he had published five chapters of *Eugene Onegin*, and by spring two more were nearly finished. In October of the same year (the autumn was always his favorite time for composition) he experienced a sudden surge of creative energy. In the course of some three weeks he wrote the whole of *Poltava*, a long romantic-heroic poem about his hero Peter the Great and the traitorous Hetman Mazepa.

Yet nothing contented him for long, and his restlessness is clearly reflected in the constant traveling from St. Petersburg to

Malinniki, the Tver estate of Aleksei Vulf, then to Mikhailovskoe, to Moscow, and back again to the capital. Wherever he went he was a welcome guest among literary friends. In Delvig's circle in St. Petersburg he was regarded as a kind of oracle, and dazzled all by his brilliant conversation. He offended, however, as often as he delighted. Unfeeling remarks, brutal frankness, and sarcasm wounded and made enemies. His high-spirited, ebullient nature had grown morose and apathetic. His thirtieth birthday was at hand and he was beginning to feel old, — that pseudo-but none the less poignant senility of a man who has reached the end of youth. Desperately he felt the need to settle down, to marry.

On one of his trips to Moscow in December of 1828 Pushkin attended a large ball. He saw there a young girl in a fluffy gown. This was the sixteen-year-old Natalya Nikolaevna Goncharova, who had recently donned long dresses for her entrance into society. Her budding charms carried with them the prophecy of enthralling womanly beauty. More than a year later Pushkin wrote of Natasha Goncharova: "When I saw her for the first time, her beauty was just being noticed in society; I loved her, my head was turned." [21] He left for St. Petersburg shortly after this eventful ball, and Natasha remained very much in his thoughts.

The capital, however, seemed less attractive than ever. Physical action always served Pushkin as a kind of antidote for moral weariness. Now his whole being cried out for physical action. Suddenly, on March 9, with one of his impulsive and characteristic gestures of despair, he fled St. Petersburg without bothering to ask the government's permission. His destination was the Russian army in the Caucasus which was fighting the Turks. But he elected to go by way of Moscow. The image of Natasha Goncharova had grown brighter in his mind.

Through a friend Pushkin quickly got himself introduced into the Goncharov household. The young Natasha was painfully self-conscious, but her girlish modesty only made her all the more attractive in his eyes. With the mother, however, he did not get along very well. Impatient of delay, Pushkin soon offered a proposal of marriage. But the mother was evasive, putting him off with the excuse that it was necessary to wait a bit, for her daughter was too young to be thinking of marriage. Discouraged, but still nourishing hope, Pushkin set out for the Caucasus on the first of May.

VIII

In the Caucasus Pushkin joined the Russian forces and played at war. In the army he met his brother and many friends among the officers. One may well imagine the surprise of the fierce Cossacks at seeing in their midst the poet turned Mars, charging along with saber, Caucasian cloak, and top hat. They took him for an army chaplain. After the capture of Erzerum Pushkin wearied of army life. Besides, General Paskevich, who was responsible for the poet, found him a distinct liability. Nor had four months of travel and martial atmosphere killed his passion for Natasha Goncharova.

At the end of September Pushkin was back in Moscow, and his first visit was to the Goncharovs. The mother behaved coldly and the daughter treated him with calculated indifference. He left for St. Petersburg with "death in my heart," as he wrote later. The Goncharovs were a poverty-stricken noble family, and the mother, given to religious mania, kept her three daughters in a pious fear of hell and damnation. Natasha was the youngest and most beautiful. Her mother had no interest in literature or literary fame, and Pushkin's rakish reputation was no recommendation in her eyes. She hoped for a wealthy, fashionable husband for her daughter.

The unhappy Pushkin resumed his disorderly life in St. Petersburg. But the city's pleasures provided no real escape. He petitioned the government for permission to go to France or Italy, and finally to China, but these requests were refused. His thoughts were filled with death:

> Each day and year of mortal pining
> There lives with me the self-same gloom,
> Among them ceaselessly divining
> The coming holiday of doom.[22]

The rumored engagement of Natasha, however, sent him scurrying back to Moscow, and since there was nothing in the rumor, he joyfully renewed his suit. Natasha's mother was now in a more amiable frame of mind. No one else had asked for her daughter's hand, largely because the family had no dowry to offer, and Pushkin was willing to forego this consideration.

At last his proposal was accepted and Pushkin's cup of joy flowed over. Yet his path was not an easy one. The Goncharovs made heavy demands upon him for money, and there were everlasting quarrels with the difficult mother. After one particularly disagreeable scene he left in despair for his father's estate of Boldino, convinced that all was over. And still worse, he now began to contrast the cares of a married man with the charms of bachelor life.

An encouraging letter from Natasha, soon after his arrival at Boldino, did much to dissipate Pushkin's deep gloom. He had expected to remain only a short time in the village, but a cholera epidemic in the region held him there for three months. It was autumn, and he spent his leisure in an extraordinary fury of composition. Besides a small cluster of beautiful lyrics, he finished *Eugene Onegin*, bringing to an end his long and arduous task of eight years. His narrative poem, *The Little House in Kolomna*[23] was written at Boldino, and also the four short dramatic scenes (*The Stone Guest, Mozart and Salieri, The Feast During the Plague, The Avaricious Knight*)[24] which are among the most brilliant of his productions. Nor did this complete the beadroll, for he also wrote his experimental prose *Tales of Belkin*[25] and the fragmentary *History of the Village of Goriukhino*.[26]

The cholera quarantine was finally lifted, and Pushkin hastened to Moscow, hoping for an early marriage. But again there were delays and quarrels with mother Goncharova. In his despair he contemplated going to Poland to fight in the rebellion that had broken out. The news of the death of his dearest friend, Delvig, added to his unhappiness. His own little world seemed to be disintegrating. All was flux and change, and he, too, was changing. He sadly wondered whether it was for the best.

At last the date of the marriage was definitely set. But the fact now failed to banish his dark doubts. The uncertainty, constant wrangling, and the mercenary aspect of all the preparations shrouded the coming event in gloom. The marriage took place on February 18, 1831, in the Great Ascension Church in Moscow. Natasha was incomparably beautiful in her bridal gown. In changing hands one of the rings fell, and during the ceremony a cross and Bible fell from the pulpit. The superstitious Pushkin grew pale and muttered: "These are all bad omens!" [27]

Despite his gloomy premonitions, Pushkin began his married life most auspiciously. After spending the winter in Moscow, the couple moved to a summer house in Tsarskoe Selo. He was deeply in love with his wife and serenely happy. During these blissful summer months he seemed to have found at last a kind of spiritual rest after years of stormy existence, wanderings, and uncertainties. As yet he had scarcely time to wonder whether his girl-bride possessed anything other than the extraordinary beauty which had first attracted him. He regarded her as a child and treated her as one. In fact, Natasha was a very ordinary young wife, entirely self-centered and eager for male attention. Her mind was extremely limited. She had no interest in poetry and hardly knew the titles of her husband's works or of the books he read. Perhaps he made a mistake in emphasizing the tremendous intellectual difference between them, for such treatment encouraged her to seek refuge in purely social activities where she could shine.

By the middle of October the couple took up residence in St. Petersburg. With an expensive household to maintain, Pushkin now found himself continually embarrassed by financial difficulties. He petitioned the tsar for readmission to the government service and a raise in rank. Both requests were granted and he was given a salary of five thousand rubles a year. Because of these favors of the tsar, enemies called him a reactionary. Although the stark problem of existence obliged him to play the part of a conservative, he remained a liberal at heart. In fact, he resented his growing indebtedness to the government and poignantly realized that it was becoming increasingly difficult to sever the silken chains that bound him to the throne.

On May 9, 1832, a daughter, Mariya, was born. Pushkin grew more serious, more concerned about the future of his family. His growing responsibilities forced him to apply himself assiduously to literary projects. Permission was granted to use the archives to write a history of Peter the Great, but this work was soon put aside for a history of the Pugachev revolt and an historical romance based on the same period. Folk-tale themes also occupied him, and he began the splendid series of popular verse tales which are among his best creations.

The kind of life his wife elected to lead, however, gave him little time to write. Natasha entered the social whirl of the capital and proved an enormous success. All the fashionable youths praised her beauty and flirted with her. Nothing seemed to concern her except dancing and being the center of attraction in the ballroom. She lived as children live — without thought or care. Her life was a series of festivities, balls, promenades, and preoccupation with her toilet. Pushkin continually worried over her flirting and the effect of this gay social life on her health. Nothing seemed to interfere with her pleasures, not even bearing children (two sons and another daughter were born). Frequently he was obliged to go to Moscow and elsewhere to conduct

historical researches, and the letters he wrote Natasha are filled
with advice and censure on the score of her behavior in the social
world. He constantly warned her not to flirt, for he did not set
any great store by her brains and tact. He fully realized the dubi-
ous position he held in St. Petersburg society, and he knew that
at the first opportunity this society would take delight in ruining
his wife's reputation and in ridiculing him. His honor he valued
more than anything in life, and Natasha's unwise flirtations bore
all the elements of tragedy.

In 1833 Pushkin was made a gentleman of the chamber by the
tsar. The honor deeply offended him. Besides being much too old
for such a position, he realized that it had been given to him
because the tsar wished to make it possible for the beautiful
Natasha to attend the exclusive court balls. He felt himself ridiculous in the eyes of the social world and yearned to get away
from the oppressive, scandal-mongering society of the capital, to
remove Natasha from the vicious influences which were destroy-
ing his married life. In June 1834, he asked to be retired from the
service. His plan was to go to the country where he would find
the possibility of bettering his financial plight and the peace
and contentment that would enable him to write. The tsar
was indignant and Pushkin withdrew this request. But his difficulties increased. Natasha's social activities finally undermined
her health. His debts were mounting steadily, and to make
matters worse the two unmarried sisters of his wife were now on
his hands. Once again, in 1835, he asked permission to retire to
the country for several years, and again the tsar made it impossible
for him to leave the service. Family cares and the many demands
on his pocket, time, and energy made him feel like a hunted man
who had no possibility of escape. And finally his cup of misery
was filled by a scandalous rumor that reached his ears. St. Petersburg high society was coupling the name of his wife with that
of a handsome officer of the Guards, Baron George d'Anthès.

IX

D'Anthès, who was the same age as Natasha, had come from France to make a career for himself in the Russian army. Tall, blond, and well-formed, he was considered the handsomest man in the regiment and one of its worst soldiers. But his pleasing disposition, witty conversation, and French gallantry made him a general favorite among St. Petersburg high society. A certain arrogance in his bearing amused those who liked him and offended some who found a special virtue in sincerity and simplicity. In his climbing tactics he had the backing of influential people, among them the Dutch minister, Baron Louis van Heeckeren, a polished diplomat with a reputation for being jesuitical, malicious, and thoroughly immoral. He legally adopted D'Anthès in 1836, but many considered their relationship highly unnatural.

D'Anthès met Natasha in 1834 and fell passionately in love with her. She flirted with him, as she did with all her admirers, but her customary passivity melted before the flame of the young guardsman. She enjoyed his youthful attention as an interesting substitute for the habitual affection of a husband whose passion she dutifully satisfied but did not encourage. There can be no doubt that she was much attracted to D'Anthès. Yet she did not submit to him, and as though to justify her innocence, she practically made a confidant of her husband in the whole affair. The love notes of D'Anthès were read to Pushkin, and she repeated his whispered compliments. D'Anthès turned up at all the social functions she attended, and his persistent wooing attracted the attention of all. St. Petersburg society hummed with the scandal and gleefully awaited the dénouement.

On November 4, 1836, Pushkin received an anonymous letter, announcing his election to "the most serene Order of Cuckolds." [28] And that same day seven or eight of his close friends received a similar letter, enclosed in an envelope addressed to Pushkin. He suspected Heeckeren, but the author has never been positively identified. There was no doubt in Pushkin's mind, however, that the anonymous letters were directly inspired by the affair between his wife and D'Anthès. His own honor and that of his wife had been sullied, and the very next day he sent a challenge to D'Anthès.

Heeckeren feared the consequences of a duel and begged for a respite of a week, which Pushkin granted. In the meantime, he brought all possible pressure to bear on Pushkin in the hope that he would withdraw his challenge. Pushkin refused. As a last resort Heeckeren declared that his adopted son was really in love with Ekaterina, Natasha's sister, and was ready to make her a proposal. (Ekaterina herself was deeply in love with D'Anthès). Pushkin was willing to accept what seemed to him a cowardly subterfuge; but a letter from D'Anthès, in which he implied that the projected marriage should not be used as an excuse for withdrawing the challenge, infuriated him, and he once again insisted on fighting. The matter was patched up with great difficulty, and only when it became clear that D'Anthès would definitely marry Ekaterina.

The wedding took place on January 10, 1837, but the unrelenting Pushkin refused to attend the ceremony. Yet, whatever motive lay behind this strange match, the marriage did not in the least cure D'Anthès of his passion for Natasha. On the contrary, he at once took advantage of his new relationship to place himself on a more familiar footing with her, and his courting grew more open and offensive. It seemed as though he were trying to prove to the social world that he was not a coward, and that he had married one sister in order to make love to the other. Once again people began to talk, and the encouragement that the thoughtless Natasha gave her lover only served to inspire more gossip. She did not seem to realize that she was running the risk of flirting away her husband's life.

The whole situation drove Pushkin into a position where he yearned for retribution. During this fatal month of January everything seemed to contrive a complete collapse of the material and emotional factors governing his life. He had reached a point where it was difficult to go on living. Despite a stupendous debt of one hundred and twenty thousand rubles, his expenses were increasing every month. At every turn he was spied upon by the police, for the government still regarded him as a suspicious person. As a gentleman of the chamber he felt himself ridiculous in everybody's eyes. He wished to retire to the country, but the tsar's favor depended upon his staying in St. Petersburg. Peace and leisure for work were denied him, and he imagined that his creative powers were failing. The magazine that he had finally been permitted to publish, *The Contemporary*, had not been well received by the critics. And now St. Petersburg high society was vastly amused because it thought that his beautiful wife was betraying him with a clever young guardsman. They laughed when they saw Prince Dolgorukov make the traditional sign of the horns behind his back. His appearance and whole personality seemed to change. Gone were his characteristic carefree manner and his spontaneous childlike laughter. For whole days he walked about the city or locked himself in his study and paced the room. He was not merely jealous of his wife; he was also jealous of his honor. His good name, he felt, belonged to Russia and posterity, and to have it dragged in the filthy mire of scandal was more than he could bear.

Finally, an incident occurred that could have but one consequence. Natasha received a note from D'Anthès in which he begged her for an interview in private. She went, but when she discovered that the rendezvous was just a subterfuge, contrived to give D'Anthès an opportunity to ask her submission, she fled the room. The next day Pushkin received an anonymous letter which informed him of the meeting. He believed the affair another trick of D'Anthès and Heeckeren, who had consistently played the pander for his son, to compromise his honor. On January 26 he wrote Heeckeren a vicious and insulting letter, filled with venom and calculated provocation. According to the standards of the time, it could have only one answer. That same day he received a challenge from D'Anthès.

The duel took place on January 27 at a snow-covered spot by Black River on the outskirts of the city. Count D'Archiac was the second of D'Anthès, and K. Danzas, an old Lyceum comrade, was Pushkin's witness. D'Anthès fired first and Pushkin fell, wounded in the abdomen. After several moments of silence he raised himself on his elbow and said: "Wait, I have enough strength to take my shot." [29] D'Anthès returned to his post and Pushkin, supporting himself on his left elbow, took steady aim. He was a dead shot. He fired and D'Anthès fell. "Bravo!" shouted Pushkin, throwing his pistol aside. The duel was ended.

Although Pushkin was seriously wounded, D'Anthès had received only a slight hurt. Pushkin was taken home and doctors were summoned, including the tsar's physician. For the next forty-five hours the poet lived through a period of terrible suffering. But he bore it all with amazing fortitude, seemingly at peace with the world, and concerned only for his wife whom he declared guiltless in the whole affair.

The news of the duel spread throughout the city like wildfire, and soon many close friends gathered at Pushkin's bedside. The tsar sent him a comforting message. Hundreds of common people stormed the house, and soldiers had to be called out to preserve order. On the 29th he grew weaker. The room was filled with anxious friends. Suddenly he opened his eyes and said to V. I. Dal: "Life is ended!" "What is ended?" asked Dal, not hearing him clearly. "Life is ended!" Pushkin repeated audibly and emphatically. "It is difficult to breathe, I am choking!" [30] These were his last words.

The authorities feared a popular demonstration and the body was secretly moved to the Royal Stables Church at midnight on January 31. Yet the word soon got around and hundreds of people appeared at the church for the funeral services. Pushkin had expressed a desire to be buried at Mikhailovskoe. On February 6, in the presence of only his old valet Nikita, his friend A. I. Turgenev, and police guards and peasants, Pushkin was buried in the graveyard of the Svyatogorski Monastery near his village of Mikhailovskoe.

Pushkin's life had been an endless discord between his inner spiritual being and the external facts of existence. All the events of his life contrived to wear him down physically and emotionally and to break the wings of his genius. The freedom that was so necessary for his creative spirit was denied him. Exile, police surveillance, government interference, and adverse material circumstances continually obstructed his efforts. He was wise in the knowledge of the human heart, but in the affairs of his own life he could be childishly naïve. Although he had many enemies, he was essentially simple and good, and those friends who loved him were aware of the beauty of his spiritual nature. The age in which he lived was a difficult one for poets, and particularly for a poet of his freedom-loving spirit. He constantly sought to escape the circumstances that were beating him down. The last duel was such an effort, and its fatal consequence was perhaps the only escape he could hope for.

HARVARD UNIVERSITY

NOTES

[1] "Iurevu" (I, 274).

[2] K. Ya. Grot, *Pushkinski litsei* (St. Petersburg: 1911), p. 221.

[3] *Vospominaniya v Tsarskom Sele* (I, 90).

[4] *Bezverie* (I, 245).

[5] *Vse prizrak, sueta* (I, 453).

[6] *Ostafevski Arkhiv Knyazei Vyazemskikh,* ed. Count S. D. Sheremetev (St. Petersburg: 1899 ff.), I, 200.

[7] P. V. Annenkov, *Materialy dlya biografii A. S. Pushkina* (St. Petersburg: 1873), p. 50.

[8] A. N. Veselovski, *V. A. Zhukovski* (St. Petersburg: 1904), see frontispiece.

[9] L. N. Maikov, *Pushkin. Biograficheskie materialy i istoriko-literaturnye ocherki* (St. Petersburg: 1899), p. 126-127.

[10] *Kavkazski plennik* (III, 94).

[11] *Bakhchisaraiski fontan* (III, 144).

[12] *Bratya-razboiniki* (III, 137).

[13] *Gavriiliada* (III, 120).

[14] *Perepiska Pushkina,* No. 169, I, 102.

[15] *K. A. P. Kern* (I, 402).

[16] *Perepiska,* No. 215, I, 302.

[17] N. I. Lorer, "Zapiski moego vremeni." Cf. V. V. Veresaev, *Pushkin v zhizni* (5th ed., Academia, Moscow: 1932), I, 203.

[18] M. A. Korf, "Zapiski," *Russkaya Starina* (1900), CI, 574.

[19] *Vospominanie* (II, 40).

[20] *Dar naprasny* . . . (II, 40-41).

[21] *Perepiska,* No. 425, II, 130.

[22] *Brozhu li ja vdol ulits shumnykh* (II, 73).

[23] *Domik v Kolomne* (III, 259).

[24] *Kamenny gost, Motsart i Saleri, Pir vo vremya chumy, Skupoi rytsar* (III, 396-467).

[25] *Povesti Belkina* (IV, 287).

[26] *Istoriya sela Goriukhina* (IV, 365).

[27] M. A. Tsyavlovski, *Rasskazy o Pushkine, zapisannye so slov ego druzei P. I. Bartenevym* (Moscow: 1925), p. 64.

[28] *Perepiska,* No. 1091, III, 398-399.

[29] A. Ammosov, *Poslednie dni zhizni i konchina A. S. Pushkina* (St. Petersburg: 1863), p. 24.

[30] P. E. Shchegolev, *Duel i smert Pushkina* (Moscow: 1928), p. 194.

PUSHKIN AND THE DECEMBRISTS

By GEORGE V. VERNADSKY

I

The first quarter of the nineteenth century was a significant period in the development of Russian civilization. It witnessed a veritable outburst of spiritual energy in various domains of life and a rapid expansion in the arts, as well as in science, literature, and education. It was the age of Vasili Petrov in physics; of Voronikhin and Zakharov in architecture; of Karamzin in history; and above all, of Pushkin in poetry.

As for the development of Russian political thought, it was primarily the age of the Decembrists. The abortive revolution of December 14 (December 26, Gregorian Calendar),* 1825, did not realize the liberal aspirations of the flower of the Russian gentry and intelligentsia of its time. It was, however, an important landmark in political development. The Decembrists were the forefathers of the Russian Revolution. To use Lenin's words, it was "the Decembrists who awakened Alexander Herzen; and it was Herzen, in his turn, who started revolutionary agitation (in the '60's)."[1]

When we speak of the Decembrists, we mean not only the actual participants in the uprising of 1825, but also the much larger circle of their sympathizers and adherents. The age of the Decembrists was characterized by the rapid spread of liberal ideas in Russia. This was primarily the result of the innate idealism of the best representatives of Russian society at the end of the eighteenth and the beginning of the nineteenth century; and it was accelerated by the influence of the ideas of the French Revolution of 1789.

* Dates quoted are the Julian Calendar unless otherwise stated.

While Russia as a whole was still a bulwark of autocracy, a land of serfdom, the ideas of French enlightenment obtained easy access to the educated *élite*. When the news of the fall of the Bastille reached St. Petersburg, people congratulated each other in the streets. Even the Grand Duke Alexander — the future Tsar Alexander I, — whose tutor was that Swiss democrat La Harpe, expressed his sympathy with the cause of the Revolution and, in fact, later criticized Napoleon for assuming the imperial title instead of remaining an officer of the Republic. The young Count P. A. Stroganov, who happened to be in Paris during the Revolution, actually became a member of one of the Jacobin "sections." He was later a close friend of Alexander I and a member of the "Informal Committee."

During the whole of his reign, Alexander I was interested in liberal reforms. In 1809, Speranski drew up a constitution, and Novosiltsov drafted another in 1820. Although neither was actually adopted, these constitutional projects resulted in some partial administrative reforms, and news of them leaked out to the people. Thus the government itself contributed to the rise of constitutional ideas.

Not only in Russia but elsewhere in Europe, liberalism was in this period closely connected with nationalism. It was again Tsar Alexander who led the Russian intelligentsia in this respect. In his mind the struggle against Napoleon was associated with both the liberal and the nationalistic idea. In his famous instructions to Novosiltsov in September 1804, which may now be regarded as the first plan for a League of Nations, Alexander suggested that the liberation of various nationalities from foreign domination should be considered one of the chief ends of the coalition against Napoleon. This aim was shared by many officers in the Russian army, who felt that in defending Russia from Napoleon they were fighting for the general cause of liberation. On their victorious homecoming in 1815, they were proud not only of their military achievements but also of their prominent role as liberators of Europe.

It was not long, however, before the conflict between the government and public opinion made itself felt in Russia. Although the government had been, in a sense, the promoter of the liberal and nationalistic movement, it now began to proceed much more cautiously. The strain of the war had been terrible. The exchequer was empty, and the newly assumed obligations of international policy required more and more attention. The upkeep of organized international peace necessitated almost as much military strength as the whole preceding series of wars. The fatal idea of organizing the army by means of "military settlements" rooted itself in Alexander's mind, and General Arakcheev became his henchman in this scheme.

Although this did not stop the tsar's constitutional projects (it was as late as 1820 that Novosiltsov's draft of a constitutional charter was completed), the tempo of reform was retarded just when public opinion was clamoring for more. Both police and army were strengthened, and the break was inevitable between the government and the nation. The liberals organized a chain of secret political societies, the beginning of that movement which led to the Decembrist Revolt.

In many cases, the masonic lodges served as a kind of preparatory school for future members of the revolutionary associations. Two main trends were noticeable in freemasonry, which had already played an important role in the intellectual development of Russia in the eighteenth century. One of these, originating in England, was toward a new rationalistic philosophy and system of ethics related to the progress of natural science. The other, which had as its chief exponents the Moscow Rosicrucians,[2] was of a more mystical nature. It was not until the reign of Alexander I that freemasonry emerged from the inactivity imposed upon it by Catherine II toward the end of the eighteenth century. It emerged with more than its old vigor, for now many of the lodges were influenced by radical French freemasonry of the Grand Orient type, which had intrenched itself in Poland and thence spread through Russia.

Masonic ritual was observed in some cases by the founders of revolutionary unions and circles, such as the Primeval Concord, founded in 1818 in the province of Poltava (South Russia) by Borisov, a *junker*, or military cadet; or such as the Union of Salvation, organized in 1817 by Colonel Muravev and Second Captain of Cavalry (later Colonel) Pestel, at St. Petersburg. These two groups became respectively the nuclei of the so-called Southern Union and the Northern Union, which were the main agencies of the Decembrist movement.

In 1818 the Union of Salvation was closed and a Union of Welfare was organized in its stead. The latter was much more moderate in both its program and its tactics, and allowed a larger quota to join its ranks. The leaders of the new Union secretly cultivated, however, the former revolutionary traditions. In order to widen the field of their influence they started a number of affiliated circles and societies, which hid their political tendencies under a devotion to the arts. One of these affiliated societies was The Green Lamp in St. Petersburg, whose avowed purpose was the promotion of literary and historical studies.

At the end of 1820 a mutiny occurred among the soldiers of the Semenovski Guard Regiment which was quickly put down by the government, but resulted in a stricter police surveillance over the liberal leaders. In consequence of this surveillance, the leaders of the movement decided, in January 1821, to dissolve the Union of Welfare, the activities of which were too much in evidence. The next move was a consolidation of the two secret groups, the Northern Union and the Southern Union.

Several different trends may be discerned in the political programs of the revolutionary leaders. Colonel Pestel, who eventually became the head of the Southern Union, was a radical leader of dictatorial type, a follower of the French Jacobins and, in a sense, a predecessor of Lenin. His aim was a democratic republic. Colonel Nikita Muravev, one of the leaders of the Northern Union, supported the more moderate program of a constitutional monarchy. Both Pestel and Muravev drafted their own plans for the future Russian constitution, but neither one was adopted officially by the group.

There was a variety of opinions among the individual members of each of the two societies. Many a future Decembrist suggested the arrest or assassination not only of the tsar but of the whole imperial family, after which a provisional revolutionary government was to be created. There was no unanimity, however, as to the social aspect of the revolution. While all the leaders advocated the abolition of serfdom, some of them were afraid of giving too much political freedom to the masses, and would not have enjoyed seeing the abolition of the imperial autocracy followed by a new autocracy of the mob.

Even more diversity of opinion was apparent among those sympathizers outside the societies. Some of the men of moderate liberal disposition were in sympathy with constitutional reform but would not at all have welcomed any violent revolution. Such persons were happily unaware of the radical tendencies of the leaders, and their loyalty was due wholly to a general spirit of opposition to the existing government.

If Alexander had hastened the realization of his constitutional projects, he could probably have satisfied many of his opponents. But he proceeded with his plans warily and with the utmost secrecy. On the other hand, while he knew of the activities of the societies through his secret agents, he did nothing to stop them.

On November 19, 1825, the tsar died of a fever in Taganrog. Since he had no children, his brother Constantine, the commander-in-chief of the Polish army, was generally considered the heir apparent. Only a few higher dignitaries of the empire were aware that Constantine had resigned the crown in favor of the next brother, Nicholas.

Confusion resulted. After receiving the news of Alexander's death, Nicholas, who was in St. Petersburg at the time, proclaimed Constantine emperor; everybody had to take the oath accordingly. Simultaneously in Warsaw Constantine was swearing fealty to Nicholas. Since there was neither telegraph nor railroad service, the brothers had to rely upon special messengers (*feldjäger*) who rode in carts. It was not until December 12 that Nicholas received Constantine's final refusal of the crown, and on December 14 a new oath was to be taken by the troops.

The leaders of the secret societies decided to take advantage of the situation, and urged the troops to refuse the second oath. Their success was rendered likely by the fact that Nicholas was not popular among the Guards regiments. Thus on December 14, 1825, several regiments refused to pledge their allegiance to Nicholas and proceeded to Senate Square with the cry of "Constantine and Constitution!"[2] Some of the soldiers, so the story goes, were under the impression that "Constitution" was the wife of Constantine.

The revolt might have been successful with better leadership. Prince Sergei Trubetskoi, the dictator-elect, failed to appear at the Square, and Nicholas had an easy victory. The Southern Union had no better luck than the Northern, for its leader, Colonel Pestel, was arrested by police agents almost on the eve of the insurrection. There was only one mutiny among the regiments of the south, and this was easily suppressed by loyal troops. All the leading members of the movement were arrested and tried by the Supreme Criminal Court. Five of the leaders were hanged, among them Colonel Pestel and the poet Ryleev. Over one hundred were sentenced to penal servitude, and many more were exiled to Siberia for a period of years.[3]

Now began the regime of police dictatorship, with the paternalistic government of Nicholas attempting to crush the spirit of liberal initiative. Thirty years later Russia paid for this autocratic victory with the humiliation of the Crimean War.

II

Pushkin, although he took no part in the Decembrist uprising, was closely connected with the liberal movement in Russia. As a matter of fact, there was no marked boundary line between the development of literature and the development of political thought. The liberal movement influenced Pushkin, and he, in turn, was a very important factor in its development. Although he was no revolutionary, many of his early poems sounded an appeal for liberal reform, and these had an appreciable effect on the liberal ideology of his day. They were mentioned specifically at the trial of the Decembrists as having influenced some of the participants, and M. Bestuzhev-Riumin testified that the liberal poems of Pushkin were distributed in manuscript form all through the army.[4]

Pushkin's liberal tendencies were in part the result of his education. As a precocious child he had devoured all the French books on his father's shelves and developed simultaneously a taste for love stories and the ideas of Voltaire. In 1811, at the age of twelve, he entered the newly founded Lyceum at Tsarskoe Selo, near St. Petersburg, and here his liberal predilections received further impetus. The Lyceum was one of the pet institutions of Alexander I and was founded during his intensely liberal phase, while Speranski was in control. Located in one of the annexes of the Tsarskoe Selo imperial palace, it was intended for the children of the nobility and was sufficiently progressive to encourage their spirit of initiative. Corporal punishment was strictly forbidden, a fact which makes the Lyceum something of a phenomenon in early nineteenth-century education. Most of the professors were of decidedly liberal spirit, — notably Kunitsyn and Monsieur de Boudry. The latter was the teacher of French and a brother of the bloodthirsty Marat himself. The students were well instructed in both French and Russian literature, and were also encouraged to try their own hand at poetry. It was in his Lyceum years that Pushkin began writing verse, and here that he found a congenial friend in Baron Delvig who was also a poet, though less talented.

The students at the Lyceum were distinguished by a spontaneous and fervent patriotism. In 1815, when most of the Guards regiments were returning to the capital after the gigantic international struggle, the students struck up a close friendship with the officers of the Hussars, whose quarters were at Tsarskoe Selo. Pushkin and some of his friends were included even in the officers' carousals, and apparently had ample opportunity to discuss political questions with them. It was just at this period that the secret societies were being formed, and many a Guards officer was imbued with revolutionary spirit. Pushkin made two friends who were members of the Union of Welfare, P. P. Kaverin and P. Ya. Chaadaev. The latter was never very active politically, but his powerful mind strongly impressed Pushkin.

In addition to his intimacy with the liberal Guards officers, Pushkin became, in his senior year, a member of Russia's leading literary club, known as the Arzamas. Russia's most prominent poets and authors belonged to this club, including the poet Zhukovski and the historian Karamzin. Its chief aims were to inculcate freedom of thought and to combat the obsolete tendencies in Russian literature. It was not a political club — some of the members being, like Karamzin, conservatives — and when new members insisted on the adoption of a liberal political program, it eventually disintegrated in 1818. But in the meantime these disagreements had given Pushkin the opportunity of meeting such prominent leaders of the secret societies as General M. F. Orlov and Colonel Nikita Muravev, who persistently brought politics into the Arzamas meetings.

At about the time of the dissolution of the Arzamas, Pushkin, together with his Lyceum friend Baron Delvig, joined another literary club known as The Green Lamp. This, as has been mentioned before, was one of the circles affiliated with the Union of Welfare. Several members of the Union were at the same time members of The Green Lamp, among them Kaverin and Prince S. P. Trubetskoi, the future "Dictator" of the Decembrists. The records that have been discovered show that the meetings of the club were devoted mostly to the reading of literary productions by the members, with occasional papers on the political situation of Russia and Europe. Some manuscript copies have been preserved among the minutes of the club, such as the alleged conversation of Napoleon with an English traveler, or *The Dream*, a paper on the future Russian constitution. There was probably a good deal of informal discussion of politics, and more often than not a noisy banquet with plenty of champagne concluded the evening.[5]

It was precisely during the years of Pushkin's membership in The Green Lamp that he wrote most of his political poems and epigrams which made him so popular among the liberals, but eventually caused his exile to South Russia in 1820. Of these the best known are *Noël* (1818), *The Village,* and *The Ode to Freedom* (1819). *The Village* presented a powerful protest against serfdom. Its concluding lines are quoted:

> Will serfdom be abolished at a ruler's nod?
> Shall I see the long-awaited dawn of freedom
> Rising above our fatherland? [6]

It is said that through the intermediary of his friend Chaadaev Pushkin communicated the text of *The Village* to Prince Vasilchikov, who showed it to Tsar Alexander. The latter asked Vasilchikov to thank Pushkin for his poem ("Faites remercier Pouchkine des bons sentiments que ces vers inspirent").

Both *Noël* and *The Ode to Freedom* were much more radical in tone and were not, of course, suitable for presentation to the tsar. Some of the lines of the *Ode* sound like a revolutionary tocsin:

> Now tremble, despots of the world!
> And you, unawakened slaves,—
> Listen, take heart, and revolt! [7]

It contained moreover a reference to the assassination of Paul, Alexander's tyrannical father, which might be interpreted as a direct warning to Alexander himself.

Noël was bitingly derisive of Alexander's liberal pretensions, which Pushkin suggested would never be realized:

> Thus spake the Tsar:
> "O my people, listen!...
> In my imperial wisdom
> I have deemed it best
> To give all human rights to men."
>
> The little child
> Leaped joyously from bed...
> "Hush," his mother said,
> "Close your eyes and go to sleep;
> You will play another time.
> That was only Papa Tsar
> Telling you a nursery rhyme." [8]

None of Pushkin's liberal poems could be printed at the time because of the censorship, but they all had a wide circulation in manuscript form. He used to read *Noël* at the informal meetings of St. Petersburg liberals. About a decade later he described these meetings in the following verses:

> Eloquent members of this intrepid family
> Were wont to meet with reckless Nikita *
> Or with the prudent Ilya. . . .**
> Lunin, friend of Bacchus, Mars, and Venus,
> Thought himself to be in France,
> And cried aloud for revolution,
> While the lonely Yakushkin caressed a regicidal knife.
> Pushkin read aloud *"Noëls"*, and the lame Turgenev,
> Loving only Russia in the world, listened silently,
> Foreseeing in these noblemen the liberators of the serf. [9]

* Nikita Muravev.
** Prince Ilya Dolgoruki

Thus, according to Pushkin's own testimony, there can hardly be any doubt that he was for all practical purposes one of the liberals of his day. He was not, however, a formal member of any of the secret societies, except for The Green Lamp which, as we have said, was affiliated with the Union of Walfare. There is evidence in some contemporary memoirs that the leaders of the secret societies would not accept Pushkin as a member because of his versatile character. They were afraid that he would not be able to keep their decisions secret. On the other hand, Pushkin did not take the liberal movement of this period too seriously:

> At first the brave conspiring over banquet wine
> Was table-talk to which the heart attended not.[10]

III

By 1820 the liberal poems of Pushkin had attracted the attention of the authorities. Count Miloradovich, the military governor of St. Petersburg, obtained possession of the manuscript of *The Ode to Freedom* and reported the matter to the tsar. Alexander must have been particularly offended by those lines of the *Ode* that referred to the assassination of his father. He was always sensitive on this point. The plotters of 1801 had had his consent for Paul's arrest, and although he had not sanctioned the murder, throughout his life he felt morally responsible for it, and he never forgave any allusion to the matter. Indeed, his enmity toward Napoleon may be traced partially to this cause, for the latter's answer to the Russian protest against the murder of the Duke of Enghien had contained a transparent hint about Paul's assassination. Under the circumstances it is not surprising that Alexander harbored a personal distaste for Pushkin during the whole of his life.

Pushkin, too, felt a keen dislike for Alexander's personality, quite apart from questions of policy. In his draft of the tenth

chapter of *Eugene Onegin* (1830) Pushkin referred to Alexander
in these words:

> Our bald hero, dauntless fop,
> Who laughed at everything
> But danger, thought Creation stopped
> The day it crowned him King.[11]

Since this prejudice existed before Pushkin's exile, when he could
hardly have had any personal motive for it, it must be explained
on purely psychological grounds. His mentality was strikingly
different from Alexander's: his passionate emotional nature had
nothing in common with the tsar's spurious sentimentality.
Alexander was an actor on the political stage; there was nothing
sincere about him, and Pushkin could tolerate anything but in-
sincerity in his fellowman. Furthermore, Alexander was primarily
interested in abstract political theories, with little taste for real
life, and a tendency toward mysticism made him, as time went on,
rather inert and apathetic. Such a man could have no claim on
Pushkin's admiration. It was Peter the Great who appealed to
him as the ideal ruler, and the two tsars had nothing in common.

Anticipating a search for his manuscripts, Pushkin burnt all
the original copies of his political verse. But when he was summoned before Miloradovich and questioned about them, he
asked defiantly for pen and paper and wrote them down from
memory. Miloradovich praised his chivalry, but this did not save
him from punishment. In his capacity of civil servant (he had a
sinecure position as a minor clerk in the Ministry of Foreign
Affairs) he was transferred from St. Petersburg to South Russia.
Although technically this was not exile, it was understood as such
by Pushkin and his friends.

He spent four years in South Russia (1820-1824), first in Kishinev (in Bessarabia) and finally in Odessa. He had also the
opportunity of traveling in the Northern Caucasus and the
Crimea, and this period of his life was significant in the development both of his poetic mastery and his liberal ideas.

Bessarabia, which had been annexed to Russia less than a decade before, was still a primitive country, but it had the advantage, for Pushkin, of being near the stage of the Greek Revolution. Although he soon became disappointed in Greek and Moldavian leaders, his liberal sympathies were at first very much stirred, and there is evidence that at one time he even contemplated joining Ypsilanti's band. The Greek uprising produced some apprehension in Russia as to possible war with Turkey, and troops were therefore stationed along the Moldavian frontier. Liberal leaders took advantage of this situation in order to spread radical propaganda among the officers of the Second Army. It was about this time that the famous Southern Union came into existence, with Pestel and Muravev-Apostol as its leaders.

Since Pushkin had been so close to the liberal leaders in St. Petersburg, it was natural that he should now renew some of the older friendships and form new ones. It may also be noted that just at this time he joined the ranks of the freemasons and was accepted into the Kishinev lodge. The legal existence of freemasonry was near its end, for in 1822 all the lodges were closed by order of the government.

As a poet Pushkin was already popular among the liberals, but now as an exile he had a new halo about him. In April 1821, he met Pestel for the first time and was greatly impressed by his personality. There is a characteristic entry in Pushkin's diary for April ninth: "I have spent the whole morning with Pestel. He is a clever man in the full sense of the word. He says, 'Mon coeur est materialiste mais ma raison s'y refuse.' We had a talk with him on metaphysics, politics, morals, etc.... His is one of the most original minds I know." [12] Although he never became very intimate with Pestel, he was on close terms with many other members of the Southern Union who gathered at Kamenka, the country estate of a Madame Davydova. Kamenka was situated on the river of the same name in the province of Kiev. This estate was not far from Tulchin (the headquarters of the Second Army) and frequently served as a meeting place for liberal army officers. Pushkin was received with warm friendship in the families of both the Davydovs and the Raevskis. The head of the Raevski family was a prominent general in the Russian army who had been a hero of the war of 1812. While not a liberal himself, he was nevertheless very tolerant, and his two sons, both brilliant army officers and Pushkin's close friends, were frankly associated with the liberals. His eldest daughter, Ekaterina, was married to General M. F. Orlov, one of the influential leaders of the liberal party. Pushkin had met Orlov several years previously in St. Petersburg, when they were both members of the Arzamas literary club.[13]

Another of Raevski's daughters, Mariya, later became the bride of Prince Sergei Volkonski. This was a few months before his arrest as a Decembrist, and Mariya followed him in his Siberian exile. She became a legendary figure for subsequent generations, and one of the most popular feminine types among the Russian intelligentsia.[14]

Pushkin, always susceptible to feminine charms, fell in love with Ekaterina and then with Mariya Raevskaya, and was spurned by each. Most of Pushkin's biographers have suggested that his love for Mariya was very profound and lasted all his life, but in my opinion there is no valid evidence for this surmise.

As a close friend of the Raevski family, Pushkin spent a good deal of time at Kamenka, and took a lively part in the gay social life there. He courted the French wife of one of the Davydov brothers, apparently with success, but he was also much interested in the political discussions which were habitual with his hosts, and together they used to drink to the success of both the Russian and the European revolutions.

It must have been after some of these political discussions that Pushkin wrote his *Dagger*, a frank defense of revolutionary terrorism. The opening stanza follows:

The Lemnian god forged thee, mighty sword,
For use of the Eternal Nemesis.
Thou art the secret guard of Freedom,
The last avenger of disgrace and tyranny.[15]

It was also during his life in the south that Pushkin wrote his
blasphemous *Gavriliada,* a satire on both idealistic love and the
dogma of the Greek Orthodox Church, which was not printed in
Russia until after the Revolution of 1917. While not in any
sense a manifestation of political liberalism, the *Gavriliada* is
nevertheless characteristic of the poet's state of mind during this
period, — irritated as he was against both State and Church.

Although he was not formally a member of the Southern
Union, Pushkin was well aware of its plans, as is shown in the
tenth chapter of *Eugene Onegin.* He had not taken the liberal
agitation in St. Petersburg from 1817 to 1820 any too seriously,[16]
but now he was forced to change his opinion. Let us quote
again from the tenth chapter:

> So it was on the icy Neva,
> But on the shadowy Kamenka,
> On the hills of Tulchin,
>
> .   .   .   .   .   .
>
> Pestel, armed against the tyrants,
> An honest war began.
> Muravev * explosively demanding action,
> While their tranquil leader **
> Trained his forces.[17]

Pushkin's stay in the south came to an unexpected end in 1824,
when he was suddenly dismissed from civil service and deported to
his father's estate in the province of Pskov (northwestern Russia),
where he was to live under police surveillance. The pretext for
this exile was apparently furnished by a letter which Pushkin
had written from Odessa and which was intercepted by the police.
It contained the remark that he was taking lessons from an

* Sergei Muravev-Apostol.
** General Yushnevski.

Englishman [18] in "pure atheism." Biographers say that a con-
tributing cause for this punishment was the jealousy of Count
Vorontsov, the governor-general of South Russia, with whose
wife Pushkin had become rather too intimate.

Pushkin was under no very strict police surveillance at Pskov,
but he felt keenly the separation from his liberal friends. He kept
up a correspondence with some of them, but of course political
subjects had to be avoided. His time was divided between literary
work (he was continuing *Eugene Onegin,* begun in Kishinev) and
love affairs. He became the close friend of a neighboring squire's
family and was a frequent visitor at their estate, Trigorskoe, one
of the typical "gentlemen's nests" of the period.

It must have been a welcome surprise when one of his closest
Lyceum friends, Ivan Pushchin, came to spend a day with him.
This intrepid visitor was now a judge in a Moscow court and, as
an influential member of the Northern Union, he was able to give
Pushkin the latest political news. Although, according to Push-
chin's memoirs, he avoided any mention of specific plans of the
Union, because his friend was not a member, Pushkin was well
enough posted to be able to fill in the blanks for himself.

IV

At the beginning of December 1825, news of the death of
Alexander I reached Pushkin. His comment was, according to
the report of a secret police agent: "At last the tyrant is no more;
let us hope that none of the family will be alive much longer."

On the evening of December 10, while Pushkin was visiting
his neighbors at Trigorskoe, a servant returned from St. Petersburg with news that the troops had been called out in the capital
and that the situation was tense (this was during the time of the
interregnum).[19] Pushkin turned pale and rushed home. He
started for St. Petersburg early the next morning, with the intention of going straight to Ryleev, who was then leader of the
Northern Union.

The revolution, in which Pushkin apparently wanted to take an active part, must have appealed to him from personal as well as theoretical motives, since it provided an escape from his exile and the promise of a free life. Of course, it was dangerous: if he joined his rebel friends he staked his life on their victory.

After driving a few miles toward St. Petersburg, Pushkin suddenly decided to give up the adventure and turn back. They say that on the way he encountered a priest and that a hare crossed his path — both very bad omens in Russian folklore. Pushkin was inclined to be superstitious, and in his state of nervous excitement it is quite possible that he took the omens seriously. At any rate, he turned back.

The next few days passed without news, and then came reports of the failure of the revolution and the subsequent governmental terrorism. Pushkin's first thought was that he would be arrested because of his friendly relations with so many revolutionary leaders. For some time he remained very quiet, burning all his manuscripts that contained any reference to the liberal movement, and not daring even to correspond with his friends. But days went by and still no police appeared at Mikhailovskoe.

Pushkin began a realistic analysis of the situation. If the government did not consider him a member of the revolutionary group, might there not be a chance for him to take advantage of the new reign by asking for a termination of his exile? Accordingly, at the end of January 1826, he decided to write to Zhukovski, a conservative poet who enjoyed the complete confidence of several members of the imperial family.

"You are quite right," answered Zhukovski (in April 1826), "in claiming that you have no direct connection with the conspiracy. However, all those who were arrested had copies of your verses among their papers, which does not seem an auspicious beginning for your friendship with the government." [20] Nevertheless, Zhukovski, as well as other influential and conservative friends, made every effort to extricate Pushkin from the impasse, and after sounding out the new tsar they found the situation far from hopeless.

It had been obvious from the first that Nicholas intended to punish the ringleaders with the utmost severity. In addition to strengthening the police, a special "Third Section" had been organized to concentrate the activities of the secret police. General Benkendorf, a Baltic German whose loyalty could be trusted, was appointed head of the Third Section and chief of the new gendarmes.

On the other hand, Nicholas wondered whether some political lessons might not be drawn from the events of December. He had a résumé compiled of the Decembrists' suggestions as to administrative, judiciary, and economic reforms, and he actually consulted these suggestions before his next administrative move. He saw, too, that the government should try to increase its moral authority by effecting some reconciliation with public opinion. Bulgarin, that sly reactionary journalist, presented Nicholas with a memorandum on the necessity of taming the "Lyceum spirit" among the liberals by courting individual leaders and heaping them with benefits. It was in this spirit that Nicholas approached Pushkin's case. Pushkin's animosity toward Alexander did not trouble him, since he himself had not been over-fond of his late brother.

On July 13, 1826 the five ringleaders of the Decembrists were hanged. Immediately after this Nicholas decided to settle Pushkin's case. Accordingly, on July 19 a special agent of the secret police was sent to the province of Pskov to gather information about Pushkin's political activities, but no traces were found of the latter's alleged revolutionary propaganda among the peasants. In fact, the only suspicious circumstance that the agent was able to unearth was that Pushkin had appeared at a public function, such as the fair at the Svyatorgski Monastery, dressed in a red peasant shirt, with a pink sash and a wide-brimmed hat, carrying an iron cane. In spite of his dislike for informal dress, Nicholas found nothing particularly dangerous in Pushkin's behavior, and was inclined to look with favor on his petition of June 1826. (Pushkin had pleaded ill health and asked permission to seek medical advice in some Russian or European center). At this juncture, however, a new circumstance arose which nearly ruined the poet.

In August 1826, the Moscow agents of the Third Section seized the manuscript of a revolutionary poem which was circulating among the army officers. One stanza read:

> Where are freedom and the law?
> Our only ruler is the axe. Tyrants are dethroned,
> But we choose executioners and hangmen for our tsars! [21]

According to the information of the Third Section, this poem was a direct reference to the Decembrist affair, and its author was Pushkin. Nicholas, who was in Moscow awaiting his coronation, had been just about to grant the poet a complete pardon when he received Benkendorf's report of this latest scandal. He decided on immediate action and sent a special messenger (*feldjäger*) to the province of Pskov to bring the culprit back post haste for a personal interview.

Apparently Pushkin's fate hung upon this interview. He was brought to Moscow on August 28 and received immediately by the tsar. It is said that Nicholas first asked him where he would have been on December 14 if he had happened to be in St. Petersburg. Pushkin answered without hesitation, "I would have been in the ranks of the rebels," [22] and Nicholas commended him for his frankness. We have no record of this conversation, but we may assume that the next question dealt with the recently discovered poem. On this point Pushkin was able to give a completely satisfactory explanation. There was no need to deny his authorship: the poem had been written before the Decembrist affair, and it referred to the French Revolution. In fact, it was dedicated to the memory of André Chénier,[23] and it had already appeared in print at the end of 1825, — with the omission of the offending stanza, to be sure, but with the censor's approval. The whole affair seemed to be just a blunder of the police.[24] Having cleared up this point, the tsar offered Pushkin his friendship, and promised him freedom from the regular censorship on condition that the poet show him all his future productions before they were printed.

Pushkin was overwhelmed at this reception and believed at once in the tsar's sincerity. His unexpected appearance in the parquet of the Grand Theater produced quite a sensation, and it was generally felt that Nicholas had behaved with extreme magnanimity. In fact, Nicholas' behavior proved to be a political masterpiece. It was only gradually that Pushkin began to realize that he had fallen into a trap. Ostensibly he was free, but actually he was the tsar's hostage under the supervision of General Benkendorf, and before long he was to be entangled in a net of suspicion, intrigue, and blackmail.

V

The tragedy of the Decembrists left an indelible impression upon Pushkin. So many of them were his close friends, and he had come very close to being one of them. Immediately after getting news of their failure, he destroyed, as we have seen,[25] all his papers relating to the activities of the secret societies. But he left us an unconscious record in his literary manuscripts.

Pushkin had one idiosyncrasy that has been invaluable to his biographers. While he was working on a poem he used to draw pictures on the same sheet of paper — faces, profiles, etc. Some of these drawings illustrate the poem, but others are far removed from his poetic creation and reveal the extraneous problems occupying his mind. Thus we are in a position to state that while starting the fifth chapter of *Eugene Onegin* on January 4, 1826, Pushkin was haunted by thoughts of revolution: the margins of two pages of this manuscript are covered with profiles of revolutionary leaders.[26] On one page we find the profiles of Pestel, Ryleev, Mirabeau and Voltaire — Voltaire being included, probably, as the father of the revolutionary movement. It is interesting to note one face that bears some resemblance to both Robespierre and Pushkin himself, giving rise to the speculation that the poet was thinking of his own participation in a future revolution, and so stylized his face to resemble Robespierre. On the next page we find profiles of Pestel, Pushchin, and Pushkin again, — but without any transmutation — Prince Vyazemski, Kiukhelbeker, and Ryleev. This preoccupation with Pestel and Ryleev — the leaders of the Southern and Northern Unions — seems to show that Pushkin had been well informed about the development of revolutionary policies, for at this time (the beginning of January, 1826) he could have had no new information about the roles of individual leaders.

Sometime at the end of January, when he was staying with his neighbors at Trigorskoe, he drew for them another series of profiles of people connected with the December uprising. There we find Ryleev, Prince Trubetskoi, and Pushchin, representing the Northern Union, and Pestel, the two Raevski brothers, and Davydov representing the Southern Union. Near the profile of Nikolai Raevski there is a picture of an unknown lady, — possibly Raevski's sister, Ekaterina Orlov, one of Pushkin's former loves. At the end of April or the beginning of May Pushkin drew another series of faces — this time Pestel, Trubetskoi and Ryleev, as well as Prince and Princess Vyazemski. At the end of July, after he had learned of the execution of the five Decembrists, there appeared in his manuscripts the picture of a gallows, with five men hanged, and the following caption: "And I could (have been hanged) as a buffoon." [27]

Trubetskoi, the dictator-elect who remained away on the fateful day of December 14, appears several times in Pushkin's drawings. Once he is shown facing the gallows, as if Pushkin were dwelling on the fact that Trubetskoi would have been hanged had he not deserted the revolutionaries. Perhaps the artist was haunted by a parallel between his own case and that of the deserter.

While he was trying to make his peace with the tsar, Pushkin did not disown his exiled friends. In addition to his efforts of intervention on their behalf — which we shall discuss later — he rendered them a real service in their isolation by sending them messages of friendliness and encouragement. On December 13, 1826, — a tragic anniversary — he sent an affectionate poem to Push-chin, exiled in Siberia. Pushchin did not receive the poem until 1828, when Madame Muraveva arrived in Siberia to join her husband, but his diary records how precious to him was Pushkin's moral support. Madame Muraveva brought the Decembrists another poem of Pushkin's, his *Epistle to Siberia*, written in 1827:

> Even in the deep Siberian mines
> You keep your proud endurance.
> Your work and your high effort
> Shall not have been in vain.
> Hope, the faithful sister of misfortune,
> Shall awaken courage once again;
> Friendship and love will speak to you
> As now my free voice reaches through stone.
> The chains will fall, and prisons be destroyed.
> Your brothers wait: we hold your swords unused.[28]

Prince A. I. Odoevski answered Pushkin on behalf of the others, saying, in effect, "The spark will start a big blaze." [29] On October 19, 1827 — the anniversary of the founding of the Lyceum — Pushkin sent greetings again to his Lyceum friends among the exiles:

> O God! Be with my friends and comfort them
>   In storms, in desert seas, . . .
> In all the gloomy chasms of the earth.[30]

A few months earlier, in July 1827, Pushkin had written of his own role in the Decembrist movement in the beautiful poem *Arion*:

The boat was holding many of us...
And I was singing to the men.
A sudden storm smashed the surface of the sea;
The captain perished with all his sailors,
And I, alone and strange, escaped to a barren shore.
Under the white cliffs I dry my clothes, singing the old songs.[31]

While Pushkin thought that the storm had ended as far as he was concerned, new clouds were gathering over his head. In May 1828, an army officer was arrested in St. Petersburg on the charge of circulating manuscript copies of an atheistic poem, and one of the copies was seized by the police. It was Pushkin's *Gavriliada*.

Summoned before the military governor of St. Petersburg, Pushkin at first denied his authorship. Then he asked permission to write a personal letter to the tsar. Although the letter was delivered to Nicholas, it has since been destroyed, and we can only surmise that it contained a frank confession. In any case, the affair was dropped by the police.

Pushkin was working on his *Poltava* when the *Gavriliada* affair broke. His anxiety did not stop his literary composition, but he was not apparently very sanguine about the outcome of the case, for on one page of the manuscript of *Poltava* we find the familiar drawing of the gallows, with the five men hanged.

A year later Pushkin decided to portray the Decembrist movement in the tenth chapter of *Eugene Onegin*. Unfortunately, he burned the manuscript in 1830 and never rewrote it. We may assume that fear of the police caused its destruction. A few fragments of this chapter remain, however, written in such an effective code that they not only escaped police censorship after Pushkin's death,[32] but they were a puzzle to the literary historians themselves until recently.[33] Pushkin had intentionally mixed the verses, writing consecutive lines in different corners of the page, and even special students of Pushkin paid no attention to these drafts until 1910, when P. O. Morozov succeeded in deciphering the manuscript. Only a small part of the tenth chapter has been saved in this way, however, — most of it having been destroyed by Pushkin — and the most significant quotations have already been given.[34]

VI

Pushkin was not content with writing about the Decembrists and sending them cheerful verses: he carried on a campaign in their behalf with the government. Immediately after he heard of the execution of the five conspirators (July 13, 1826), he resolved to do what he could toward saving the others. "The hanged are hanged," he wrote realistically to Vyazemski on August 14, "but hard labor for one hundred and twenty friends, brothers, and comrades is a terrible thing";[35] and he expressed his hope that the coronation of Nicholas I would bring them pardon.

But the coronation brought pardon only to Pushkin himself, and now he tried to use his new friendship with Nicholas in order to get his friends' sentences commuted. Methodically, in a series of poems beginning with the *Stanzas* of December 22, 1826, he urged the tsar to reprieve the Decembrists.

The *Stanzas,* for which Pushkin was severely criticized by the liberals, opened with a parallel between the Decembrist uprising and the mutiny of the Streltsy at the beginning of Peter the Great's reign.

> I see a future filled with glory...
> Was not the shining reign of Peter
> Begun in shame and bloodshed? [36]

Since Peter the Great was Pushkin's hero, the parallel was meant to be especially flattering. Pushkin concluded his poem by reminding Nicholas that his renowned ancestor may have been severe in suppressing treason, but that he was not vindictive toward his enemies — a statement which may seem a trifle over-enthusiastic.

> Take pride in family likeness;
> Be in all things as your forefather:
> Firm and untiring in vigilance,
> In mercy indefatigable.[87]

In 1828, Pushkin wrote another poem, entitled *To My Friends,* in which he defended himself against the accusations of the liberals that he had become a court flatterer. He pointed out the fact that a flatterer would never intervene in behalf of those who were under the tsar's disfavor.

Before long, apparently, Pushkin began to doubt Nicholas' sincerity with regard to himself as well as to the others. Part of the poem *Oprichnik* (the bodyguard of Ivan the Terrible), written in the same year as the epistle *To My Friends*, pictures sixteenth-century Moscow after Ivan's terrorism, and may have reflected some of Pushkin's secret thoughts.

Although he continued now and then to express his admiration for the tsar, there was always an admixture of doubt. A poem, *The Hero* (1830), is a characteristic example. It was written on the occasion of Nicholas' arrival in Moscow during the cholera epidemic. (Cholera was then considered as contagious as the plague). *The Hero* is a dialogue between the poet and a friend. The poet expresses his admiration of Napoleon for shaking hands with his plague-stricken soldiers during the Levant campaign. The friend warns him that this is a legend rejected by historians, and the poet answers thus:

> Let us cling to our illusions of glory,
> For they are more true than facts;
> Take not his great heart from the hero
> Lest you reveal but a tyrant.[88]

This was probably intended as a warning to Nicholas.

All Pushkin's poetical interventions in favor of the Decembrists were useless, but he could not help repeating them from time to time, since they seemed to him part of his moral obligation toward his friends. Again in 1830 Pushkin wrote a poem called *Peter the Great's Feast*, emphasizing his belief that Peter's greatest joy was to pardon the guilty. While hardly true historically, this was again intended primarily for official consumption.

A few months before his death Pushkin wrote his celebrated *Monument*, in which he asserted his claim to immortality. The following lines may be quoted here:

> Long will the people remember me
>
> . . . .
>
> For in this cruel age I have glorified Freedom,
> I have invoked mercy toward the fallen.[39]

VII

In the preceding sections we have dealt chiefly with the personal aspects of Pushkin's attitude toward the Decembrists. No less important was his attitude as an historian or political philosopher. Imbued with the liberal spirit in his youth, Pushkin in the last decade of his life became a conservative. A few signs of this change were apparent even before 1825, and made it easier for the poet to conclude a truce with the tsar in 1826. The shift to the conservative camp was accelerated by the benevolent friendship which Nicholas offered. However, we must remember that although Pushkin became a conservative he never became a reactionary. Until his death he valued individual rights and individual freedom, and he struggled desperately against Nicholas' henchmen for his own freedom of thought and research. But now, a monarchy limited by aristocracy, and not a democratic revolution seemed to him the best remedy for despotism.

On the other hand, even before 1825, Pushkin had not been an implacable radical, in spite of the fact that his poems were so popular among those of the left wing. Leaving aside his dislike for the personality of Alexander I, his earlier poems may be considered rather moderate from the point of view of political theory.

A passage in his *Ode to Freedom* (1819) [40] is particularly characteristic:

> Sovereigns, do you forget the law which crowned you?
> An Eternal Law requiring your obeisance,
> As you demand it from the people.[41]

His poetry was apparently directed against the reactionary "naturalistic" theories of state sovereignty which flourished in France and Germany in the first two decades of the nineteenth century. According to these theories, the ruler's authority was founded on force (as an expression of Nature) and not on the law. Such were, for example, the views of Ludwig von Haller, the noted Swiss student of government (whose first volume, *Restoration of Political Science*, was published in 1816), or the French reactionary philosopher, the Marquis de Bonald.[42]

However, while opposing reactionary political theories, Pushkin did not subscribe to the idea of the *contrat social* which was so popular with the leaders of the French Revolution. He believed that the law was not only superior to the will of sovereigns but to the people as well:

> Woe to that nation
> Where the law is trampled under foot
> By people or by king.[43]

The lawlessness of revolutionary terror was repulsive to Pushkin. To quote his description of the execution of Louis XVI:

> No law, no mercy speaks in protest.
> The criminal axe descends...
> Behold! The murderer's purple
> Has covered the shackled Gauls.[44]

The same motif is again emphasized in his *André Chénier* (1825).

While taking part in the political discussions of radical leaders in South Russia, Pushkin must have sometimes wondered whether the victory of Pestel and his associates would not mean a regime of terror like that in France. On the other hand, he grew rather pessimistic about the people's readiness for liberal ideas, and sometimes revolutionary propaganda seemed to him futile because of their indifference. This discouragement is plainly expressed in his poetic comment on the *Parable of the Sower* (1823):

> Sowing seeds of freedom in the desert,
> I went too soon before the morning star,...
> And I shall reap but mockery and hatred.
> Graze on, happy people!
> The cry of liberty will not awake you;
> No troubling sound will stir your peaceful herds.[45]

After the failure of the Decembrist uprising Pushkin's political conservatism rapidly increased. He was now almost certain that even in the event of their victory the rebels would not be able to control the forces of revolution, nor produce an ordered society. There would have been merely a repetition of the terror and dictatorship of France. He doubted whether a social upheaval would benefit Russia, whose civilization seemed to him essentially aristocratic. What would become of his country after the ruin of her upper classes?

The possibility of violent revolution in Russia haunted Pushkin until his death. In fact, most of his literary work after 1825 was devoted to a study of the problem, chiefly from an historical point of view. Thus, for example, the plot of *Poltava* is concerned with the Cossack uprising of Hetman Mazepa against Peter the Great. Recently some of Russia's literary historians have even tried to interpret *Poltava* as a symbolic picture of the Decembrists, but I think there is insufficient evidence for such an interpretation. In 1829 or 1830 Pushkin, as has already been mentioned, wrote the tenth chapter of *Eugene Onegin*, containing scenes from the revolutionary movement in Russia up until 1825.

In 1830-1831 the Polish uprising occurred, followed by the mutiny of several Russian regiments in the Novgorod military settlement. Both these events produced a tremendous impression upon Pushkin. It was soon after this that he began work on the history of the Pugachev uprising of 1773-1774, a peasant revolt which was suppressed only with the utmost difficulty by Catherine II's generals. Pushkin finished his history in 1833, and in the same year wrote his *Captain's Daughter*, a charming novel which also dealt with the Pugachev revolt. While studying the historical background of peasant revolution in Russia, Pushkin never forgot the possibility of a political revolution led by the radical intelligentsia, of which both Radishchev and the Decembrists might be considered the forerunners.

It is with such associations in mind that we must approach Pushkin's poem *The Bronze Horseman*, which he wrote in October 1833, and which may be considered in some respects his poetic masterpiece. The title refers to the equestrian statue of Peter the Great by Falconet which stands in Senate Square, St. Petersburg, and which was for Pushkin the symbol of imperial Russia. The poem itself is a history of the St. Petersburg flood of 1824, and begins with the founding of the city at the mouth of the Neva by Peter the Great. It is, in a sense, a hymn to the glory of the empire. But Pushkin sees clearly that Peter has reared his empire on the very edge of an abyss, with the forces of nature and social revolt constantly threatening to pull it down.

> O mighty king of Fate!
> Curbing Russia with an iron bit,
> You brought her to a plunging stop
> Upon a crumbling precipice.[46]

It is only natural that Pushkin, while meditating on the possibilities of revolution, should have foreseen a time when the horseman would be cast down from his horse. Among his manuscript drawings of 1829 — about the date of the tenth chapter of *Eugene Onegin* — we find this precise thought: a picture of the horse of Falconet's monument without the horseman. The drawing is characteristic enough. In my opinion it reflects Pushkin's vision of what would become of Russia in case of the success of the Decembrists.

One theme of *The Bronze Horseman* is the personal tragedy of Eugene, a poor *chinovnik* (civil servant), whose fiancée has been drowned in the flood. Eugene goes mad and holds Peter the Great — the founder of the city — responsible for her death. Standing before Falconet's monument, he brandishes his fist at the emperor, and then to his terror he sees the figure of Peter start toward him. He flees through the city streets, hearing the Bronze Horseman's footsteps behind him all the way. In the morning Eugene is found dead on the roadway. The story of Eugene is but one motif of the poem. The main philosophical theme is the conflict between the State and the spirit of opposition — between imperial autocracy and revolution.

The description of the flood of 1824 must have reminded the contemporary reader of the events of 1825, since the waves of the Neva, attacking the lofty buildings of St. Petersburg, were for Pushkin symbolic of human crowds in revolt against peace and order. And he was almost literally quoting from his own description of the Pugachev uprising, which he believed would be re-enacted in case of a revolution:

> Thievish waves plunder the houses, climbing to the windows,
> As brigands plunder a village, — looting, breaking, slaughtering.
> Everywhere is blood and violence.[47]

Other symbolic touches find their way into the poem: for example, it was in Senate Square that Eugene was caught by the flood, and there he unsuccessfully defied the Bronze Horseman:

> Now Eugene's mind was clear...
> Again he saw the waves that crowded in revolt;
> He knew the lions and the Square.[48]

And of course that Square had served as a stage for the Decembrist revolt. If Pushkin was unable, because of imperial censorship, to mention this revolt in so many words, the reader would then be able to complete the analogy for himself.

The poem is, of course, much more than a commentary on the

Decembrists, not only because the full meaning of a true poetic work can never be explained by its subject-matter alone, but also because *The Bronze Horseman* — almost more than any other of Pushkin's poems — contains a wealth of allusive background which must be grasped for its full appreciation. But if we accept as one aspect the symbolic interpretation outlined above, then *The Bronze Horseman* stands as Pushkin's poetic comment upon the events of December 14, 1825.

YALE UNIVERSITY

NOTES

[1] V. I. Lenin, "Pamyati Gertsena," *Polnoe sobranie sochineni* (2 ed., Moscow: 1929), XV, 468.

[2] On European freemasonry in the eighteenth century see Bernard Faÿ, *Revolution and Freemasonry* (Boston: 1935); for a study of freemasonry in Russia see A. N. Pypin, *Russkoe Masonstvo,* ed. G. Vernadsky (Petrograd: 1916); G. Vernadsky, *Russkoe Masonstvo pri Ekaterine II* (Petrograd: 1917).

[3] For a study of the Decembrists see A. Kornilov, *Modern Russian History* (New York: 1924), chapters XII-XIV. The most important collection of sources is *Vosstanie Dekabristov* (Leningrad: 1925). See also V. I. Semevski, *Politicheskiya i obshchestvennyya idei Dekabristov* (St. Petersburg: 1909).

[4] *Vosstanie Dekabristov,* I, pp. XVII, 430. Cf. also P. E. Shchegolev, *Pushkin* (St. Petersburg: 1912), pp. 224-236.

[5] Cf. P. E. Shchegolev, *Pushkin,* pp. 1-21; B. L. Modzalevski, "K istorii zelenoi lampy," *Dekabristy i ikh vremya* (Moscow: 1928), I, 11-61.

[6] *Derevnya* (I, 284).

[7] *Volnost* (I, 270).

[8] *Noël* (I, 533-534).

[9] B. Tomashevski, "Desyataya glava *Evgeniya Onegina,*" *Literaturnoe Nasledstvo* (Moscow: 1934), p. 398.

[10] *Ibid.,* p. 400.

[11] *Ibid.,* p. 392.

[12] *Iz Kishinevskogo Dnevnika* (VI, 372).

[13] See section II.

[14] The poet Nekrasov glorified Princess Mariya Volkonskaya in his poem *Russian Women.* This is available in a translation by Juliet M. Soskice (World's Classics, Oxford University Press).

[15] *Kinzhal* (I, 317).

[16] See section II.

[17] B. Tomashevski, "Desyataya glava *Evgeniya Onegina,*" p. 399.

[18] The name of the Englishman, as quoted by Annenkov (Pushkin's first biographer), was Hunchison. According to Annenkov's information, Hunchison later returned to London and became rector of a church there. Cf. P. V. Annenkov, *Pushkin v aleksandrovskuiu epokhu* (St. Petersburg: 1874), p. 270.

[19] See section I.

[20] *Perepiska,* No. 248, I, 340.

[21] *André Chénier* (I, 395).

[22] M. A. Korf, "Zapiski," *Russkaya Starina* (1900), CI, 574.

[23] P. E. Shchegolev, *Pushkin,* pp. 266-306.

[24] The unfortunate army officers who copied Pushkin's poem and apparently referred it to the Decembrists' cause were tried and demoted to the ranks.

[25] See section IV.

[26] See A. Efros, *Risunki poeta* (Academia, Leningrad: 1933), pp. 318 ff.; "Dekabristy v risunkakh Pushkina," *Literaturnoe Nasledstvo* (Moscow: 1934), pp. 923-946.

[27] Tetrad 2368, list 38; cf. also A. Efros, *Risunki poeta,* pp. 221, 356.

[28] *V Sibir* (II, 19).

[29] Cf. I. A. Kubasov, *Dekabrist A. I. Odoevski* (St. Petersburg: 1922), p. 73. In 1900 this quotation suggested to Lenin the motto of the Social Democrat magazine, *Iskra* ("Spark"), a publication that played an important role in promoting the revolutionary movement.

[30] *19 Oktyabrya, 1827 g.* (II, 25).

[31] *Arion* (II, 23). Arion was a Greek poet of the fifth century B.C. According to legend, when he was robbed and thrown into the sea by Corinthian sailors, a dolphin became enchanted by his singing and carried him to shore.

[32] Pushkin's papers were sealed by order of the tsar, and General Dubelt of the Third Section was assigned to assist Zhukovski in examining them. The remains of the tenth chapter of *Eugene Onegin* aroused no suspicion, and General Dubelt simply added them to the files of Pushkin's manuscripts.

[33] B. V. Tomashevski, "Desyataya glava *Evgeniya Onegina*," pp. 378-420.

[34] See sections II and III.

[35] *Perepiska,* No. 264, I, 364.

[36] *Stansy* (II, 17).

[37] *Ibid.*

[38] *Geroi* (II, 96).

[39] *Pamyatnik* (II, 190).

[40] See section II.

[41] *Volnost* (I, 270).

[42] Cf. V. Valdenberg, "Priroda i zakon v politicheskikh vozzrenyakh Pushkina," *Slavia* (1925-1926), IV, 63-81.

[43] *Volnost* (I, 271).

[44] *Ibid.*

[45] *Svobody seyatel pustynny* (I, 353).

[46] *Medny vsadnik* (III, 294).

[47] *Ibid.* (III, 288).

[48] *Ibid.* (III, 294).

PUSHKIN AND MICKIEWICZ

By Arthur P. Coleman

I

Sometime between September 8 and October 24, 1826,[1] during the period when the ceremonies attendant upon the coronation of Tsar Nicholas I helped somewhat to dispel the gloom caused by the disaster of the Decembrist Revolt of the previous winter, there came together in Moscow two of the most illustrious of all Slavic poets — the Pole, Adam Mickiewicz, and the Russian, Alexander Pushkin. They were within six months of the same age,[2] and each had won acclaim for his verses among his own compatriots.[3]

The meeting of these two poets resulted in a friendship whose importance, however much investigated, continues to fascinate the student of comparative literature. Mickiewicz's influence on Pushkin has often claimed the attention of Russian scholars, but the Poles have been the principal investigators. The names of these scholars constitute a distinguished roll.[4] Outstanding in the field is our own contemporary, the eminent Professor Wacław Lednicki. Through the patient efforts of these men, especially through the work of Lednicki, the many details of the Pushkin-Mickiewicz friendship have gradually been unearthed and clearly set forth. Yet, declares Professor Lednicki himself in his latest study, *Przyjaciele Moskale,* published in Kraków, 1935: "All this does not alter the fact that the Russian period of Mickiewicz, even to this day, awaits exhaustive and objective working over." [5]

To the fundamental groundwork of these scholars this brief study can add little. My task will be simply to set down the facts which have already been revealed and in such a way that this article may serve as a kind of introduction to that investigation which some dispassionate scholar may one day produce — a detailed and thoroughgoing examination of the works of Mickiewicz for traces of Pushkin's influence.

II

Startlingly alike, upon superficial observation, are the outward circumstances of the lives of Pushkin and Mickiewicz up to the time when they met: their age, which was almost the same; their similar position in the social hierarchy of their respective countries; their exile at the end of their school days because of liberal utterances and writings, and for sentiments directed in each case against the tsarist regime. Even the sources from which each derived his inspiration were often identical: both were inspired by the Oriental charm of South Russia, by high-spirited women, especially women of Polish origin, and by Byron. They were both early attracted by ideas of liberty and progress and patriotism. Yet the two poets were meteors discharged from mutually hostile planetary systems. They were, in the words of Mickiewicz: "Two Alpine crags, born one, which hidden streams had riven wide since birth." [6]

What were the two young men like when they met in Moscow in the autumn of 1826? The year following that fateful September 1826 was the period of Alexander Pushkin's greatest popularity. His lustre was as yet undimmed by literary polemics or by adverse judgment upon the employment of his talents. His dramatic emergence from a long exile, with the poetic fruits of that exile already well-known or in his hand, set Pushkin up at once as the reigning literary lion.

As for Mickiewicz, he calls himself, months later when he met Pushkin in St. Petersburg: "a pilgrim, newly come from out the west, an alien, little known, a victim of the tsarist rule." [7] Before Adam Mickiewicz had left his homeland because of the charges of the tsar's agent, Novosiltsov, he had been molded into a vital and heroic pattern by strong forces. In the first place, he had been born in that special and distinct part of the old Polish Commonwealth which was known traditionally as Litwa. Litwa, at the turn of the century, as always, was somewhat isolated from the world of affairs by its magnificent forests, isolated, that is, to the extent that it was not and never would be in danger of losing its special characteristics, yet not so isolated as to be out of touch with world currents. Of these currents Litwa was always intimately aware through the cosmopolitanism radiating from its universally-minded and widely-traveled nobility.

The society of Litwa was homogeneous, with its roots deep in the soil. It loved that soil so passionately that it made Poles everywhere love it with an equal passion. Like the true New England Yankee, the Pole of Litwa scarcely understood how anyone could endure life anywhere else in the world or breathe any other air than that which caressed his native forests and lakes and meadows. Though the Litwa of Mickiewicz's birth identified itself completely with the whole of the old Polish Commonwealth, though it never ceased to feel that Warsaw was its capital even when Warsaw was in alien hands, still the Polish land of Litwa remained in a sense distinct. A certain sentiment which was both heroic and passionate clung to the very name "Litwa."

In the second place, Adam Mickiewicz had passed through a memorable experience during his thirteenth year, when Litwa had been shaken in the summer of 1812 by the passage over its quiet roads of the Grand Army of Napoleon I. In Napoleon Litwa imagined it had found its redeemer. Already this magician had wrested from Prussia the trunk of the old Polish Commonwealth, and created out of it in 1807 the Grand Duchy. Might he not, the Poles of Litwa prayed, restore to that trunk the good right arm of Litwa which Russia had torn away? Through the ecstasy of that brief hope Mickiewicz passed while he was still a boy studying in the Dominican school in his native town of Nowogródek. The radiance, the intoxication which filled all Litwa as the army advanced, even through Nowogródek itself, never left Mickiewicz during his whole life. His last and greatest poem, *Pan Tadeusz,* is a monument to the persistence of that hope, even thirty years after the event:

> O spring! Happy is he who beheld thee then in our land!
> Thou memorable spring of war, spring of creation!
> O spring, how we beheld thee as thou wert, blossoming
> With grain and with grasses, glittering with men in arms,
> Crowded with doings, pregnant with hope!
> I see thee as thou wert, thou lovely phantom of my dreams!
> I who was born in slavery, chained in swaddling bands,
> But one such spring in all my life have I seen.[8]

Mickiewicz passed through a remarkable university experience. During the actual years of his undergraduate study (1815-1819), the University of Wilno was indeed the oven in which much of the intellectual bread of all Poland was baked. The fact that its curator was the one-time adviser to Tsar Alexander himself, Prince Adam Czartoryski, bespeaks the enlightened and cosmopolitan nature of its guiding spirit. A galaxy of professors no less enlightened made up its faculty. The University of Wilno was, moreover, a breeding ground of the highest patriotism and manly virtue. Here more than anywhere lingered the afterglow of Litwa's ecstasy of 1812. The hopes of Polish freedom then enkindled were kept alive by student groups, and to such groups Mickiewicz naturally belonged. Even in the days when one of Mickiewicz's colleagues, Antoni Górecki, carried away by the current hope that Alexander might become Poland's savior, could write that "they reverenced Alexander as the second God," [9] yet the youth of Wilno did not deceive themselves as to the ultimate aim of their strenuous self-cultivation: dedication to the cause of Polish liberty. It was only the avowed friendliness of Alexander for Poland that restrained student activities from assuming, for the moment, an anti-Russian character. But their attitude gradually changed. No sooner had Mickiewicz completed his undergraduate work in the summer of 1819 than Novosiltsov, Russia's imperial commissioner in Poland, had completed a system of espionage and coercion which was soon to affect decisively the young poet's life. By the spring of 1820 the youth of Litwa had become aware to what end this system was leading. In April 1820, Franciszek Malewski, one of Mickiewicz's lifelong friends, wrote: "There is simply and without malice a marked tendency to Muscovitize this country. For a long time I could not fall asleep (after realizing it), and many things kept buzzing in my head." [10] The effect of the new policy was to turn the activities of the students into political channels, channels they had previously only skirted. By the school year 1821-22, which Mickiewicz spent in Wilno doing graduate work, his comrades had reoriented their thinking, and all their activities had acquired a political cast. Martyrdom was inevitable. For martyrdom these students had long prepared themselves with eyes wide open and with the high courage of the true religious martyr. In 1823 Mickiewicz was arrested; in the autumn of 1824 he was deported from Litwa to Russia.

Two years later, when Mickiewicz fell under the influence of Pushkin and his coterie, the Polish poet was not the same person who on a dismal October day had been hustled away over the forbidding white plains that were the "road to Russia." [11] Russia had changed the raw and hotheaded young man. His association in St. Petersburg with that rare personality, his compatriot Joseph Oleszkiewicz, and with certain of the future Decembrists had broadened his thinking. He had come to realize the universal nature of the struggle his own Litwa was waging against tyranny and darkness, and that struggle now seemed to take on a mystical quality. Then his sojourn in South Russia, following the winter in St. Petersburg, had not only broadened but it had also matured him. It had done what Litwa could never have done: wrenched him from provincialism and religiosity and thrown him into the wide world. In South Russia for the first time he met intimately a brilliant company of cultivated and cosmopolitan persons, most of them of Polish origin and many of them women. In South

Russia, moreover, he was confronted by nature in one of her most lavish and voluptuous moods, a manifestation of nature strange and stimulating to the Pole from Litwa. The response of Mickiewicz to the charms of interesting people and of gorgeous nature is completely recorded in the *Crimean Sonnets.* They constitute a permanent evidence of the deepening and enriching effect of the South Russian experiences upon the poet's sensitive personality.

When he met Pushkin, Mickiewicz had been in Moscow almost a year, having come to that city from South Russia just about the time of the ill-fated Decembrist uprising in 1825. As the atmosphere of Moscow during these months was heavy with dread and apprehension, so was the life of the Polish exile heavy, dull, lifeless, and uneventful — he gravitated between his duties in the office of Prince Golitsyn and his literary activities. Socially, Mickiewicz mingled only with the small circle of his Polish friends, most of them friends of the old Wilno days. The warm, interesting, and talented person whom both Litwa and South Russia had molded had not been discovered behind the mask of "Lithuanian cold and timid continence." [12]

III

It was the publication of the *Crimean Sonnets* by a Moscow press late in the summer of 1826 that opened a new life for Mickiewicz. Later the *Sonnets* were to create, as Mickiewicz wrote to his friend Antoni Odyniec in Warsaw, a "stir, with parties lining up *pro* and *contra.*" [13] They had scarcely been published when their author began to be noticed. First Nikolai Polevoi, editor of the *Moscow Telegraph,* took him up. Through Polevoi Mickiewicz was introduced into the best literary circles of Moscow. One of the most fashionable and stimulating places where the *literati* were accustomed to meet was the *salon* of Princess Zinaida Volkonskaya. This charming woman frequently invited Mickiewicz, and the pleasure he took in the company of this *salon* was immortalized in the poem *To a Grecian Room,* among whose lines is the one in which the poet describes that room as "half the way to paradise." [14] It was inevitable that, moving in such a company, Mickiewicz should meet Pushkin almost immediately upon the latter's emergence from the enforced retirement in which he had been living on his own estate at Mikhailovskoe until about two months before Mickiewicz had left his native land.

Consider the obstacles to friendship that the poets had to overcome before a true kinship of spirit could be established. Pushkin had already taken the first step along a road of silence and of compromise — for which Mickiewicz was forever to condemn him. On September 8, Pushkin had come to Moscow at the tsar's express command after six years of exile. To Mickiewicz it never seemed right that the voice that had rung so clearly in *The Dagger*, and in those other youthful poems of revolt, could be silenced. He could never condone, only forget, the step Pushkin had just taken. This we know, for six years later Mickiewicz was to direct venomous words against the poet for his backsliding.[15] Pushkin, on his part, had a lifetime of hatred toward his country's most ancient enemy to overcome. He had been born with an inherited contempt for Poland, and every experience of his life had militated against his ever deviating from that contempt and hatred.[16]

Yet between Mickiewicz and Pushkin there occurred the same phenomenon that had happened two years before in South Russia in the case of Pushkin and Count Olizar, a Polish poet who, like Mickiewicz, was also a burning patriot. That phenomenon Pushkin records in a poem which begins: "Singer! Since ancient times our races twain have striven," and which further on contains the lines:

> The fire of poetry
> Makes friends of hostile hearts;
> Through the song of joy
> Our mutual hatred sleeps,
> And blessings rise;
> Over the heart is spread
> A covering of peace.[17]

Pushkin loved Mickiewicz, as he wrote himself in the famous lines beginning, "He lived among us...",[18] and his image continued to haunt him, even after Mickiewicz had been gone from Russia a number of months. This we know from the sketch Pushkin drew of himself and Mickiewicz in his manuscript of *Hasub* toward the end of 1829 or early in 1830.[19] That he did not entirely trust Mickiewicz's affection for himself we are led to suspect from the second line of the poem just quoted: "Ill-will toward us he nourished in his soul"; and from the four lines he once wrote on another occasion, which run:

> I do not trust the honor of a gambler,
> The love for Russia of a Pole;
> I question the word of a German official,
> And doubt the friendship of a Gaul.[20]

The friendship of Pushkin and Mickiewicz was the natural flying together of two sympathetic personalities with common literary tastes. Both were interested in actual work in hand — Mickiewicz in finishing his *Wallenrod*, Pushkin in making known his *Boris Godunov*, which had been practically completed at Mikhailovskoe. It may have been at one of the evening literary gatherings, during which Pushkin read *Boris Godunov* to his friends, that the two poets were for the first time introduced. It was certainly at one of three homes, either at that of Prince Peter Vyazemski, of Sergei Sobolevski, or of Dmitri Venevitinov, moving spirit in the soon-to-be-started *Moscow Messenger*, that the first meeting took place.[21]

During the first brief stay of Pushkin in Moscow after his exile (September 8 to early November, 1826), the poets did not see a great deal of each other, though their names were linked, and we know that on October 24, at a dinner of the *Moscow-Messenger* group, toasts to both of them were proposed.[22] It was during the second visit of Pushkin to Moscow, and especially during February and March of 1827, that Mickiewicz spent a good deal of time in his company. Though exact and uncompromising in his literary judgments, Pushkin was satisfied with the work of Mickiewicz, and his acclaim of it contributed much to Mickiewicz's increasing literary reputation. Pushkin became so interested in *Wallenrod*, which by this time Mickiewicz had completed, that he later translated part of it.[23] All this interest was intensely flattering to Mickiewicz and appreciated by him. He wrote to his friend, Antoni Odyniec, in Warsaw, apropos of Pushkin's translation of his *Wallenrod*: "The Russians extend their hospitality even to poetry, and through their graciousness toward me, translate me."[24] In March 1827, Mickiewicz again wrote to Odyniec: "The strongest prop (of the new *Moscow Messenger*) is Pushkin. Of him I'll write more fully later. Now I'll only add that I know him and that we often meet. Pushkin is almost the same age as I, two months younger, in conversation very witty and lively; he has read a good deal and is well acquainted with the new literature; of poetry he has pure and lofty conceptions. He has written recently the tragedy *Boris Godunov*. I find many of its scenes historical in character, well thought out, and extremely beautiful."[25]

Pushkin's best episode in *Boris Godunov,* the tavern scene near the border of Lithuania, must have appealed to Mickiewicz, and he must have shared the current enthusiasm for the "revolutionary" step Pushkin had taken in *Godunov*: employment of the Russian tongue for "romantic" tragedy. The two poets had a good deal in common just at this moment, since each stood, in his own way, in the van of the struggle which romanticism was waging with classicism.

During this time relations between the poets reached the point at which they dared banter each other. One day Pushkin saw Mickiewicz approaching him on the street and shouted: "Out of the way, deuce, the ace is coming." Mickiewicz retorted: "The deuce of trumps will beat an ace!"[26]

That Pushkin had a high regard for Mickiewicz is illustrated by numerous incidents. One day when K. A. Polevoi had come looking for Mickiewicz at Pushkin's, the latter launched into a burst of praise for the Pole. He remarked: "Not long ago Zhukovski said to me, 'Do you know, brother, he will get the better of you?' And I replied, '*Will* get the better of me? He already has.'" [27] His esteem for Mickiewicz is shown also by his habit of consoling himself for being duped by Mérimée's *La Guzla* with the thought that Mickiewicz too had been taken in: "C'est donc en très bonne compagnie, que je me suis laissé mystifier?" [28]

The common debt to Byron for certain of their poetic impulses prompted Mickiewicz to present to his Russian friend a copy of Byron in English, with the dedication in his own handwriting: "Mickiewicz, an admirer of you both, presents Byron to Pushkin." This constitutes one of the monuments to the friendship of Pushkin and Mickiewicz in Moscow.[29]

In May 1827, Pushkin left Moscow, but Mickiewicz stayed on at the old routine in Prince Golitsyn's office almost a year longer. Several well-known translations belong to this Moscow period, the most charming of these being the Petrarchan stanzas beginning, "O clear, sweet, limpid waters," which Mickiewicz wrote at the villa Ostafevo which belonged to his good friend, Prince Peter Vyazemski. Neither this nor the translations he made at this time from Shakespeare and from Goethe show traces of Pushkin. It was a time, however, when, as Professor Borowy says, "Mickiewicz's ideas of poetic diction and construction were strengthened by his frequent intercourse with Russian connoisseurs and artists. His new works testify to a growing craftsmanship, united with a deepening insight into the world." [30]

Two original poems from this period may be found to owe some of their style to Pushkin. This is a problem for the specialist to solve. In the ballad of the Ukraine, entitled *Czaty* (*Guards*), and in the ballad of Litwa called *Trzech Budrysów* (*The Three Sons of Budrys*), there is both a new form and a new spirit. In the ballad of the Voivod who had trouble with his sentries, and in the one about the three brothers who, wherever they went

a-conquering, always brought home a Polish bride, there is a
new note of humorous gaiety, and the lines skip along, rippling
with merriment. Perhaps the gay, brilliant, sophisticated society
in which Mickiewicz was moving had begun to invade his poetry,
as it certainly had, according to his friend Oleś Chodzko, his
manners.[31] Or perhaps there is in these verses more direct evidence of the lightening hand of Pushkin. It is perhaps significant
that these two poems alone, of all Mickiewicz's writings after the
poets met, appealed sufficiently to Pushkin to impel him to translate them.[32] At any rate, Pushkin did translate them both [33] (into
rather careless Russian, it must be admitted), when he was at
Boldino in 1833, the very autumn when he created his masterpiece, *The Bronze Horseman*. Having left Moscow, Pushkin did
not return to that city during Mickiewicz's sojourn there.

The Polish poet's stay in Moscow was interrupted by a brief
visit to St. Petersburg in December 1827 and early January 1828.
Pushkin was then living in the capital. Glad as he was to make
this trip, in order to wind up the matter of *Wallenrod* and the
censor, Mickiewicz was unsettled by it. His reception in St.
Petersburg was so cordial, such a series of ovations, and the pros-
pect of spending an eternity in Moscow with any outlet for his
talents denied him (as in his request for permission to publish
a journal in Polish) — all this was so barren of enchantment that
he dreaded to go back to his prison. The determination to get to
St. Petersburg and from there — dared he hope it? — abroad, grew
apace within him.

A carnival party at Marja Szymanowska's during the first week
of April 1828, in the course of which Mickiewicz appeared as a
Spaniard, dressed half as a lady, half as a gentleman,[34] and a dinner given for him by the literary men of Moscow on the twenty-
eighth are among the final leaves in Mickiewicz's memory-book
of Moscow.[35] He left the city for St. Petersburg on the twenty-
second of the same month, never to return to the scene of his
first Russian triumphs.

St. Petersburg meant renewal of friendly relations with Pushkin. On April 27, some days after Mickiewicz's arrival in the
city, we know from a letter of Prince Peter Vyazemski that there
was a party which included the two poets. "Three days ago,"
wrote Vyazemski on the thirtieth, "we spent an evening and a
night with Pushkin, Krylov, Khomyakov, Mickiewicz, Pletnev,
and Nikolai Muchanov. Mickiewicz improvised in French prose
and astonished us not by the arrangement of his sentences but by
the richness and poetry of his thoughts. Mickiewicz compared
his thoughts and feelings, clothed of necessity in a foreign language, with inflammable materials which burn beneath the earth's
surface and have no crater through which to erupt. His improvi-
sation had an amazing effect. Mickiewicz alone was entirely
composed, and all listened to him with trembling and with tears.
And what would it have been like if such thoughts had been
set forth in the form of exquisite poetry!" [36]

Literary "routs" were evidently held with considerable regularity in St. Petersburg during that spring of 1828, and at these
Mickiewicz continued to be a favorite guest. One of the larger
affairs of the season was a *soirée* at Count Laval's to which Mickiewicz went with Prince Peter, and at which were present both
Griboedov and Pushkin. On this occasion Pushkin read *Boris
Godunov* aloud, as he had done more than once in Moscow.[37]

One of the gathering-places of the Pushkin group was the apart-
ment of Baron Delvig. Here, according to Madame Kern, Mickiewicz was often seen. Her description of him has nothing in
common with the notion that the poet was a kind of Polish Ham-
let: "My, how kind and friendly he always was! And what an
unusual being! Whenever he came it was always gay. I do not
recall that he often met Pushkin, but I do know that he was respected and loved by both Pushkin and Delvig. What was there
so clever about him? He was so tender, good-hearted, adapting
himself so graciously to everyone, that all were transported by his
presence. He would often sit beside us, relating tales to us which

he was just putting together, and he was interesting to us each and all."[38]

Madame Kern's uncertainty concerning the frequency of Mickiewicz's meetings with Pushkin is considerably dispelled by the evidence adduced by Professor Lednicki to show that during the spring months of 1828 the old Moscow habit of Pushkin and Vyazemski and Mickiewicz was revived, for the three took long walks about the city. On May 25, they even made a trip to Kronstadt, and after it enjoyed a gay supper in the company of other literary men, including Griboedov.[39]

It was during this period of Mickiewicz's closest association with Pushkin that he translated a fragment from his *Vospominanie,* just written, which he called *Przypomnienie (Remembrance).* Translated freely into English verse, these lines go:

> When night spreads out its shadowed silence
>   Upon the noisy day,
> Then sleeps the dumb and peaceful city,
>   Its clamor put away;
> And all men sleep but one: in darkness
>   Dreams return to me;
> Dark serpents of remorse are summoned
>   By crowding memory,
> And I reread my life with loathing —
>   I read it bitterly
> And vainly: little serves my weeping
>   To wash out tragedy.[40]

It is highly probable that the longing expressed by Pushkin was regret over his lost moral freedom, a freedom he had sacrificed to freedom of motion. Certain scholars also suggest that in these stanzas is a strain of envy for the moral freedom Mickiewicz still retained while he was physically a prisoner of the tsar.[41] It may be Pushkin's way of saying he was sorry that he could be no *Faris,* knowing no fear of external obstacles, surmounting them all by the strength of his will and the flying course of his imagination. For this was the time when Mickiewicz was dreaming of, and finally achieving, his proudest poem of defiance.[42]

We have seen how Mickiewicz repeatedly had a share, along with Pushkin's other literary friends, in launching *Boris Godunov*. During the creation now of the seventh chapter of that other long work of the 'twenties, *Eugene Onegin,* Mickiewicz knew Pushkin well, for, this chapter was being written in the spring of 1828. Years later, in his Paris lectures, Mickiewicz was to refer to *Onegin* as a work which would always be read with pleasure among Slavonic peoples, and analyzed it as a portraiture of the poet Pushkin himself.[43] Whether or not the genesis of *Pan Tadeusz* in Mickiewicz's mind goes as far back as these days in the company of Pushkin, whether, indeed, *Pan Tadeusz* owes anything concretely to *Eugene Onegin* with respect to its conception, style, and characters, etc., is a problem that must be considered. The rural atmosphere of both poems is identical, and it is possible, as Professor Krzyżanowski points out, that the character of Telimena owes something to Mickiewicz's Russian sojourn, if not, indeed, directly to Pushkin. So far no words of Mickiewicz expressing indebtedness to Pushkin's *Onegin* have turned up. Professor Pigoń, an authority on the sources of *Pan Tadeusz*, has given no credit to Pushkin, if, indeed, any should be given. This is to be expected, since Professor Pigoń is not a Russian scholar. But, in the words of Professor Krzyżanowski: "One may not assert that there is no influence of Pushkin, for that is still a field for research."[44]

The last of Pushkin's works which Mickiewicz knew in Russia was *Poltava,* called in its pre-natal stages *Mazepa.* In *Poltava* Mickiewicz had a certain vested interest, for when the idea of this heroic poem had scarcely been conceived, Pushkin laid out before Mickiewicz his plan for a work about the Cossack hetman, and "ardently and sincerely tried to lead him into the world of his own opinions to prove he had made a thorough study of the principal hero of the poem."[45] Mickiewicz's work with Pushkin over *Poltava* and the discussions it gave rise to concerning its hero, Peter the Great were destined to bear fruit later in one of Mickiewicz's important works, the *Introduction to Forefathers' Eve, Part III.*

On May 15, 1829 Mickiewicz left Russia for good, having been enabled to accomplish this long-desired end through the efforts of Vyazemski, Pushkin, and other Russian friends. So was brought to a close a period in the Polish poet's life which Professor Kallenbach calls one of "enormous evolution of spirit,"[46] and which Professor Windakiewicz declares was "the most peaceful and the most pleasant in his life," the one which "brought out his creative energy and helped him to a swift maturity," and which widened his hitherto "provincial" outlook.[47] It was a period, moreover, that helped to make of him the "powerful" man that Kozlov describes.[48] In the development of Mickiewicz during this Russian period we have seen that Pushkin had no small part. The numerous evidences of the Pole's concrete influence on Pushkin's work, which Professor Tretiak has so assiduously traced, are undoubtedly balanced by similar concrete evidences of Pushkin's influence on Mickiewicz's work. The discovery of these facts however, would require much research.[49]

IV

In 1829 both the Polish poet who left Russia and the Russian poet who remained entered upon new ways of living. For both the divorce from the old ways was crucial: in Pushkin's case the months immediately following Mickiewicz's departure were the last period of bachelorhood; for Mickiewicz they were months crowded with new scenes, new associates, new interests, and finally a renewed faith.

Two events rapidly widened the rift between the Pushkin of the 'twenties and the Pushkin of the 'thirties. The July Revolution in Paris, which did not touch Mickiewicz (he was traveling in Switzerland at the time), crystallized Pushkin's long-maturing, yet long-wavering nationalism and legitimism. Parliamentarianism of the current French brand was distasteful to him, and the accession of Louis Philippe displeased him not only in principle but in practise, for it meant the downfall of a friend of Russia, Charles X. At the same time, Pushkin's marriage in February, 1831, had brought with it the obligation to provide an assured income. Economic necessity thus became a factor in ending for him the period of compromise which the 'twenties had been. He had to make the choice between the principles for which the Decembrists had stood and died and out-and-out devotion to the tsar. In the tsar's service lay security and a steady income. The other course meant at best insecurity and discomfort, at worst exile or death. A growing distaste for liberalism, accelerated by the spectacle of the way liberalism worked out in France, coupled with the pressure that drives a family man, made of Pushkin during the 'thirties a servant, to all appearances, of the tsar.

The Polish Uprising of 1830, coming on the heels of the July Revolution, made it impossible for Pushkin to think of deviating from his chosen path. For the Polish Uprising let loose upon the western world such rivers of venom toward Russia and toward everything Russia stood for, that even the most wavering national-ist would have felt it necessary to rise in defense of his native land.[50] Between Pushkin and Mickiewicz it provoked a bitter exchange of polemics — a bitter harvest but a creative one: from Pushkin, a trilogy of anti-Polish poems, from Mickiewicz, the *Introduction to Forefathers' Eve, Part III.* One may also con-sider Pushkin's *Bronze Horseman* a by-product of these polemics.

July 1831 marked the high point of sympathy in Western Europe and America for Poland's cause. French intervention with an armed force seemed not improbable. The Poles, moreover, were holding their own against the cholera-ridden armies of Russia. In the middle of that terrible month conditions in Russia were, as Pushkin wrote, "worse than in 1812." It was at this point that Pushkin delivered himself of his first answer to the universal cry of hatred that was rising abroad: the poem which he called, *To the Shade of the Commander*. It was dedicated to Kutuzov, Prince of Smolensk and hero of Borodino. A couple of weeks later, on the second of August, when Pushkin was staying at Tsarskoe Selo, he wrote the second of his anti-Polish poems, *To the Calumniators of Russia*. Still a month later, on the fifth of September, immediately upon receiving news of the fall of Warsaw, Pushkin wrote the third in this sequence, *The Anniversary of Borodino*. The second and third of these poems, together with a poem by Zhukovski, were published at once under the title, *The Taking of Warsaw, Three Poems*.

This collection, animated by a fanatical glorification of Russia and her historic role, together with rank vilification of Poland, had great success in Russia. It was circulated abroad, for although in general Pushkin was little known outside Russia, universal interest in the Polish Uprising caught up everything connected with it. Mickiewicz heard of the publication in Dresden, where he was stopping during the final months of 1831 and the early part of 1832.[51]

Mickiewicz's answer to Pushkin was a short group of verses appended to Part III of his *Forefathers' Eve*. It was addressed *To Moscow Friends*:

Do you out there remember me? How many times I dream
Of all those friends of mine, their deaths, their exiles, their imprisonments,
And think of you; your foreign faces have the rights
Of citizens within my reveries.

Where are you now? Ryleev's noble head —
My brother's head — by tsarist edict
Hangs suspended to a shameful tree...
May those who slay their prophets be forever cursed!

That hand Bestuzhev once stretched out to me —
Poet, soldier, seer — that hand, from pen and weapon
Torn, and harnessed to a barrow by the tsar,
Today is carving in the mines beside some Polish hand.

In exile you are spared the sterner punishment
Of brothers who are chained to office —
Your free souls have not been shackled to the tsar,
Nor on his doorstep do you beat out flattery!

One of you with mortgaged tongue is celebrating this,
Rejoicing even in the martyrdom of friends;
In my own nation, sprinkled with my very blood,
He boasts of his accursed work in tsardom's service.

If unto you from far away, from nations that are free,
These mournful strains should reach your north
And speak aloud above your ice-bound plain,
Oh let them herald freedom, as the cranes announce the spring!

Know me by my voice. As long as I was shackled,
Crawling silent as a snake, I fooled the despot.
But to you the secrets deep within me I revealed.
To you I always had the open clearness of a dove.

Now my chalice pours out poison over all the world,
Corrosive, burning, is the venom of my speech.
Bitterness, distilled from tears and blood of my own land,
O let it bite and burn — not you, but all your chains!

If one of you complain, for me his plaint would seem
Only the angry barking of a dog, so long
Accustomed to his painful collar, that at last
He turns against the man who would deliver him.

Through all the bitterness and disappointment of these stanzas, Mickiewicz never "identified the tsarist government with the nation, for he deeply loved his Russian friends and was oppressed with sorrow at the way the great Pushkin had changed his front before the 'gendarme of Europe,' Nicholas I," [52] writes Professor Pollak, and with this we can agree. Yet the personal attack against Pushkin in stanzas four and five is a pointed and a scathing one.

Pushkin saw *Forefathers' Eve, Part III* in the autumn of 1833, when his friend Soboloevski brought him at Boldino the four-volume Paris edition of Mickiewicz's *Poetic Works*. Pushkin's

answer to Mickiewicz's personal attack was the charming poem
entitled simply "M," which he wrote in August 1834:

> He lived among us; ill-will toward us
> He nourished in his soul; while we,
> We loved him. Peaceful and benevolent,
> He listened to our conversations;
> With him we shared our purest daydreams
> And our songs. He saw beyond us;
> From the heights he looked on life
> And saw a time when nations,
> Having put aside their quarreling,
> Would be united in a single harmony.
> We listened greedily to what the poet said.
> And then he went away, and with him
> Went the blessing of us all...
> But now his verses fawn upon the noisy rabble,
> He sings of hatred. From afar his well-known voice,
> Malevolent now, comes to us! O God, return
> Thy peace unto his maddened soul! [53]

To which personal controversy Mickiewicz's final contribution
must be added: the last words of the article he wrote in the Paris
Globe after Pushkin's death, signing it simply "A Friend of Pushkin": "I knew Pushkin well, and for a considerable time regarded
him as a person possessed of a character impressive but sometimes light, yet always sincere and noble and generous. His
faults seem to belong to the environment and the society in
which he lived, but whatever was good in him arose from his
own heart."[54]

V

When Pushkin read Mickiewicz's *Forefathers' Eve, Part III,*
in the autumn of 1833, he must have found in its long *Introduction* haunting traces of himself and of the conversations he had
had with the Polish poet, especially the conversations to which
their work over the manuscript of *Poltava* had given rise. As the
poem *Poltava* represents Peter the Great as a glorious hero, so the
Introduction portrays him as a satanic hero. Both pictures arose

from the gropings of the two poets toward an understanding of the meaning of Peter the Great, a figure whose overwhelming importance in Russian history Pole and Russian alike realized.[55]

In its scheme the *Introduction to Forefathers' Eve, Part III* is a gradual unrolling before the bewildered eyes of a foreigner (Mickiewicz) of the Russian panorama in the year 1824. The endless, windswept, *kibitka*-ridden road across the wilderness toward Russia cries out to the foreigner that here is a land bare and waste and soulless. Not only in the drifted plain does he read this meaning, but in the eyes of the few lonely individuals whom he meets along the way he sees the same emptiness:

> I meet people with stout shoulders,
> Men with broad breasts and sturdy necks,
> Like all the trees and animals of the north,
> Full of vigor, full of health and power.
> But the face of every one is like their land,
> An empty, wide, and savage plain.

At length the foreigner discovers the source of this country's barrenness: the very capital itself, St. Petersburg, a monument to a despot's freakish wilfullness:

> In ancient Greek and Roman times
> Men built their homes beneath the sanctuary of some god,
> Above nymph-haunted spring, 'midst groves —
> Or on high mountain tops sought haven from their enemy.
> So was Athens built, so Rome and Sparta.
> Then later in the Gothic age beneath some baron's tower
> Where the people all around could find protection,
> Huts would rise, pressed tight against the walls,
> Or, buttressing the banks of navigable streams,
> Towns would grow up, matching the slow progress of the centuries.
> Some deity has elevated all these cities,
> Some reason of defense or industry.
> But what beginnings had this Russian capital?
> Whence among these Slavic thousands rose the will
> To creep into these corners, the place of their tenancy,
> These corners raped so newly from the sea and from the Finn?
> Nor fruits nor bread afford this bitter soil,
> Its very breezes carry only snow and rain —

Too cold or yet too hot the skies are here,
Unchangeable and fierce, like despot's whim!
The people did not wish it — the marshes here allured
The fancy of the tsar, and he set out to found
A city not for men but for himself: a monument to vanity.
Into the depths of fluid sands and marshy swamps
He bade them sink a hundred thousand piles
And trample down the bodies of a hundred thousand men,
Earth having fallen on the bodies of the serfs,
Then he harnessed other generations
To his wagons and his ships,
To carry wood and shining stone
From distant lands, from chaos of the seas.

At length, behind the soulless plain and the presumptuous capital, the foreigner discovers the one who animates it all: Peter the Great himself, embodied in the equestrian statue by Falconet which Catherine had caused to be erected.

It is at this point that Pushkin enters the picture, for in his company the foreigner imagines himself to be contemplating the figure of Peter.[56] Arm in arm the two friends stand there in the twilight dew. They gaze at the terrible figure above them. Then in a quiet voice the Russian poet breaks the silence:

Unto the first of tsars, to him who did these wonders,
The second, a tsarina, had this great Colossus built.
Here the tsar, poured out in bronze in Titan form,
Is seated on the back of bronze Bucephalus,
And here stands waiting to effect an entrance on his steed.
Knowing that Peter would repine on native Russian soil,
They sent beyond the sea, they tore from Finland's coast
This granite hillock: at the Lady's word...
.   .   .   .
The hillock now is ready; now he flies, this tsar of bronze,
Knout-armed, bedraped in Roman toga...
Now his steed is leaping on the granite walls...
Rearing his head he stands upon their very edge.

Far away from the Russian capital the Polish poet now discovers a far different kind of ruler than the Colossus before him:

Marcus Aurelius, the "darling of the people," like Peter himself immortalized in stone:

> A fair and mild and noble brow has he,
> And on it shines the wish that all may prosper.
> One hand is lifted solemnly as if to bless
> The subjects thronging round his feet.
> The other hand rests lightly on the rein
> Wherewith he curbs the gallop of his steed,
> As though a crowd of people have been standing in his path
> Crying, "Caesar, and our father, has returned!"
> Slowly he rides, as if to let the favor
> Of his glance rest equally on all.
> His charger lifts his mane, his eyes flash fire,
> But well he knows he bears a precious burden,
> Bears the father of a million children,
> Wherefore he checks the frenzy of his pace...
> The children may approach, may see their father,
> His horse treads evenly the even road,
> As though advancing into immortality.

Then comes the conclusion, and the dread:

> With Peter now — the rein hangs loose,
> You see him flying, charging down the road,
> As if he'd leaped upon the precipice's very edge,
> And now the frenzied horse were lifting up his hoof. . . .
> Uncurbed by hand of tsar he gnashes at the bit. . . .
> You think he must plunge down and dash himself to pieces;
> Yet there for centuries he stands, leaping, but never falls,
> Like a cascade that flows from solid granite,
> Poised, that frozen hangs above some deep abyss.
> But when the sun of liberty shall once shine out,
> And western winds begin to thaw these people,
> What will happen to this mad cascade of tyranny?

Here is the heart and kernel of the *Introduction*. The next section, "Military Review," simply underlines the vanity of the tsar, the subservience of the Russian folk and the sycophancy of court and army. The final chapter, "The Day before the Petersburg Flood, 1824, Oleszkiewicz," opens with a beautiful description of the day before the Neva overflowed so disastrously. It sweeps on to a dramatic conclusion in which the mystic Oleszkiewicz foretells the doom that is certain to befall the emperor and the imperial city. The one who wears the mantle of tsardom in the day of destruction is Alexander I, easily identified by the description of him which Oleszkiewicz gives in the first two lines:

> Sunk in tyranny — he who once was human —
> Abandoned by the Lord to slow corruption,
> He has driven from him like an evil thing
> His last resource of conscience.
> He will reach yet greater heights of pride,
> Till Satan trample all his arrogance.
> In thy stead, O tsar, thy humblest subjects
> Will receive the blows of heaven's wrath...
> As lightning... sears the valley first
> And strikes the guilty last of all.
> Fallen asleep in brawling drunkenness,
> They will not awake. Poor dead skulls,
> Sleep on, until His anger burn you out!
> . . . .
> I hear the herald winds, scarecrows of the sea,
> Thrusting from the ice-fields.
> I hear... the ocean break its fetters,
> Run wild and kick and bite the loosened ice-blocks...
> Now swells its dripping neck to very heaven:
> A single chain still holds... it back...
> That too they will unweld... I hear their hammers' beat.

When Mickiewicz put into the mouth of Pushkin the text of his long sermon on tyranny, which the *Introduction*, taken as a whole, contains, he was reaching down into his memory for a Pushkin he had known in the spring of 1828 in St. Petersburg, to a Pushkin with whom he had often taken such walks as described in "Before the Monument of Peter the Great," to a Pushkin who had discussed with him plans for an heroic poem on Peter the Great's triumph over the Swedes at Poltava.

To make the monument of Peter the symbol of tyranny was a distortion of Falconet's purpose, but to put in Pushkin's mouth such words of criticism concerning his imperial hero was no dis-

tortion of Pushkin's ideas and sentiments. Mickiewicz knew
Pushkin well and he was thoroughly aware of his dualistic attitude toward Peter. Though he had watched Pushkin build up
his hero to divine proportions in such lines as:

> And then, inspired from heaven,
> Resounded the voice of Peter:
> "For the cause, with God!" From out the tent,
> Surrounded by a swarm of favorites
> He comes. His eyes are shining,
> His movements swift and splendid.
> And he is all. Like God's own thunderstorm
> He goes,[57]

yet he knew Pushkin to be still of the mind he was in 1822 when
he had written in his notes, "Peter I did not concern himself with
popular freedom, the inescapable consequence of enlightenment,
but relied on his own power and looked with contempt upon the
people even more perhaps than did Napoleon." [58] Mickiewicz
knew that to Pushkin Peter was a combination of God-given ability and satanic cruelty. In their conversations concerning Peter
we can detect the very genesis of Mickiewicz's interest in the great
tsar and in his theory that he represented the Russia he, as a friend
of humanity and as a Pole, most regretted.

Professor Lednicki suggests that the other emperor who appears
in "Before the Monument," Marcus Aurelius, may owe his position here in antithesis to Peter to one of the youthful works of
Pushkin, a work called *To Licinius.* To define this possible debt
of Mickiewicz to Pushkin is a problem in research.[59]

This much is clear, at any rate: the *Introduction to Forefathers'
Eve, Part III,* is Mickiewicz's answer to the anti-Polish trilogy of
Pushkin; and for the Pushkin who appears in the *Introduction,*
as well as for certain of the concepts therein, Mickiewicz is indebted to a genuine literary friendship that no "ancient enemy"
could ever destroy.

Pushkin saw *Forefathers' Eve, Part III,* as we have said before, in the autumn of 1833. He was at Boldino that autumn, finishing up his *History of the Pugachev Rebellion*. Between the sixth of October and the middle of November, in a frenzy of creation, he wrote the masterpiece of his lifetime: *The Bronze Horseman,* which we have indicated owed a certain debt to Mickiewicz's *Introduction*. Those who are familiar with *The Bronze Horseman* and who have followed in this study our excerpts from the *Introduction*, will have discerned certain startling similarities. This question of direct indebtedness in not within the province of this work. Professor Lednicki is of the opinion that Pushkin's indebtedness to Mickiewicz has been overemphasized, and he is especially certain that Pushkin never intended *The Bronze Horseman* to be primarily a piece of polemics with the Polish friend whose memory still haunted him and of whose freedom he was, in a mystical sort of way, jealous. A certain indebtedness to Mickiewicz, however, Professor Lednicki is willing to concede. He says: "It was Mickiewicz who created a concept of St. Petersburg as a revelation of the poverty of Russian civilization and at the same time of its tragedy, of St. Petersburg as a symbol of extortion, slavery, parasitism and degradation." This concept Pushkin introduced into Russian literature in his *Bronze Horseman*, and it became "the starting-point of all the poetry and literature about St. Petersburg which the second half of the nineteenth century produced, most of it motivated by dislike, critical appraisal, offense, skepticism, and finally fear of the capital...." [60]

We do not know what Mickiewicz thought about *The Bronze Horseman*, or whether he ever saw it. It was not allowed to be published until four years after Pushkin's death, in the year 1841. At this time Mickiewicz was in Paris, lecturing at the Collège de France. In his personal life the Polish poet was falling more and more deeply under the influence of the mystic Towiański, to the destruction of his artistic and literary judgment. In his lectures on Russian literature in the Collège, Mickiewicz never mentioned *The Bronze Horseman*. In none of his lectures does Mickiewicz give any hint that his old friend, like himself, had seen the menace lurking behind the shining Colossus, or that he had premonitions as terrible as his own of the fall of the "Babylon of the north."

The nature and extent of Mickiewicz's friendship with Pushkin and its importance in his life we have seen rather clearly. The weight of his indebtedness to the great Russian still remains to be exactly evaluated. For the moment Mickiewicz himself has the final word in those famous opening lines of "Before the Monument of Peter the Great" in the *Introduction to Forefathers' Eve, Part III*:

> Two youths were standing in the twilight dew,
> Arm linked in arm, one cloak about the two.
> One a pilgrim from the west but newly come,
> Unknown, by Tsarist edict driven forth;
> The poet of the Russian folk, the other one,
> Already famous for his songs through all the North.
> They had not known each other long,
> Some days, — yet friendly ties so soon were strong.
> Their spirits twain transcended obstacles of earth,
> Like two great Alpine crags, born one,
> Which, riven by deep-hidden streams since birth,
> But little heed the Enemy's dull roar,
> As each toward each their craggy summits soar.

COLUMBIA UNIVERSITY

NOTES

[1] Wacław Lednicki, *Przyaciele Moskale* (Kraków: 1935). See chapter, "Puszkin-Mickiewicz, Mickiewiczowy Nekrolog Puszkina," pp. 20-22.

[2] Mickiewicz was born in Nowogródek in Poland, December 24, 1798 (OS); Pushkin in Moscow, May 26, 1799 (OS).

[3] Pushkin especially for his *Ruslan and Liudmila*, published in 1820; Mickiewicz especially for his ballads, his famous *Ode to Youth*, and his *Grażyna*, a tale in verse of Litwa and the Teutonic Knights.

[4] The bibliography of Mickiewicz-Pushkin is large. I list here only the works of the outstanding scholars who have been concerned specifically with the interplay of the two personalities, and all of these, it appears, are Polish. Of their works only the ones bearing directly on the subject are mentioned:

Vladimir Spasowicz, *Mickiewicz i pomnik Piotra Wielkiego*, in *Pisma*, Vol. II (St. Petersburg: 1889), pp. 225-290.

Józef Tretiak, *Mickiewicz i Puszkin* (Warsaw: 1906).

Alexander Brückner, "Mickiewicz i Puszkin," *Przegląd warszawski* (1922, Nr. 12, Sept., 1922), pp. 336-339.

Ignacy Chrzanowski, "Mickiewicz i Puszkin," in *Z epoki romantyzmu* (Kraków: 1918).

Wacław Lednicki, "Mickiewicz en Russie," *Revue de l'Université de Bruxelles* (1929), Vol. 34, No. 2, pp. 318-333.

———— *Aleksander Puszkin, Eugenjusz Oniegin,* przłożył L. Belmont, opracował W. Lednicki, Bibljoteka Narodowa (Kraków: 1925).

———— *Aleksander Puszkin* (Kraków: 1926). See especially chapter, "Z historji poetyckiej przyjaźni," pp. 162-226.

———— *Pouchkine et la Pologne, à propos de la trilogie antipolonaise de Pouchkine* (Paris: 1928).

———— *Jeździec Miedziany,* opowieść petersburska Aleksandra Puszkina, translated by Julian Tuwim into Polish verse with an introduction and critical essay by Lednicki (Bibljoteka Polska, Instytut wydawniczy, Warsaw: 1932).

———— Przyjaciele Moskale (Kraków: 1935). In this work, scattered through the notes, will be found a complete bibliography of all works that in any way touch on this subject.

Articles in other languages than Polish on Mickiewicz-Pushkin are:

L. Léger, "Mickiewicz et Puszkin," *Revue de Paris,* 1898.

E. Lo Gatto, "Mickiewicz e Puszkin," *Studi di litterature slave* (Roma: 1925).

Juljan Krzyżanowski, "Mickiewicz and Pushkin," *Slavonic Review,* Vol. VI, No. 18 (March: 1928), pp. 634-645.

[5] W. Lednicki, *Przyjaciele Moskale,* p. 13.

[6] Lines of Mickiewicz in first stanza of *Przed pomnikiem Piotra Wielkiego,* for which see Kallenbach's edition of Mickiewicz's works (no date), IV, p. 185.

[7] *Przed pomnikiem Piotra Wielkiego.*

[8] *Pan Tadeusz,* XI, 11. 71-78 (Kallenbach, *Mickiewicz,* III, 195-196).

[9] Józef Tretiak, *Bohdan Zaleski,* I, 87 (quoted by St. Pigoń in the work cited immediately below).

[10] St. Pigoń, *Do podstaw wychowania narodowego* (Lwów: 1920), p. 128.

[11] See Mickiewicz's own description of this "Road to Russia" in the Introduction to *Forefathers' Eve (Dziady)* III; Kallenbach, *Mickiewicz,* 175-178.

[12] See Lednicki ("Mickiewicz en Russie") for a description of Mickiewicz at this time.

[13] Letter to Odyniec, June, 1827, *Dzieła wszystkie* (Pini and Reiter, Lwów), X, 212.

[14] See lines of last stanza of *Na pokój grecki,* Kallenbach, *Mickiewicz,* II, 200.

[15] See p. 93 of this article.

[16] Obvious reasons for Pushkin's hatred of Poland are, of course, the fact that he was a Russian; his friendship for Karamzin, and for Princess Golitsyna, a bitter hater of Poland; his contempt for the Polish cult of Napoleon, whom he and his native land hated equally, etc. A long discussion of Pushkin's anti-Polish sentiments is found in "Polskoe vostanie po pismam Pushkina k E. M. Khitrovo," in *Pisma Pushkina k Elizavete Mikhailovne Khitrovo,* 1827-1832 (Leningrad: 1927), pp. 257-299.

[17] *Grafu Olizaru* (I, 487).

[18] *On mezhdu nami zhil* (II, 240).

[19] Abram Efros, *Risunki poeta* (Academia, Leningrad: 1933), p. 299.

[20] A. S. Pushkin, *Sobranie zapreshchennykh stikhotvoreni* (Ladyzhnikov, Berlin: 1902?), No. 49, p. 94.

[21] See Note I, and reference.

[22] W. Lednicki, *Przyjaciele Moskale*, p. 24.

[23] Pushkin translated the introduction to *Wallenrod*, somewhat indifferently, in Petersburg in 1828, and his translation was published in the *Moscow Messenger* in 1829, part I, p. 181.

[24] Moscow, March 22, 1828, *Dzieła wszystkie*, X, 234.

[25] *Ibid.*, X, 212.

[26] P. A. Vyazemski, *Polnoe sobranie sochineni, ed.* Count S. D. Sheremetev (St. Petersburg: 1878-1887), VI, 309. Quoted by Gessen and Modzalevski, *Razgovory Pushkina* (Moscow: 1929), p. 85.

[27] K. A. Polevoi, "Zapiski," *Istoricheski Vestnik* (1887), No. 4, p. 53.

[28] Gessen and Modzalevski, *Razgovory Pushkina*, pp. 297-298.

[29] W. Lednicki, *Przyjaciele Moskale*, p. 27.

[30] Wacław Borowy, "Pan Tadeusz," *Slavonic Review*, XIII, 402.

[31] In a letter to Tomasz Zan in Orenburg, April 3, 1828, Mickiewicz wrote from St. Petersburg "Oleś Chodzko was much surprised at me for my present appearance; my even disposition he admired and my ease of meeting people, which formerly I did not have." See *Dzieła Wszystkie*, X, 236-237.

[32] *Konrad Wallenrod* can not be considered as belonging to the poet's Pushkin period, though the finishing touches were put to it after the two had met.

[33] For Pushkin's translations of these poems see *Voevoda* and *Budrys i ego synovya* (II, 157, 159).

[34] Cf. Vladimir Chodasiewicz, "Nowe dane o Mickiewiczu w Rosji," *Wiadomości Literackie* (Warsaw: November 18, 1934), No. 47, p. 3. This article quotes from several of the letters of Prince Vyazemski discovered in the archives at Ostafevo since the Revolution. The information used here is from a letter written to his wife on April 8, 1828, from Moscow.

[35] This dinner is well known to all students of Mickiewicz, and is the one at which a silver cup, engraved with the names of those present, was given him as a souvenir of his Moscow sojourn. See letter to Odyniec, St. Petersburg, April 28, 1828, *Dzieła Wszystkie*, X, pp. 240-241.

[36] Letter of Vyazemski of May 2, 1828, quoted by Chodasiewicz in the article cited in note 34.

[37] See Lednicki, *Przyjaciele Moskale*, p. 27, and Chodasiewicz, "Nowe dane o Mickiewiczu w Rosji."

[38] "Vospominaniya A. P. Markovoi-Vinogradskoi (Kern)," in L. N. Maikov, *Pushkin: Biograficheskie materialy i istoriko-literaturnye ocherki* (St. Petersburg: 1899), p. 254.

[39] Cf. Lednicki, *Przyjaciele Moskale*, p. 26.

[40] For the Polish version, see Kallenbach, *Mickiewicz*, II, p. 283; for the Russian original see, *Vospominanie* (II, 40).

[41] A. I. Yatsimirski points out in reviewing Tretiak's *Mickiewicz i Puszkin* (*Vestnik Evropy*, Sept.-Dec., 1907, p. 745), that Tretiak is of the opinion that Pushkin's sadness in *Vospominanie,* and in other poems from this period, is due to a comparison of his own state with that of Mickiewicz.

[42] See translation of this into English verse by Noyes and Parish, *Konrad Wallenrod and Other Poems* (University of California Press: 1925), pp. 77.

[43] Cf. *Dzieła wszystkie*, VI, 283.

[44] Professor Krzyżanowski was so kind as to guide and advise most generously the work of my Polish research assistant in Warsaw during the preparation of this article. Anything I may quote from him is not from his published works, but from conversations my assistant had with him, either in person or over the telephone.

[45] Lednicki, *O Puszkine i Mickiewiczu, Słów kilka* (Kraków: 1924), p. 10. *Poltava* was published in March 1829, and when it came from the press Mickiewicz was one of the first to receive a copy.

[46] Kallenbach in his introduction to his edition of Mickiewicz's works, p. XXVI.

[47] Quoted from Stan. Windakiewicz, *Życia i dzieła* (Kraków: 1935), by Marja Rzeuska in her review of this work in *Wiadomosci Literackie*, No. 35, 1935, p. 4.

[48] See Kallenbach's introduction, p. XXVI.

[49] Józef Tretiak, *Mickiewicz i Puszkin* (Warsaw: 1906).

[50] The best summary of this anti-Russian sentiment is Lednicki's in his *Pouchkine et la Pologne* (Paris: 1928). As for the American evidence of it, I have come across a good deal in a recent examination of newspapers from 1830-1831, and shall embody the results in an article in the near future.

[51] Vladimir Spasowicz, *Sochineniya* (St. Petersburg: 1913), p. 226.

[52] Roman Pollak, "Mickiewicz e la Russia" in *La Cultura* (Rome: 1924-1925), VI, 357.

[53] *On mezhdu nami zhil* (II, 240).

[54] Kallenbach, *Mickiewicz*, IV, 332.

[55] *Dziady III*, in Kallenbach's *Mickiewicz*, IV, 71-205.

[56] When Professor Lednicki wrote his *Aleksander Puszkin* in 1926, he was inclined to agree with Brückner's hypothesis that the poet with whom Mickiewicz stood before Falconet's monument was Ryleev. By 1932, when he published his introduction to, and critical study of, *The Bronze Horseman* to accompany Tuwim's translation of it into Polish verse, Lednicki had come to the conclusion that the poet could be none other than Pushkin himself. To this opinion he still holds. In reviewing Lednicki's study of 1932 in the *Rocznik literacki* for 1933, Bluth inclines to agree with Lednicki's discarded hypothesis, the Ryleev theory. The Russian scholar Ciawkawski is in agreement with Lednicki concerning Pushkin's identity. From internal evidence we can hardly doubt that Pushkin is indeed the one whom Mickiewicz means.

[57] *Poltava* (III, 236).

[58] Quoted from Pushkin's *Historical Notes* by Lednicki in the third chapter of his Introduction to Tuwim's translation of *The Bronze Horseman*.

[59] Suggested by Lednicki in his Introduction to Tuwim's translation.

[60] Lednicki, Preface to *Przyjaciele Moskale*.

PUSHKIN'S SENSE OF MEASURE

By Alexander Kaun

Pushkin's phrase concerning the gifted and versatile Lomonosov, namely, that he "was our first university," [1] may not have been intended as an unqualified approval of his extraordinary career. The multiple contributions of the fisherman's son to Russia's nascent culture were amazing, but of course he was not equally proficient as chemist, physicist, mineralogist, astronomer, historian, grammarian and poet — not to mention hobbies such as building and installing machines, executing mosaics, or working on inventions, some of which anticipated Franklin. Certainly Lomonosov's grandiloquent odes impressed Pushkin as the indifferent efforts of a poetaster.[2]

Like Lomonosov, Pushkin was endowed with a versatile genius, though not in quite so many fields. What saved him from rivaling a "university," or in plain words, from the unevenness and occasional crudeness of a Jack-of-all-trades (often the fate of pioneers) was his inherent sense of measure. Practically everything touched by Pushkin's pen, not excepting the puerilities of his early teens, had the felicity of right proportion. His historical writings, for example, when we consider the paucity of available material, have, on the whole, stood the test of time. The leading historian Kliuchevski was gratified with Pushkin's intuitive historical sense.[3] Kireevski made use of his studies in Russian folklore; [4] and Professor Vsevolod Miller praised his ethnographic contributions in no uncertain terms.[5] It is in the purely literary field, however, that we are struck by Pushkin's breadth and mastery. There is hardly a branch of literature in which he failed to excel. Not only did he try his hand at every known form of imaginative verse and prose, but he also shone as a literary critic and historian, as a journalist, as a writer on poetics, and on language and grammar. In the words of Valeri Briusov: "It would be an easy matter to reconstruct the whole history of literature, from its very sources to the early part of the nineteenth century, from Homer to Victor Hugo and Alfred de Musset, by Pushkin's notes and letters, by his scattered comments in verse and prose." [6]

Pushkin's sense of measure is most impressive in the face of the multifarious influences exerted upon him by men and books. Acclaimed by the press and flattered by literary celebrities while still a schoolboy, he nevertheless showed great discrimination in selecting the proffered laurels. Moribund pseudo-classicism beckoned to him in the person of the grand old Derzhavin, who "gave us his blessing" [7] while he was still in the Lyceum. Even more alluring were the encouragement and friendship of the younger leaders, the sentimentalist Karamzin and the romanticist Zhukovski; but these congenial embraces he also managed to shake off before long. Yet, while freeing himself from such influences, he kept aloof from those who took delight in dethroning his idols. He chided young friends who spoke disrespectfully of their erstwhile master, Zhukovski: "Why bite the breast of the nurse the moment you have cut your teeth?" [8] In the apprenticeship stage he spurned nothing that would contribute to his literary development.

When Pushkin left school in 1817 a bitter controversy was raging between the followers of Admiral Shishkov and those of Karamzin concerning the proper language of literature. Shishkov championed the superiority of Church-Slavic over the language of the common people, as well as over the Frenchified speech of cultivated Russians. Karamzin, touched by the "new sensibility" of Western Europe, found himself cramped by archaic Church-Slavic, and began to use the spoken language of his contemporaries. Pushkin naturally joined the Karamzinists in the fight against pedantry but soon left them behind. He realized that Karamzin did not go far enough, since the language he defended was not that of the people but of the *salon* — the affected speech of noble ladies and gentlemen which was heavily saturated with gallicisms antedating the French Revolution. Pushkin waged a vigorous campaign in behalf of the language which he himself used with unequaled power and beauty: the autochthonous speech of the people, tempered, on occasion, by the dignity of Church-Slavic, and modernized by western, notably French, importations.[9]

As to the influence of books on Pushkin, a mere perusal of the incomplete catalogue of his library gives an idea of what an omnivorous and thorough reader he was.[10] If we add to these volumes the vast French library of his father, most of which he had read before he learned to use his Russian language, and the well-stocked school library and the State Archives where he spent many busy hours, we may gauge his extraordinary familiarity with literary compositions from the Bible to Washington Irving. Pushkin was the first professional man of letters in Russia, and by this is meant not only that he largely supported himself and his family by his pen: the whole realm of literature, regardless of time and place, was treated by Pushkin as his native province. Besides his national masterpieces, the vast range of his output, so remarkable for the brief span of his active years, echoes almost every literature. In translations and parodies he embraced the Orient and the Occident: the Bible and the Koran, Anacreon and Xenophanes, Juvenal and Horace, Tacitus and Dante, Hafiz and nameless Arabs, Tatars and Chinese. Modern Europeans are generously represented — Shakespeare and Ariosto, Voltaire and Chénier, Parny and Musset, Byron and Walter Scott, Ossian and Goethe, the Lake Poets and Bulwer-Lytton, songs of Spain, Portugal, Finland, and of various Slavic lands, and even a curious bit from America.[11] In these, and many other foreign pieces, Pushkin invariably reveals his "omnihuman" (Dostoevski's epithet[12]) faculty of breathing life and authenticity into every place or period that he touched.

What is the meaning of Pushkin's avid reading and borrowing? He was too much alive to be suspected of having been a bookworm. Nor is there any need to recall his wealth of ideas and abundance of creative imagination in order to dismiss the notion that he was an imitator through lack of originality. Pushkin was a professional man of letters, as vitally curious about the work of fellow craftsmen as an alert scientist is about the experiments of his colleagues; for roaming through world literature he took delight in transmuting into his own speech whatever struck him as fresh and beautiful in form or approach. A number of fragments found among Pushkin's papers, bits of translations or attempts at versifying prose (e.g., Batiushkov's version of Ariosto's *Orlando*), were hardly intended for publication; they were the author's laboratory tests. Thus, in translating the beginning of Voltaire's *Pucelle,* or a monologue from Alfieri, or lines from the Lake Poets, he was probably inspired by a desire to try his ability at Russifying foreign talent. One must remember that in both form and content Russian literature was still in its groping stage. He performed the chores of a pioneer, but he did the work so lovingly that an experiment was transferred into a work of genius.

The effect of Shakespeare and Byron on Pushkin will be discussed presently. Here I wish to point out how communion with books often impelled the poet to emulate, excel, or differ from the original, or to start off on something only casually connected with it. Though prejudiced against the sonnet, he was attracted by its form, and his reading of Wordsworth prompted him to compose three perfect sonnets.[13] On the other hand, it was probably Wordsworth's poem, *Gypsies,* with its somewhat priggish contempt of "such torpid life" of the "wild outcasts of society," that caused Pushkin to counter it with his nostalgic *Gypsies,* the lines of which are charged with envy for the carefree "happy tribe." His indebtedness to Coleridge was also variable; among other things he probably owed him the title of his *Table Talk,* the idea of the "Improvisatore" in his *Egyptian Nights,* and the epigraph to

Anchar.[15] Bulwer-Lytton's *Pelham* certainly suggested the fragment, *A Russian Pelham,* which only in part is reminiscent of the original. Pushkin must have borrowed some of Walter Scott's narrative methods for his *Tales of Belkin,* though a contemporary critic hinted that the stark simplicity of the *Tales* was in imitation of Washington Irving.[16] It is more than likely that the idea for his unsurpassed *Little Tragedies* came to him while reading Barry Cornwall's *Dramatic Scenes*.[17] An untraced "Armenian legend,"[18] the Apocrypha, Voltaire, and Parny probably combined to provide him with the incentive for his charming but blasphemous *Gavriliada.* Readings in Tacitus and Aurelius Victor suggested the atmosphere for the glorious lines on Cleopatra in *Egyptian Nights*.[19] It was natural for Vuk Karadjić's collection of Serbian folk ballads to encourage his interest in Slavic lore, and to suggest the meter for his *Tale of the Fisherman and the Little Fish.* Like Mickiewicz, he responded enthusiastically to Prosper Mérimée's *La Guzla,* and he translated the poems as authentic, and published them as a part of his *Songs of the Western Slavs.* So profoundly natural was the Russian rendition that even after *La Guzla* proved to be a clever hoax,[20] Pushkin's *Songs* remained fresh and genuine.

One could go on citing examples of the way in which Pushkin transformed his borrowings by passing them through the alembic of his own genius, but one more case may suffice. *A Feast During the Plague* is a translation of scene IV from John Wilson's *The City of the Plague.* Apart from the general superiority of Pushkin's verse and his effective restraint, the Russian version contains two practically original poems which eclipse the rest of the composition by their power and beauty. I refer to the lyric song of Mary that takes the place of Wilson's lengthy and arid *Mary Gray's Song,* and more particularly to Walsingham's *Hymn to the Plague,* substituted for the original *Song of the Plague.* The haunting grimness of the *Hymn* reduces the *Song* to a cold intellectual exercise.

Much has been written concerning Pushkin's debt to Shakespeare and Byron; he readily acknowledged this himself. The English authors served as important milestones in Pushkin's literary development, but there is no need to exaggerate their influence. In his formative years he imbibed deeply of French literature. The early influence of Boileau, Corneille, Molière and Racine had a much deeper effect on him than that of their successors, however great may have been his devotion to later French writers. At the beginning of his career, these seventeenth-century French masters still held practically undisputed sway over Russian letters, especially the drama. Though he later outgrew them, and on occasion resented their tyranny, it is certain that they helped form his literary taste, and it is probably to them that he owed the classical precision and clarity of his style. But, restive and eager for new forms, he was continually exploring every source within sight and reach. By the end of his teens he discovered the English and found them more congenial and timely than the French. To be sure, his first passion, Byron, came to him second hand, in a French prose version. Before long, however, he mastered the English language [21] sufficiently to appreciate the Lake Poets and his most valuable discovery, Shakespeare.

Pushkin's infatuation with Byron lasted only a few years. Young, passionate, iconoclastic, and an exile to southern, exotic Russia, he was naturally drawn to the personality of Byron. The latter's Eastern poems had lent a decided flavor to Pushkin's *Prisoner of the Caucasus, The Bakhchisarai Fountain,* and *The Gypsies.* Traces of "Byronism" may be found in a number of other poems. The subject of *Poltava* must have been suggested by *Mazeppa,* and the form of *Eugene Onegin* by *Don Juan.* The quotation marks are used advisedly, since the essential feature of Byronism, a demonic hero, is rather lamely presented by Pushkin. Even in his three most "Byronic" poems, the Prisoner was felt by Pushkin himself to be unromantically sensible,[22] Girei, of the *Fountain,* brought laughter to his intimate friends,[23] while Aleko

of *The Gypsies* displays all the shallowness of sham individualists
and rebels. He made use of Byron's technique and found kinship
in his lighter moods, his whims and raillery, but Pushkin's sense
of measure, his classical balance, militated against exaggeration
and pose. At the very outset, his Byronic characters were notice-
ably toned down, and gradually they were subjected to an ironic
treatment. In his most mature work, *Eugene Onegin,* the notion
of a "Muscovite in the cloak of Childe Harold" has the humor of
a local incongruity.

Much deeper and lasting was the effect of Shakespeare on Pushkin. Russia was not quite ready for Shakespeare,[24] and Pushkin
had to "discover" him and to discard in his favor a heap of well-
nigh canonized authorities. In the light of Shakespeare's broad
understanding of human nature, Byron paled into a monotonous
egocentric who had "conceived only one character — his own —
and had endowed each of his personages with one trait or another
of his own." [25] At the same time he found Shakespeare's creations
both more natural and more humanly complex than those of the
French masters. In a fragment, *On the Drama,* he gave resolute
preference to the robust and at times pungent speech of Shakespeare's men over the mincing artificiality of Racine's.[26] As
against Molière's personification in each character of one certain
passion or vice, he saw in Shakespeare "living beings instinct
with many passions, many vices; their variegated and multiple
characters evolved before the spectator by the force of circumstances." [27] Such views were both new and bold for followers of
the French tradition. He had the temerity to state his "deep
conviction" that for the Russian theatre were "suited the popular
laws of the Shakespearean drama, and not the court conventions
of Racine's tragedy." [28] Accordingly, with his *Boris Godunov*
he introduced the refreshing breeze of Shakespeare into the stale
Russian drama. With all the drawbacks of the play (precisely
as a play), one must remember its revolutionizing mission of
shattering the pomposity and the Procrustean conventions of the

pseudo-classical drama. Admittedly, Pushkin followed Shakespeare in his "free and broad delineation of character," as well as in "simplicity." [29] The stiff Alexandrines he replaced by blank verse, even by occasional prose, and he did not hesitate to juxtapose tragedy and comedy, palaces and roadhouses, crowned heads and vodka-swilling hoboes.

It is doubtful whether Pushkin took seriously the Virgilian prophecy of his brilliant contemporary, Mickiewicz: *"Tu Shakespearus eris, si fata sinant."* [30] His sense of measure precluded exaggerated self-importance, for he would hardly have aspired to be anyone but himself. Even Shakespeare was no absolute to him. Pushkin helped himself lavishly to the master's treasury. *Boris Godunov* bristles with Shakespearean phrases and ideas. Had his life not been so stupidly cut short, he might have carried out his intention of writing three sequel plays, by way of a Russian "Chronicle." [31] Yet he seasoned all his borrowings with a grain of salt. What suited Elizabethan England might sound out of place in nineteenth-century Russia. To be sure, in *Godunov* and elsewhere he did his best to present his characters with historical truth, and perhaps for that very reason he parted company with Shakespeare, whose "lictors retain the manners of London aldermen." [32] Shakespeare fanatics may regard as blasphemy the suggestion that Pushkin excels his master in economy of means. Compare, for intensity of effect, Shakespeare's lengthy monologues and dialogues with Pushkin's deliberate brevity and concentration. Nearly every scene or passage in *Boris Godunov* that is reminiscent of *Richard the Third* or *King John* or some other Shakespeare play is by comparison more compactly dramatic. Such a phrase in *Godunov* as "The crowd is speechless," to cite one example, tells as much to the imagination as the Duke of Buckingham's copious lines to the effect that the citizens "spake not a word." [33] In his *Little Tragedies* Pushkin went even further in practicing laconism; the shortest of these, *Mozart and Salieri,* represents a marvel of dramatic economy of means.

A suggestive case in point is Pushkin's *Angelo*, an attempted improvement on *Measure for Measure*. Why did Pushkin choose this play? It has been lamented and apologized for by most critics, from Johnson and Coleridge to Swinburne and Brandes. Sir Arthur Quiller-Couch pronounces *Measure for Measure* "a great play — in parts — and in despite that its parts do not fit." [34] Pushkin must have reacted in the same way. He was drawn to this play, began to translate it, gave up the task, and finally embarked on a modified version, partly in narrative form. What *Angelo* meant for him can be seen from a passage in a fragmentary note where he compares this character with Tartuffe: ". . . Molière's hypocrite courts his benefactor's wife — hypocritically; assumes guardianship over the estate — hypocritically; asks for a glass of water — hypocritically. Shakespeare's hypocrite pronounces sentences with vain severity, but in accordance with justice; he justifies his cruelty by the grave considerations of a statesman; he tempts innocence with powerful and luring sophistry, not with a funny mixture of piety and flirtation. Angelo is a hypocrite because his overt actions contradict his secret passions. What depth there is in his character!" [35]

Attracted by this character, and annoyed by the gaucherie of a fellow craftsman, Pushkin composed *Angelo*. Whatever its merits, *Angelo* is free from the main faults of *Measure for Measure*, from its coarse bawdry, crude comedy, top-heavy parallelism of actors and scenes and glaring superfluities. In *Angelo* the action moves smoothly and swiftly and with finer motivation. Overboard have gone such dispensable and rather confusing characters as Escalus, Abhorson, the Barnardine, Elbow, Pompey, Mistress Overdone, and others. The Duke is burdened with years and experience, and is spared the ordeal of making "Oh, so sudden" a proposal to Isabella in the last scene. Lucio is less of an improbable nuisance on the stage, and Isabella less of a soulless prig. Above all else, Angelo is portrayed as a man of inner contradictions, caught in tragic conflict with himself and less obviously mean and unscrupulous. The piece is thus given psychological probability and a fluent structure, both of which elements have been questioned in *Measure for Measure*.

Shakespeare undoubtedly helped Pushkin to find himself and to bring out that psychological realism which had been inherent in him throughout his literary wanderings. Like Russia, Pushkin was a late comer in western civilization. Like Russia, he benefited from the absence of deeply rooted traditions and the resultant ease of adoption, especially with regard to technique. Pushkin's sense of measure taught him how to enrich his native letters with the finest jewels of world literature. At the same time his national genius continues to be the cornerstone of literary Russia. So national, in fact, is his genius, that to feel Pushkin fully one must be born in Russia. This is unfortunate, for not only is Pushkin largely untranslatable, but even those foreigners who read him in the original often miss the essence of that genius.

THE UNIVERSITY OF CALIFORNIA

NOTES

[1] *Puteshestvie Moskvy v Peterburg* (VI, 114).

[2] Cf. *ibid.* See also *O predislovii g-na Lemonte k perevodu basen I. A. Krylova* (V, 15-16).

[3] *Russkaya Mysl* (Moscow: June, 1800), I, 22, *passim; ibid.* (February, 1887), VIII, 291-306.

[4] Kireevski received from Pushkin a large collection of village songs. According to Buslaev, Pushkin warned Kireevski that some of the songs had been composed by himself, but Kireevski failed to discover the "forgeries." See *Vestnik Evropy* (October, 1891), X, 637.

[5] V. Miller remarks: "Pushkin's services for Russian ethnography are indubitable"; *Pushkin kak poet-etnograf* (Moscow: 1899), p. 54.

[6] *Moi Pushkin* (Moscow: 1929), p. 204.

[7] *Evgeni Onegin*, VII, ii (IV, 157).

[8] *Perepiska*, No. 121, I, 168.

[9] For various scattered remarks on this subject by Pushkin, see the critical articles in the sixth volume of his works. An interesting study of the subject may be found in V. V. Vinogradov's *Yazyk Pushkina* (Moscow: 1935).

[10] Cf. B. L. Modzalevski, "Biblioteka Pushkina: bibliograficheskoe opisanie," *Pushkin i ego sovremenniki* (St. Petersburg: 1910), vols. IX-X. Additional material may be found in L. B. Modzalevski's "Biblioteka Pushkina," *Literaturnoe Nasledstvo* (Moscow: 1934), XVI-XVIII, 985-1024.

[11] *Dzhon Tenner,* signed "The Reviewer," in Pushkin's *Sovremennik* (St. Petersburg: 1836), III, 205-256. Number 1423 of Pushkin's library gives the title of the book he used for this article: *Mémoires de John Tanner, ou trente années dans les deserts de l'Amerique du Nord,* traduits sur l'édition originale publiée à New York . . . Paris, 1835 (cf. B. L. Modzalevski, "Biblioteka Pushkina," p. 346). The original was published in New York in 1830, being notes of the illiterate author dictated to Edwin James. In 1831 Tocqueville bought the book from Tanner.

[12] Speech at the unveiling of Pushkin's monument at Moscow in 1880: Dostoevski, *Dnevnik pisatelya za 1880: Pushkin.*

[13] *Sonet, Poetu,* and *Madonna,* all of which were composed in 1830. Pushkin's dislike of the sonnet was noted in his early poem *Poslanie k Galichu* (1815), and in another poem *Frantsuzskikh rifmachei surovy sudiya,* in which he addresses Boileau: "Thou hast overpraised the worth of the sonnet." (II, 238). See B. V. Tomashevski, *Pushkinski sbornik* (Moscow: 1922), p. 220.

[14] Pushkin's *Tsygany* (1830) — not to be confused with his long poem *Tsygany,* composed in 1824 — had as its subtitle, "From the English." N. V. Yakovlev suggests that Pushkin was inspired by Wordsworth's *Gypsies* and Bowles' *The Gypsy Tent* to write a poem of contrasting sentiments (*Pushkin i ego sovremenniki,* XXXVI, 63-70).

[15] The epigraph reads: "It is a poison tree that, pierced to the inmost, Weeps only tears of poison." This was borrowed from Coleridge's *Remorse* (act I, scene 1). Pushkin had a copy (No. 762; B. L. Modzalevski, "Biblioteka Pushkina," p. 198) of the 1829 Paris edition of *The Poetical Works of Coleridge, Shelley,* and *Keats.* It must have been in the same edition that he read Coleridge's the *Improvisatore* (pp. 222-224). Under No. 760 of Pushkin's library is listed *Specimens of the Table Talk of the late Samuel Taylor Coleridge,* London, 1836. To be sure, he also had William Hazlitt's *Table Talk* (No. 974; B. L. Modzalevski, "Biblioteka Pushkina," p. 2461), but as N. V. Yakovlev has pointed out (*Pushkin v mirovoi literature,* Leningrad, 1926, pp. 139-140), the anecdotal form of Pushkin's *Table Talk* resembles more the work of Coleridge than the essays of Hazlitt.

[16] Cf. N. A. Polevoi (*Moskovski Telegraf,* 1831, No. 2), whose statement is quoted by Vinogradov, *Yazyk Pushkina,* p. 358.

[17] Pushkin translated several poems of Cornwall and began *The Falcon.* Shortly before his last duel he requested A. O. Ishimova to translate for his *Sovremennik* several dramas by Cornwall. On his deathbed he expressed concern about these translations. Five of *The Dramatic Scenes* did appear in the posthumous issue of the *Sovremennik* (No. 8), with the publisher's note: "One may say that in Pushkin's literary life Barry Cornwall was his last interlocutor." Cf. *Pushkin i ego sovremenniki,* XXVII, 5-28.

[18] *Gavriiliada* ii. 136-137 (III, 124).

[19] Pushkin erroneously regarded Aurelius Victor as the author of *De viris illustribus,* where he came upon a striking passage about Cleopatra. In the "Preliminary Fragments" to *Egyptian Nights* Pushkin has Aleksei Ivanovich remark about that passage: "What is notable is that in this place the dry and tedious Aurelius Victor equals Tacitus in force of expression: 'Haec tantae libidinis fuit, ut saepe prostituerit: tantae pulchritudinis, ut multi noctem illius morte emerint.' " (*My provodili vecher na dashe u Knyagin D,* IV, 713). Pushkin was reading this fourth-century writer along with Tacitus; the subject is discussed by M. Pokrovski,

"Pushkin i rimskiye istoriki," *Sbornik statei posvyashchennykh V. O. Kliuchevskomu* (Moscow: 1909), p. 485.

[20] Mérimée's interesting letter about his hoax, with apologies to Pushkin, has recently appeared in full, *Literaturnoe Nasledstvo*, XVI-XVIII, 758-765.

[21] The question of Pushkin's mastery of the English language is discussed by V. Zhirmunski, *Bairon i Pushkin*, (Leningrad: 1924), pp. 326-327, and by M. Tsyavlovski, *Pushkin i ego sovremenniki*, XVII-XVIII, 48-73, and by others. M. E. Iuzefovich states that Pushkin pronounced English as Latin, having learned the language without the help of a teacher, but that in 1829 he translated Shakespeare by sight faultlessly ("Vospominaniya," *Russki Arkhiv*, March 1880, pp. 444-445).

[22] Letter to Prince V. P. Gorchakov: "The character of my Prisoner is a failure; this proves that I am not good for a hero of a romantic poem" (*Perepiska*, No. 27, I, 36). See also a letter to P. Vyazemski (*Perepiska*, No. 48, I, 68).

[23] See Pushkin's *Zametki o rannikh poemakh* (VI, 315).

[24] See Chapter VIII of Ernest J. Simmons' *English Literature and Culture in Russia, 1553-1840* (Cambridge, Mass., 1935).

[25] Draft of letter to N. N. Raevski: "Ce Byron qui n'a jamais conçu qu'un seul caractère . . . (et c'est le sien . . .) ce Byron donc . . . a partagé entre ses personages tel et tel trait de son caractère; son orgueil à l'un; sa haine à l'autre, sa mélancolie au troisième etc., et c'est ainsi que d'un caractère plein, sombre et énergique il a fait plusieurs caractères insignificants. . . ." (*Perepiska*, No. 184, I, 248).

[26] *O drame* (VI, 81).

[27] *Shailok, Andzhelo i Falstaf Shekspira* (VI, 340).

[28] *Nabroski predisloviya k Borisu Godunovu* (VI, 303).

[29] *Ibid.*

[30] Quoted by Ivanov-Razumnik, *Istoriya russkoi obshchestvennoi mysli* (St. Petersburg: 1908), I, 108; also by V. Briusov, *Moi Pushkin*, pp. 168-169.

[31] L. N. Maikov, *Pushkin* (St. Petersburg: 1899), p. 330.

[32] *O drame* (VI, 82).

[33] *King Richard the Third* (III, vii).

[34] Introduction to Cambridge edition of *Measure for Measure*, 1922, p. XLI.

[35] *Shailok, Andzhelo i Falstaf Shekspira* (VI, 340).

PUSHKIN'S PROSE WRITINGS

By George Z. Patrick

The prose works of Pushkin owe their importance to the fact that they represent the fruits of a period in which his creative powers and poetic insight had expanded to full maturity. All of them were written during the years 1827-36 when the author, having freed himself from foreign influences, came closer to Russian life, grasped its spirit, its problems, divined its ideals. This consideration alone justifies the closer examination of Pushkin's prose which, if not of the same quality as his poetry, occupies a rightfully prominent place in Russian literature.

Two forms of expression are distinguishable in a survey of these prose writings: historical novels and imaginative stories. In his historical novels the author dealt with three important periods: the time of Peter the Great in *The Negro of Peter the Great*; the reign of Catherine II, in *The Captain's Daughter*; and that of Alexander I in *Roslavlev*.

In these novels is presented a real and typical atmosphere of the particular time described; the narrative contains no exaggeration of detail and no false coloring of the background. Pushkin well understood the past which he reproduced, penetrating to the very core of the period in a faithful picture of its moods and trends. Always he attempted to reduce the peculiarities of the past to terms of everyday life, as if to show that those quaint and unusual incidents, which from a distance of ages seem to be out of the ordinary, are in reality nothing but logical, natural manifestations of daily routine.

Between 1824 and 1826 Pushkin was obliged to spend two years "like a hermit," on his country estate of Mikhailovskoe, and it was during this interval that he turned his attention to historical writings. In Russia, as well as in Western Europe, the early part of the nineteenth century was noteworthy for an awakened interest in historical research. As in practically all European countries under the influence of romanticism, Russian poets found a fertile field in themes borrowed from national life. This stimulus, heightened by a natural reaction against outworn pseudo-classicism, led to the appearance of divers works which were based on a study of the folklore of various ethnographic groups. In the purely literary field the well known historical novels of Walter Scott called forth in Russia a number of similar works by Zagoskin (1792-1853), Lazhechnikov (1792-1869), and others. These writers, considered in their own time as the Russian Walter Scotts, are now almost forgotten, while Pushkin is still recognized as a model for such recent historical productions as Aleksei Tolstoi's *Peter the First*.

The Negro of Peter the Great, first of the historical group, was published in 1827, and Abram Hannibal, the hero of this unfinished novel, was one of Pushkin's ancestors. The work bears unmistakable traces of the author's profound historical perception, and its most striking attribute is its perfect objectivity. Before us there unfolds a dispassionate, cool, and even narrative of actual historical incidents and persons. Life in St. Petersburg in the eighteenth century is described so vividly that it stands out in bold relief. Imperceptibly the reader is carried away by this picture of the past and almost feels himself breathing the very air of a bygone period.

The character of Peter the Great plays a large part in the novel, and the tsar is portrayed against the background of everyday life. One learns of his industry, his activity, his simplicity, and of the unassumed manner of his dealings with his subjects. Particularly colorful are the scenes of Peter's meeting with his godson, the negro Abram, recently come from France; of the assembly where the tsar, amidst clouds of tobacco smoke, plays chess with a Dutch skipper; and that of the sovereign's call on the boyar Gavrila Afanasevich R. (Rzhevski). With a few masterly strokes the author unfolds the spiritual make-up of the nobles of Peter's Russia, their haughtiness, their crass ignorance, and their superstitious dread of enlightenment. Despite their opposition to the policies of Peter, they bow down in abject fear before the will of their stern master. Even in his most rebellious mood, Gavrila Afanasevich passively submits to the order that his daughter marry the young African. Though humiliated and hurt by the proposal, Rzhevski could not think of protesting openly before the tsar.

The character of Abram is barely outlined and, on the whole, rather vague. `After having lived in Paris for several years, the African arrives in St. Petersburg disillusioned, with a broken heart, and his faith in love and happiness shattered. His wounds somewhat healed, he begins to look for a quiet haven of family life, and decides to marry a Russian girl.

Pushkin interrupted his work on this novel, for he appears to have contemplated a radical change in the plot. But he never returned to it. In sum, *The Negro of Peter the Great* presents to the observer a realistic picture of the time with all its lights and shadows.

In 1832 and 1833, while collecting material for a history of Peter the Great, which he never lived to complete, Pushkin happened to discover some valuable documents belonging to the Pugachev uprising (1773-1775). Since the details of this revolt were but little known to his contemporaries, Pushkin thought of presenting a full account of the rebellion, basing his story on official sources and reminiscences of the survivors of that troublous period. In the course of his reading of the dry, formal archives, his poetic fancy wove from the naked unadorned facts a rich and colorful pattern with lifelike participants presented against a real background of the Pugachev rebellion. The fruits of such interaction of analytical study and poetic imagination were: *The History of Pugachev Rebellion*, published in 1834, a brilliant historical monograph, and *The Captain's Daughter*, which appeared in 1836 in the *Contemporary*, a magazine edited by Pushkin himself. For a closer acquaintance with the place of action, and in order to absorb local color, Pushkin had previously toured the provinces of Kazan and Orenburg, gathering on his way various legends in connection with the topic in which he was interested.

The Captain's Daughter is the most remarkable prose novel of Pushkin. Its historical and literary settings are complete and delightful, and for its artistic quality it must be placed high among the author's masterpieces. There are no hastily written or clumsy passages in it; every scene, almost every word, is fully justified by the requirements of the plot and the descriptive elements. Grinev's dream and the brief picture of the snow-storm (Chapter 2) reveal the great poet whose imagery, economy, and brilliant style are perfection itself. But the chief merits of the novel lie again in the author's amazing ability to grasp the spirit of the historical period he describes, and in the realistic picture he gives of life in the homes of the Russian nobility at the end of the eighteenth century.

The Russian literary critic Apollon Grigorev called *The Captain's Daughter* a "Family Chronicle." Indeed, this novel is to a great extent devoted to an account of the lives of two families: the Grinevs and the Mironovs. Pugachev and his rebellious followers are introduced into the story for a brief period to bring death and destruction into the peaceful, patriarchal existence of such families, and then they vanish again. The traces of ruin and devastation soon effaced, life takes again its usual course, and in place of the perished Mironovs comes the family of the young Grinevs. Even when looked upon as merely a record of Russian eighteenth-century family life, *The Captain's Daughter* stands in the first rank and may justly be considered a forerunner of Aksakov's *Family Chronicle* and of Tolstoi's *War and Peace*.

In picturing the life of the Grinevs Pushkin introduces us to that milieu which molded the moral and spiritual traits of such men as Peter Grinev, the hero of the novel. Throughout his life Peter follows his father's moral code: "Watch over your honor while you are young." There are many blunders and mistakes in young Grinev's life, but he does nothing for which he will be ashamed of in old age.

Of particular interest are the character sketches of Captain Mironov, of Mariya Ivanovna his daughter, of Savelich, and of Pugachev.

Captain Mironov, a henpecked husband, drags out a wretched existence under the constant supervision of a strong-willed wife who manages not only her household but also the entire fortress of Belogorsk. His only concern is to come out, clad in nightcap and flannel dressing gown, to drill his men for a few minutes before dinner. Even in this soldierly routine the captain proved ineffectual, for he cannot, no matter by what effort, teach his soldiers which is the right-hand side and which the left. Yet in time of distress one sees this simple soul in all the glory of undaunted courage, in all the greatness of an indomitable sense of duty. In the face of death he cannot resort to deception, and he fearlessly calls Pugachev a thief, a rebel, and an impostor. To Captain Mironov, as to old Grinev, military service is not a road toward personal career and riches, but the sacred duty of every able-bodied man. His conviction of duty to the throne has in it a trace of abstract idealism.

With a very fine touch does Pushkin portray Mariya Ivanovna, Captain Mironov's daughter. A simple Russian girl, kindhearted and modest, she is sincere in her affections and wholly free from affectations or mannerisms. Her portrait is drawn with such precision and delicacy that it is hardly inferior to that of Tatyana in *Eugene Onegin*. Tatyana may appeal more to the imagination, her sad and pensive face so romantic as to be entirely captivating. But the modest face of Mariya is framed in such a halo of purity and poetry that she rightly takes her place among the best feminine portraits in Russian literature.

The portrait of Savelich is also one of Pushkin's best. His character lives to illustrate the simple relations between serfs and their masters. In the old servitor Pushkin does not defend the institution of serfdom which he hated, for he understood very well the baneful influence the bondage of the peasants had upon the life of Russia. "Shall I ever see a people liberated and bondage broken by orders of the tsar?" — exclaims the poet in *The Village*. At the same time his treatment of relationship between masters and serfs, based on common bonds of mutual understanding, is just and unbiased.

Savelich, concerned especially with Peter Grinev's well-being, is at times a rather comical figure. His simplicity and naïveté appear ridiculous. But his boundless devotion, his humility, and, at the same time, his sense of human dignity inspire both author and reader with sympathy toward this faithful servant. In the portrayal of Savelich Pushkin reveals his keen insight into the soul of the common people.

With equal efficacy Pushkin represents the character of Pugachev as a combination of ruthless cruelty and mercy. To gratify his vanity and ambition Pugachev, the would-be Peter III, destroys all in his path and tramples upon his victims. Yet sparks of gentleness and humane feelings flicker in this dark savage soul. Not only does he remember kindness, but on occasion repays it generously. In gratitude he saves the lives of Peter Grinev and his fiancée because the young man had been kind to him at some earlier time.

The Captain's Daughter is written with such knowledge of Russian life and manners of the eighteenth century, with such understanding of the various aspects of the Russian character that it charms the reader on the hundredth perusal.

The third historical novel *Roslavlev* is, like *The Negro of Peter the Great*, unfinished. The author's intent in this undertaking was to present a picture of Russian society at the time of the national war of 1812, a picture more faithful than that given by Zagoskin in his book *Roslavlev, or The Russians in 1812* (1830). In the fragments of Pushkin's *Roslavlev* the character of a public-spirited young Russian woman, Polina, resembles that of Turgenev's Elena, heroine of *On the Eve.*

To the second group, that of imaginative writings, belong *The Tales of Belkin,* five short, rapidly told stories: *The Shot, The Snow Storm, The Lady-Rustic, The Station Master,* and *The Coffin Maker.* They were written in the autumn of 1830, when Pushkin, because of a quarantine during a cholera epidemic, was confined for three months in Boldino, one of his country estates. Pushkin ascribes *The Tales* to a certain Ivan Petrovich Belkin, a man of pathetic candor, naïveté, and simplicity. These attributes in the alleged narrator seem to serve as a justification for the self-effacement of the real author, a device which Pushkin considered essential to a good story-teller.

Belkin represents a goodly half of Pushkin's own spiritual make-up. There is a great similarity in their biographies (Belkin's fictitious biography appears in the preface to *The Tales*). The year of Belkin's birth is 1798 and that of Pushkin's is 1799. They both delight in their nurses' fairy tales, which they heard in their childhood, and reinterpret in their mature days. They both feel that they have a great deal to learn after leaving the school bench. Each plans to write a solemn epic poem and a tragedy dealing with the reign of Rurik (Pushkin's *Vadim*); and when these plans end in failure, they turn to ballad writing (Pushkin's *The Bridegroom, The Drowned Man*). At one time they looked rather disdainfully upon prose writing, but gradually they take it up and busy themselves with collecting material for historical narratives.

This does not mean that the personality of Belkin should be identified with that of Pushkin. The goodnaturedness and artlessness of Ivan Petrovich, his sympathetic and humane dealings with the downtrodden, his common sense and ready wit, his longing for a wider education, and his love for the country life — all this has been borrowed from the author. But the latter has far outstripped Belkin's artlessness and circumscribed naïveté. In

Pushkin's character Belkin's traits are apparent; but so are some of Onegin's. That is why Pushkin is neither the one nor the other. Toward his two most important literary characters, Onegin and Belkin, Pushkin's attitude is quite objective. He judges them by the dictates of poetic truth.

The best of the five *Tales* are: *The Station Master* and *The Coffin Maker*, in which is painted vividly the simple life of people belonging to the lower social stratum. The realistic characters and their environment are drawn with painstaking care, without distorting the actual conditions or embellishing the sordid scenes of the life of the lowly.

In *The Station Master* the author relates the sad fate of an humble man whose only daughter runs away from home with a passing hussar and subsequently becomes his mistress. Her father, to whom Dunya had been the only joy and solace in his old age, grieves for a long time over her disappearance. At last, having learned that she is living in St. Petersburg, he seeks her out. He sees her amidst the luxurious surroundings of a rich home. However, the meeting is cut short by Dunya's lover who rudely turns out the old man. And the poor station master goes back to his post to drink himself to death.

Pushkin can measure the sufferings of the station master without resorting to Karamzin's lachrymose sentimentalism in his *Poor Liza*; and the sad fate of the lonely old man fills the reader with genuine pity. The story begins in a humorous strain, but as it nears its conclusion tears can be discerned through the laughter, and the entire tone of the narrative is suffused with warmhearted, wistful sadness. In *The Station Master* Pushkin reveals himself as the precursor of such important realistic stories as Gogol's *The Cloak* and Dostoevski's *Poor Folk*. It will be remembered that the clerk Devushkin, the hero of *Poor Folk*, praises Pushkin's story very highly and pities the lot of the station master.

The main characters of *The Coffin Maker* are poor artisans: Prokhorov, the coffin maker, a morose and melancholy man,

breaks his customary silence only to scold his daughter; the shoe-
maker Schultz, who considers his friend's trade more profitable
than his own because "the living can do without shoes but the dead
cannot do without coffins"; and the watchman Yurko, solemnly
pacing back and forth near his watch house, carrying his axe and
wearing a gray coat of mail. This story is focussed upon the simple
ways of the common folk, and may justly be regarded as one of
the first prose writings in Russian literature in which reality and
an unalleviated humdrum existence are treated with great skill.

There is an opinion current among Russian literary critics that
The Chronicle of the Manor of Goriukhino is a parody on either
Karamzin's *History of the Russian State* or on Polevoi's *History
of the Russian People*. Such a view seems to be erroneous, for this
Chronicle is related also by Belkin, who in character is neither
capable nor desirous of resorting to a deliberate parody. *The
Chronicle of the Manor of Goriukhino* is partly an innocent farce,
partly a satire ridiculing the "half-baked" intellectuals who take
upon themselves the performance of a task beyond their strength.
The style of the work is solemn, pompous, and stilted and, in the
opinion of Belkin, most becoming to an historical narrative. As
a true scholar Belkin appends a list of sources to his monograph:
1. A collection of calendars in 55 parts, with extremely brief and
clear entries, such as: "May 6: it snowed, Trishka was beaten for
drunkenness; May 9: the brown cow died, Senka was beaten for
drunkenness; May 11: clear weather, caught three hares"; 2. The
chronicle of Goriukhino's deacon, "acquired for a measure of
oats"; 3. Oral accounts of human privations; 4. The data of the
census. Moreover, the *Chronicle* deals with certain episodes typical
of serfdom: the master's stern demand for a double amount of the
quit-rent; the meetings of the village commune, so stupid, absurd;
recruiting; peasant family life in which at first the wives beat their
husbands and then the husbands take their turn in venting their
wrath upon their better halves; fisticuffs, drunkenness, and bouts
— all of which testify to the retarded state of cultural development

in Pushkin's Russia. The comic aspect and the drollness of the story become particularly striking where the solemn style of the narrative becomes obviously incongruous and irrelevant to describing the most commonplace occurrences and trivial things. In spite of all the naïveté of Belkin's narrative, one becomes convinced that he not only knows the humble people but has a deep love and sympathy for them. Here Pushkin appears as a brilliant and witty satirist.

The Queen of Spades, another of Pushkin's prose masterpieces, has a feature in common with The Coffin Maker, in spite of the totally different social background and status of the characters. The element common in both stories is that tinge of fantasy which makes them somewhat akin to the tales of Hoffman and, in Russian literature, to Lermontov's Fragment from a Story and Gogol's The Portrait and The Nose. In The Coffin Maker, this touch of fantasy is limited only to the unpleasant dream of Prokhorov. In The Queen of Spades it pervades the entire story and looms over the whole plot like some mysterious and fatal curse. Accordingly, the tone of these two is quite different. The first is written in a playful, humorous style; the latter runs in a cold, dry, and relentless vein, just as cold and harsh as the hero Hermann himself.

Dubrovski is the story of a young officer whose father is ruined by his wealthy and greedy neighbor, Troekurov, to whom all the local authorities are completely subservient. To avenge himself young Dubrovski becomes a highway robber, introduces himself into the house of Troekurov as a French tutor, but forgoes his revenge because of his love for his enemy's daughter. This tale presents a sordid picture of Russian rural conditions and of Russian legal procedure under Catherine II. The two noblemen, Troekurov and Vereiski, both bullies, are impressive creations in Pushkin's portrait gallery.

In all his prose stories except the historical ones, Pushkin seems to have been more interested in masculine types than in feminine.

What he says of Olga in *Eugene Onegin* is merely a reaction from what he had seen in many Russian families: the triviality and spiritual vacuity of young provincial misses bored him to distraction. The following sarcastic lines from *The Lady-Rustic* illustrate this particular viewpoint:

"Those of my readers who have never lived in the country cannot imagine how charming these provincial young ladies are! Brought up in the pure air, under the shadow of the apple trees of their gardens, they derive their knowledge of the world and of life chiefly from books. Solitude, freedom, and reading develop very early within them sentiments and passions unknown to our town-bred beauties. For the young ladies of the country the sound of the post-bell is an event; a journey to the nearest town marks an epoch in their lives, and the visit of a guest leaves behind a long and sometimes an eternal recollection."

All the young ladies in Pushkin's non-historical works serve as mere illustrations of this general characterization. Each heroine may have her own idiosyncrasies, but all are distinguished by their sluggish intellectual life. Much more diversified are the author's masculine characters — Troekurov, the Dubrovskis, Vereiski, the Berestovs, Silvio, Muromski — whose individual traits are so conspicuous that it is impossible to generalize concerning them.

Kirdjali, a character sketch of a Bulgarian brigand at the time of the Greek revolt, is of little importance.

Mention should be made also of *The Egyptian Nights* and *The Russian Pelham,* both unfinished. In the first, Pushkin tried to point out how little poetry was appreciated by his contemporaries. In the second, the author planned to present a realistic picture of that society in which he found himself upon the completion of his studies at the Lyceum of Tsarskoe Selo.

As a poet Pushkin still stands unrivalled in Russia. As a prose writer he surpasses only his predecessors, and at the same time indicates a wider field to those who follow. His prose writings lack the limpidity, the ease, and the musical rhythm of his verse;

their value lies chiefly in the simplicity of style and in the anticipation of Gogol and the Russian realistic school.

There is an idle tradition that Pushkin is the father of the Russian literary language. In reality Lomonosov, Sumarokov, Radishchev, Derzhavin, Karamzin, and others before him contributed greatly to its development. It is true that none of these authors wrote with such sweetness, grace, and facility. For Pushkin, endowed with a finer linguistic sense than all his predecessors, was able to employ archaic expressions, neologisms, and vulgarisms without making them appear out of place or too stilted. Pushkin's contribution to literary Russian lay in his choice of simple language, interspersed with the popular vernacular, through which vehicle he revealed all the beauty of the native tongue and made it accessible to all his readers.

THE UNIVERSITY OF CALIFORNIA

BIBLIOGRAPHY

Bondi, S. M., *Novye stranitsy Pushkina* (Moscow: 1931).
Grigorev, A. A., *Sochineniya* (St. Petersburg: 1876), I, 230-304.
Grossman, L. P., *Etiudy o Pushkine* (Moscow: 1928).
Lerner, N. O., Proza Pushkina (Petrograd: 1923).
Lyatski, E. A., *Pushkin Povestvovatel v Istorii Pugachevskogo Bunta* (Prague: 1929).
Povarin, S., "Russki Pelam Pushkina," *Sbornik statei istoriko-filologicheskogo fakulteta S. Peterburgskogo Universiteta* (St. Petersburg: 1900).
Pushkin, A. S., *Polnoe sobranie sochineni* (Moscow: 1934), vols. IV-V.
Simmons, E. J., *English Literature and Culture in Russia, 1553-1840* (Cambridge, Mass., 1935), chapters V-VII, IX.
Vinogradov, I., "Put Pushkina k realizmu," *Literaturnoe Nasledstvo* (Moscow: 1934), XVI-XVIII, 49-90.
Yakubovich, D. P., "Iz zametok o Pushkine i Valter-Skotte," *Pushkin i ego sovremenniki* (Leningrad: 1930), XXXVIII-XXXIX, 122-140.

THE FOLK TALES OF PUSHKIN

By Victor de Gérard

I

Critics are not lacking who deny to Russia a Romantic Movement commensurate in extent and significance with the corresponding movement in Western Europe. But it would be hard to describe the brilliant period between 1800 and 1840 with any adjective other than "romantic," and the literary production over these years can bear comparison with the best of Western Europe. Although the West profoundly influenced the inception and development of Russian romanticism, this influence ultimately resulted in a literature whose chief aim was to reflect the life and idealism of the Russian people. Through the efforts of young Russian romantic writers the subservience to French, German, and English models, which had been so complete throughout the eighteenth century, eventually ceased.

As is well known, one of the chief aspects of European romanticism in the various countries was an intensified interest in national antiquities, and this interest was as fruitful in a literary way in Russia as it was in England and Germany. The Ossianic poems and Scott's historical romances inspired Russian writers to take an interest in the past of their own country. "Investigators began to burrow into the forgotten repositories of ancient manuscripts," says one critic, "seeking records of Slavic antiquity. Soon the famous *Tale of Igor's Raid* was brought to light, and in an article Karamzin immediately compared it to the 'beaux morceaux d'Ossian.' [1] Scandinavian, German, and English ballads were read, and several translations were made of Percy's *Reliques*. Collectors began to search the unusually rich store of Russian folklore in an effort to find their country's past as honored in literature as Ossian's Scotland." [2] Karamzin's famous *History of Russia* began to appear, Zhukovski wrote ballads on national themes, and after the publication of Zagoskin's *Iuri Miloslavski* in 1829 a whole series of historical novels quickly developed.

One of the most significant phases of the new movement was the deep interest taken in Russian folklore. In fact, the transition from a dilettantish curiosity in popular tales to a solid scientific study was made in 1831 in the investigations and collections of P. V. Kireevski. And soon other serious students of popular lore were busily engaged in collections and scientific studies.

The field was extraordinarily rich. In no country in Europe are these strange tales of the simple people found in greater abundance than in Russia. For centuries the great gray masses have passed on by word of mouth their stories of monstrous, irrational incidents, of the metamorphosis of men into beasts and beasts into men, of a childlike belief in all the fantastic adventures of the handsomest of heroes and the most beautiful of heroines, of the tallest of giants and the tiniest of dwarfs. The printed book is the unconscious annihilator of the oral folk tale, and the unusual richness of Russian popular tales is no doubt to be attributed largely to the relative slowness with which sophisticated literature has made its way among the illiterate rural masses. From nearly every section of the vast country, folk tales have been collected, and these fanciful stories have become as definite a part of the national literary heritage as the productions of professional authors. Furthermore, to an unusual degree folk tales have profoundly influenced Russian poetry, ballet, and opera. And it was through the genius of Pushkin that the folk tale was first brought to the attention of Russian readers as suitable material for artistic treatment.

II

Folk tales * have an inevitable charm for children, but on Pushkin as a child they made a very deep impression which remained

---

* The Russian *skazka* is more properly translated "folk tale" rather than "fairy tale," for the fairy as understood in Western Europe does not exist in Russian folk literature.

in his memory years after. His childhood was not happy, largely owing to an irresponsible mother and father who neglected him as a moody, recalcitrant youngster. In his position as an ugly duckling in the household, the boy eagerly sought the comfort of his old nurse, Arina Rodionovna. A good deal of nonsense has been written about this woman which has only served to conceal the essential traits of her nature. Arina was a freed peasant woman whose loyalty, earthy wisdom, and efficient service gave her the position of a privileged domestic in the Pushkin household. Perhaps because he was an unloved child, Arina made a special favorite of the young Pushkin. Like most peasant woman, her tenacious memory was furnished with a seemingly endless store of folk tales which she herself had doubtless heard as a girl in the village. The little Pushkin eagerly looked forward to those evenings when his parents would go off to a ball, for then he could expect a story-telling hour. When he had been tucked away in bed, Arina would enter, and in a whisper tell her tales of marvels and adventures until the enraptured boy fell asleep. Pushkin never forgot these memorable evenings or the charming tales he heard, for they were among the few pleasant recollections of his childhood. Years later he recalled in verse these "secret nights," the wondrous tales, and his nurse, "the kind friend" of his wretched youth.[3] Even thus early Arina Rodionovna awoke in him a love for the folklore of his native land which was to inspire some of his best poetry.

When he went to the Lyceum in 1811, Pushkin took with him his interest in folk tales, and already the artistic feasibility of using these stories as subjects for literary treatment occurred to him. It was here that he began his poem *Ruslan and Liudmila*, which he did not complete, however, until 1820. The poem is based on a folk tale of the beautiful princess who is stolen away on her marriage night by the wizard Chernomor and, after many fantastic adventures, is finally rescued by her hero-husband, Ruslan. But it is interesting to observe how at this stage in his literary development the young poet subordinated the essential folk nature of the tale to a variety of other elements. Pushkin was still very much under the influence of his French masters, such as Voltaire and Parny. *Ruslan and Liudmila* is encrusted with a ballet-like *décor,* and with the malicious humor, mocking irony, and cold sensualism of French eighteenth-century erotic poetry. In this sophistication the genuine folk elements all but disappear. But it must not be forgotten that *Ruslan and Liudmila* won for Pushkin his first literary fame.

The next four years of Pushkin's life were a period of exile, wandering, and disillusion. It was the "Byronic Period" of his literary development, and in his Southern verse tales he was concerned with themes that had little relation to Russian reality. He submitted to the wave of romanticism that had begun to penetrate Russia from the West. During his stay of four years in Kishinev and Odessa, Pushkin did not evince any particular interest in the folk literature of his own country. However, he was somewhat attracted by the peculiar quality of popular Moldavian and gypsy songs, and he made an effort to learn these languages. His well-known lyric, *The Black Shawl,*[4] and the haunting song of Zemfira in *The Gypsies*[5] owe something to Pushkin's interest in Moldavian and gypsy folk material. Generally speaking, however, the dominating personality of Byron and his flaming poetry exercised a strong influence on Pushkin throughout this period, and most of the lyrics and verse tales he produced between 1820 and 1824 are shot through with this influence. Yet he was rapidly reaching literary maturity, and the time was soon at hand when he would put Byron behind him and aspire to themes that were peculiarly Russian and to a poetic style essentially his own.

III

In 1824, the government discharged Pushkin from the service and ordered him to leave Odessa for his mother's village of Mikhailovskoe in the province of Pskov. In this country exile he spent two years, and the period is of the utmost significance in his literary development. He seemed to feel that his apprenticeship stage had come to an end and that he could now create, as he told Nikolai Raevski. His romantic Southern verse tales were subjected to a cold evaluation and dismissed as immature. A new awareness of his own country and its people turned his attention to the reality of Russia's past and present as material for poetry. The two works which claimed most of his attention at Mikhailovskoe, *Boris Godunov* and *Eugene Onegin*, are emphatically indicative of this new interest. Pushkin was making the transition natural to his poetic genius — a transition from romanticism to realism. And a very important phase of this new preoccupation with Russian reality was a lively interest in the Russian peasantry, its language, traditions, superstitions, and folk literature.

In 1826, Pushkin defined this new interest in a fragmentary article: "There is a form of thought and feeling, a mass of customs, beliefs, and usages belonging exclusively to every people. Climate, mode of living, and beliefs give to every people a special physiognomy which is more or less reflected in the mirror of poetry." [6] And in his relation to this popular material Pushkin's attitude was a twofold one — that of the ethnographer and the literary artist. In the village of Mikhailovskoe he loved to visit the peasant huts and talk with the serfs. He was interested in their curious superstitions, popular cures, and their rich earthy language, many words and phrases of which became part of his own poetic vocabulary. At the fairs of the neighboring Svyatogorski Monastery he fraternized with the common people and joined in the songs of the beggars on the church steps. Several years later in trips to Kazan, Orenburg, and Simbirsk which he made in order to collect material for his *History of the Pugachev Rebellion* and *The Captain's Daughter*, he spent much time in conversation with the natives in an effort to obtain the local color of popular traditions. And in these works all this ethnographical interest is clearly reflected in the attention he pays to proverbs, folk songs, and popular beliefs. At times he even catches the very flavor of the folk language.

One of the most important influences in this renewed interest in folklore was once again his old nurse. During most of his exile in Mikhailovskoe Arina Rodionovna was his sole companion. At night, when he grew weary of his literary labors, Pushkin would call upon Arina to amuse him with folk tales drawn from her endless store. He listened to them far into the night, and a few he took notes on in his huge copybook. His reaction to these *skazki* is clearly indicated in his letters at this time. He wrote to his brother from Mikhailovskoe: "Do you know what I do? Before dinner I write my memoirs, I eat late; after eating I ride horseback, and in the evening I listen to folk tales — and I make up for the insufficiencies of my damnable education. How charming are these folk tales! Each one is a poem!" [7] And shortly after this letter he wrote to a friend: "At night I listen to the folk tales of my nurse, the original of Tatyana's nurse." [8] It may be remembered that Tatyana's nurse in *Eugene Onegin* is able to charm her young mistress as old Arina charmed her master.

With the eye of a literary artist Pushkin saw more in the folk tales than mere narratives of wondrous adventures. He saw that they constituted the literary heritage of the simple, illiterate Russian peasant, and that they were the repositories of centuries of popular traditions, beliefs, customs, and earthy wisdom. "Young writers," he advised, "read the folk tales of the common people in order to perceive the nature of the Russian language." [9] And again he advised: "A study of the old songs, folk tales, etc., is necessary for a complete understanding of the nature of the Russian language. Our critics scorn them in vain." [10] In a letter to Pletnev he tells how impatiently he awaits the latest ballads of Zhukovski, and then adds: "Russian folk traditions are not in the least inferior in fantastic poetry to the Irish and German folk traditions." [11] Pushkin, however, was not alone in Russia at this time in recognizing the essential worth of the song and story of the folk. But he was the first to recognize the possibilities of this material for artistic handling in the language of sophisticated literature. And above all, he possessed precisely that artistic intuition which enabled him to retell these stories in verse without losing any of the peculiar charm of the originals.

IV

It was at Mikhailovskoe that Pushkin first attempted the faithful reworking in verse of a Russian folk tale. This is *The Bridegroom* (1825) [12] which he heard from the lips of Arina Rodionovna. All the glitter, the irrelevancies, and the subjective interpolations of *Ruslan and Liudmila* are entirely eschewed in this poem. It is the story of the bridegroom who loses his beautiful enchanted bride, Natasha. The poem is written in an eight-line ballad stanza, which Zhukovski preferred, and it moves swiftly and simply to its tragic conclusion. The great critic Belinski said that in this poem was a "thousand times more of the Russian spirit" than in *Ruslan and Liudmila*. In this judgment the critic was correct, but in *The Bridegroom* Pushkin is more the experimenter in handling a folk tale in verse. He had not yet perfected his medium.

In the next six years Pushkin underwent many changes of fortune. It was not until after his marriage in 1831 that he once again returned to the folk tale. The summer of this year he spent with his young wife at Tsarskoe Selo, and frequently of an evening Gogol and Zhukovski visited the newly married couple. The conversation often dwelt upon literary matters, and a competition between Pushkin and Zhukovski was proposed in writing folk tales. In this competition Pushkin versified two popular stories, *The Tale of Tsar Saltan* and *The Tale of the Priest and of His Workman Balda*.[13] The first of these is certainly one of the best of all his folk tales. Although it is likely that he heard it from his old nurse, recent investigations have shown pretty conclusively that for some of its elements he may well have been indebted to published Western European folk-tale collections.[14] Pushkin had access to such collection to a much greater extent than is commonly supposed.

The Tale of Tsar Saltan is a well-known folk story, and exists in many variants in Russia and in countries of Western Europe.[15] It is the story of Tsar Saltan who marries the youngest of three daughters. While he is away at war the two sisters and their wicked mother lie to the tsar that his wife has given birth to a monstrous creature. The wife and child are set adrift in a cask, and are finally rescued by an enchanted swan-princess. Merchants bring tidings to Saltan of a marvelous prince Gvidon and his kingdom over the sea. His desire to visit his unknown son is twice frustrated by the wicked sisters and their mother. But with the aid of the enchanted princess, who regains her human form and marries Gvidon, the tsar and his wife and son are brought together.

Pushkin kept very closely to the subject-matter of the tale as it exists among the folk. The only important variation he made is in modifying the ending. In the folk versions the wicked sisters and mother are punished; Pushkin has Tsar Saltan forgive them. By this time Pushkin had come a long way in his understanding of the inherent qualities of folk tales. In *The Tale of Tsar Saltan* he completely identifies himself with the spirit and execution of folk literature. There is an artlessness in the folk tale which is often beyond the powers of the sophisticated literary artist to imitate. Indeed, very few authors who have undertaken to write tales and ballads in the spirit of the folk have been able to simulate the peculiar qualities of their models. In the ballad Sir Walter Scott is perhaps the only English author who has ever imitated this form so successfully that it is really difficult for the expert to distinguish between Scott's version and the folk product.[16] And the skill of Walter Scott in this respect depended in a large measure upon his thorough knowledge of folk literature and his artistic comprehension of its inner laws. Pushkin had just such a comprehension. He had learned to move about with sureness in this world of complete fantasy, careful in the significant aspects never to subordinate the artlessness of the folk to the sophisticated rules of art. The impersonality of the narrator is strictly preserved; the moral is never preached but unfolded by incident. The story moves on with the customary folk iteration as by its own volition, irrespective of human significance, and with a logic all its own. Throughout it has the crude humor of the folk, varied by touches of simple irony. All these qualities are to be found in Pushkin's splendid rendering of *The Tale of Tsar Saltan*. His purpose was to turn into a finished work of art a folk tale that had long been on the lips of the people, purging it of its crudities, while never essentially violating the folk spirit of the original. *The Tale of Tsar Saltan* is flawless in execution, one of Pushkin's most perfect creations.

The Tale of the Priest and of His Workman Balda is, in its story element, quite a contrast to *Tsar Saltan*. It has less of the magical and timeless quality of the latter and more realistic and rough popular humor. Its source is distinctly oral, and in one form or another it has many analogues in international folklore. It is the story of the strong servant who performs difficult and sometimes preternatural tasks for a ridiculous wage which, however, usually results in the undoing of his taskmaster. The peasant Balda is hired by a priest for a year's labor, at the expiration of which time Balda will receive his promised wage of three raps on the priest's head. When the time arrives for his wage, the priest tries to cheat Balda by proposing an impossible task. But the peasant turns the tables on the priest, who duly receives three ruinous blows on the head.

The poem was not published in Pushkin's lifetime, for he realized that calling the priest a "porridge-head" and the scant ceremony with which he treated the cleric in the tale would hardly pass the censor. In fact, before Zhukovski would print it in 1840, after Pushkin's death, he felt it necessary to turn the priest into a merchant. Yet this attitude of mockery toward the parish priest is an authentic touch, well supported by village practice. The language of the tale is rich in pure folk expressions, and the rough-and-tumble movement of the story is admirably supported by the uneven lines and unusual rhyming.

In 1833 Pushkin completed two more folk tales in verse, *The Tale of the Dead Princess and the Seven Champions* and *The Tale of the Fisherman and the Little Fish*.[17] Although the former story is well known in popular lore, Pushkin's version contains incidents and details which do not turn up in any of the analogues of the tale in Russian collections. The story bears a close resemblance to the German analogue *Schneewittchen*, and contains other features which turn up in the stories in the Grimms' *Kinder-und Hausmärchen*. Since Pushkin knew very little German, the notion that he may have used the collection of the Brothers Grimm was given little support by critics. Recently, however, it has been noticed that Pushkin's library contained a partial French translation of the *Kinder-und Hausmärchen* in which may be found the very stories which seem to have contributed to *The Dead Princess*.[18] In fact, there can be little doubt that, although the basis of Pushkin's version was a Russian tale that he had heard, he supplemented this by borrowing from *Schneewittchen* and other German *Märchen*.

The Tale of the Dead Princess is the familiar story of the king's daughter persecuted by an envious stepmother. After being miraculously rescued by the Seven Champions in the forest, she is once again tricked by the wicked stepmother who beguiles her into eating a sleep-producing fruit. And the princess, of course, remains in her death-like sleep until rescued by her prince charming. Pushkin has not been so successful in this tale in eliminating story-elements which are not of a pure folk nature, and the plot does not develop with the directness of *Tsar Saltan*. Nor has it the same formal perfection as the earlier tale. Yet, in the invocations of the stepmother to her mirror, and particularly in the passage where the hero calls upon the sun, moon, and wind to help him find his betrothed, we have poetry of a very high order.

As Pushkin's versified folk tales appeared, they were greeted with scorn by the "democratic" critics, who regarded them as insipid nonsense, and censured the poet for concerning himself with such trifles. *The Tale of the Fisherman and the Little Fish,* however, was accorded a mild measure of praise by these critics. Hostile as they were, it was difficult for them to deny this particular tale some charm, for it is altogether one of his best efforts in this genre. Pushkin's notes of the tales told him by his old nurse contain no mention of *The Fisherman and the Little Fish.* Variants of the story exist in Russian folklore, but with one exception, none is particularly close to Pushkin's version. This exception is a tale in Afanasev's great collection [19] which is so close to Pushkin's that early investigators were convinced that both had derived from the same source. But the more probable solution, as Maikov pointed out, is that Pushkin's version is the source of the tale in Afanasev.[20] What has led the investigators astray in the hunt for the source is the complete Russian localization of Pushkin's version. "Pushkin has charmed us with the brightness and moral purity of this native story," wrote one Russian critic, "and by virtue of his own artistic craftsmanship he has transformed this rough diamond of the folk into a brilliant of the clearest water." [21] In reality, it has now been pretty definitely established that the source was once again the *Kinder-und Hausmärchen* of the Brothers Grimm.[22] Always a cosmopolitan in literature, Pushkin manifested this quality in folk literature as well as in sophisticated literature, and the popular tales of Western Europe, as those of his own land, deeply interested him.

The Tale of the Fisherman and the Little Fish is widely known. As a reward for releasing a golden fish, the poor fisherman is allowed to wish for anything that he may desire. He wishes for nothing, but his shrewish wife promptly sends him back to ask for a trough. Dissatisfied, she sends him back again and again —

for a cottage, a palace, for a kingdom, and finally to be queen of the ocean. At this last desire the little golden fish is silent, and the fisherman returns to find his greedy wife reduced to her former poverty.

Here Pushkin is entirely successful in preserving all the characteristics and flavor of the folk tale, and despite its foreign source the story is thoroughly Russian in spirit. The peculiar iteration of the folk method of narration acquires a highly artistic mock-epical turn in the finely-balanced verse. The crude speech of the old fisherman is pleasantly convincing, and the naïve folk humor altogether delightful, as when the old man first hears the golden fish speak — and in Russian:

> Three and thirty years he'd fished,
> Yet had never heard a fish talking.[23]

Pushkin's last folk story was *The Tale of the Golden Cock*[24] which he wrote in 1834. It is a tale well known in popular lore. The golden cock, presented to the king by a eunuch, warns by his crowing of the danger of invading enemies. The theme of the mortal combat between the king's sons is worked in, but the connection with the main plot is not skilfully made. However, the combat does bring the old king in contact with the strange and beautiful princess whom the eunuch demands as his promised reward for the gift of the golden cock. The king refuses to give up the princess, and strikes the eunuch dead with his scepter. Whereupon the golden cock alights on the king's head, kills him with one peck, and vanishes from the land. And Pushkin characteristically concludes:

> Though my story be not true,
> Lads, let it be a lesson to you.[25]

The source of *The Tale of the Golden Cock* had defied all students of Pushkin until a recent investigator proved rather conclusively that it was taken from a French translation of no less a book than Washington Irving's *The Alhambra*.[26] This French version was found in Pushkin's library.[27] Pushkin's version has become particularly well known to foreigners through the delightful operatic adaptation by Rimsky-Korsakov. In general *The Tale of the Golden Cock*, in its adherence to pure folk elements, is the weakest of all Pushkin's attempts in this genre. He introduces names and action which are foreign to popular usage. The eunuch and the exotic Princess Shamakhan are distinctly non-popular elements. However, the charm of the story is hardly lessened by these interpolations. Its temper is sharp, the movement swift, and the cock, although scarcely a Chaunticleer in characterization, is portrayed as a very human sardonic bird that will stand no nonsense. On the whole, the story has the sting of real irony which increases its intellectual, though diminishes its universal appeal.[28]

V

The extent of Pushkin's interest in folk literature is by no means fully indicated by the works already mentioned in this article. Throughout the whole body of his productions there is manifested a deep knowledge and artistic appreciation of all those popular customs, traditions, superstitions, proverbs, games, tales, and songs which are commonly summed up by the one word "folklore."[29] In many short poems, in *Eugene Onegin, The Tales of Belkin, Dubrovski*, and in other works we have numerous examples of his familiarity with popular lore which he employs for literary purposes. In his *Songs of the Western Slavs*[30] he turned a number of short poems, which he found in Mérimée's *La Guzla*, into the Russian epic meter, thinking that they were genuine Slavic folk songs. His beautiful but fragmentary folk drama *Rusalka*, although based on a foreign motif, is steeped in the haunting, eerie atmosphere of Russian folk poetry. And any superficial analysis of Pushkin's language will at once indicate how much he was indebted to the popular language of the people. Pushkin opened the door to the rich treasure trove of Russian folklore, and by his immortal poetic versions of folk themes he stimulated many students and Russian artists to interest themselves in this fascinating field.

HARVARD UNIVERSITY

NOTES

[1] *Pisma N. M. Karamzina k I. I. Dmitrievu* (St. Petersburg: 1866), p. 474.

[2] E. J. Simmons, *English Literature and Culture in Russia 1553-1840* (Cambridge, Massachusetts: 1935), p. 186.

[3] Cf. *Zimni vecher, Son,* and *Nyane* (I, 236-237, 418; II, 202).

[4] *Chernaya Shal* (I, 301).

[5] *Tsygany* (III, 174).

[6] *O narodnosti v literature* (VI, 19).

[7] *Perepiska,* No. 101, I, 140.

[8] *Ibid.,* No. 112, I, 154.

[9] *Otvet na statiu v 'Atenee' ob 'Evgenii Onegine'* (VI, 38).

[10] *Polemicheskie i grammaticheskie zametki* (VI, 310).

[11] *Perepiska,* No. 535, II, 237.

[12] *Zhenikh* (I, 403).

[13] *Skazka o tsare Saltane* (II, 277); *Skazka o pope i rabotnike ego Balde* (II, 307).

[14] Cf. M. K. Azadovski, "Istochniki skazok Pushkina," *Pushkin Vremennik* (Akademiya Nauk, Moscow: 1936), pp. 150-156.

[15] For a discussion of the variants see N. F. Sumtsov, *A. S. Pushkin, Issledovaniya* (Kharkov: 1900).

[16] For this information I am indebted to E. J. Simmons.

[17] *Skazka o mertvoi tsarevne i o semi bogatyryakh* (II, 318); *Skazka o rybake i rybke* (II, 311).

[18] Cf. M. K. Azadovski, "Istochniki skazok Pushkina," pp. 143-149.

[19] Cf. A. N. Afanasev, *Narodnye russkie skazki* (Moscow: 1873), Nos. 39 and 40.

[20] See V. Maikov, " 'Skazka o rybake i rybke' Pushkina i ee istochniki," *Zhur. Min. Nar. Prosv.* (1892) V, 154.

[21] Vs. Miller, cited by M. K. Azadovski, "Istochniki skazok Pushkina," p. 137.

[22] *Ibid.,* pp. 136-143.

[23] *Skazka o rybake i rybke* (II, 311).

[24] *Skazka o zolotom petushke* (II, 334).

[25] *Ibid.* (II, 340).

[26] Cf. A. A. Akhmatova, "Poslednyaya skazka Pushkina," *Zvezda* (1933), No. 1.

[27] Excellent English translations of the five folk tales studied in this article have been made by Oliver Elton, *Verse from Pushkin* (London: 1935), pp. 78-148.

[28] For a discussion of the literary qualities of Pushkin's folk tales, see the notes of N. O. Lerner in S. A. Vengerov, *Pushkin* (St. Petersburg: 1907-1915), VI, 412-415, 418-419, 444-445, 454-455, 467.

[29] For an excellent study of Pushkin as a folklorist, see N. Trubnitsyn, "Pushkin i russkaya narodnaya poeziya" in Vengerov, *Pushkin,* IV, 52-72.

[30] *Pesni zapadnykh slavyan* (II, 116).

EUGENE ONEGIN READ TODAY *

By Dorothea Prall Radin

Full of enthusiasm for Eugene Onegin, I once read the first
stanzas to a friend of mine unacquainted with the poem and the
author except by name. They start:

> My uncle's life was always upright
> And now that he has fallen ill
> In earnest he makes one respect him:
> He is a pattern for us still.
> One really could not ask for more —
> But heavens, what a fearful bore
> To play the sick-nurse day and night
> And never stir beyond his sight!
> What petty, mean dissimulation
> To entertain a man half dead,
> To poke his pillows up in bed,
> And carry in some vile potation,
> While all the time one's thinking, "Why
> The devil take so long to die?"

When I looked up, it was to see an expression of surprise and
rather extreme disapproval on my hearer's face. "That the greatest poem of the greatest poet of Russia!" she said. "Why, it's
nothing but society verse!"

Like a true apologist, I explained that I probably had not picked
out the best parts, and turned to the pleasant opening of the second
chapter: **

> The place in which Onegin languished
> Was a delightful country spot
> Where lovers made for simpler pleasures
> Would have been grateful for their lot.

* The quotations from Eugene Onegin have all been taken from the author's
complete rendering of the poem which has been published by the University of
California Press, 1937.

** Pushkin divided *Eugene Onegin* into eight "chapters," for he preferred to regard the work as a novel in verse.

> The manor house itself was set
> Apart beside a rivulet,
> Cut off by hills from every storm.
> Before it, flowery, golden-warm,
> Meadows and cornfields stretched away,
> And cattle cropped the grassy land,
> And hamlets shone; while near at hand
> The great neglected gardens lay
> Where wistful dryads came and made
> Their refuge in the deep green shade.

When my auditor still showed no admiration, I read her the description of the coming of spring at the beginning of Chapter VII:

> Now driven by the sun of springtime
> From off the neighboring hills, the snow
> Runs sweeping down in muddy rivers
> To flood the meadows far below,
> And nature, sleepy, smiling, clear,
> Salutes the morning of the year.

> The sky is dark with shimmering blue,
> And one can still see clearly through
> The woods, just touched with greening down;
> The bee has left its waxy cell
> To stock anew its citadel,
> The motley fields no longer drown;
> The cattle low, the nightingale
> Already wakes the silent vale.

"It's pretty," my visitor said.

I tried another justification. After all, this was only a translation that she was hearing. Perhaps there were no lines of just the nineteenth-century romantic glamor of

> Helen, thy beauty is to me
> Like those Nicean barks of yore,

nor even quite like

> Ah, what avails the sceptred race,
> Ah, what the form divine!

But if one were to choose more fairly from narrative verse contemporary with Pushkin's, from *Childe Harold*, for instance, to which *Eugene Onegin* is so often compared, and take the lines:

> There is a pleasure in the pathless woods,
> There is a rapture on the lonely shore,
> There is society where none intrudes
> By the deep sea, and music in its roar,

then I am not at all sure that Russian ears hearing the original would not find many of the more lyric stanzas of *Eugene* comparable to Byron's. Such a stanza is the one in the first chapter beginning:

> O blue waves of the Adriatic,
> O Brenta, river of my choice.

Another is the third stanza of Chapter VII:

> Perhaps we do not see with gladness
> The leaves returning springs restore,
> Because with each new forest murmur
> Old losses rise in us once more;
> And when we see that nature wakes
> Again, our puzzled thinking makes
> The contrast to our dying years,
> With no rebirth as springtime nears.
> Or in some poet's revery
> Perhaps some long-past spring will rise
> Again in dreams before our eyes,
> And in its thrilling light we see
> A distant country, fair and bright,
> A wonder moon, a magic night.

There is even more of Byron's quality in the lines where the poet says of his Muse that she

> — galloped with me like Lenore
> Past moon-lit rocks; and on the shore
> Of Taurus by the midnight seas
> She often led me by the hand
> To hear the crashing ocean and
> The whispering Nereides
> And the eternal waves whose choir
> Extols the Universal Sire.

The English lacks magic, and of course it has not the clouds of glory which cadences recollected from our childhood trail. But even so, the mood and the pictures retain some of their elegiac charm.

Here I left the argument, defeated, but I continued it in my own mind. Was it translation that was to blame? I thought not; for when I first read *Onegin* it was in a mediocre English version, and yet I found it impressive. What are the unforgettable parts? One of them is certainly the scene at the theatre:

> The house is full, the boxes glitter,
> The pit is like a seething cup,
> The gallery claps with loud impatience,
> The curtain rustles — and goes up.
> There, half of air and all aglow,
> Obedient to the magic bow,
> Circled by nymphs in lovely bands,
> Istomina, resplendent, stands.
> Balanced on one toe, tremulous,
> She slowly whirls the other round,
> Then with a sudden leap and bound,
> Flies as if blown by Aeolus.
> She winds, unwinds, and light as feather,
> In mid-air beats her feet together.

There is the description of Eugene's private room, where the disciple of exacting fashion was dressed, undressed, and dressed again. The refinements of London and the elegancies of Paris, brought across the Baltic in exchange for Russia's timber and tallow, in this room

> Of our philosopher were seen —
> The seer and sage just turned eighteen.
>
> Pipes from Stamboul with stems of amber,
> Bronzes and porcelain *en masse,*
> And, that enjoyment of the pampered,
> Perfumes in flagons of cut glass.
> Steel files and combs elaborate
> And scissors curved and scissors straight,
> Brushes with thirty odd details,
> Some for the teeth, some for the nails —

When at last Eugene

> ... sallied forth
> After three hours before the glass —
> For so three hours at least would pass —
> 'T was like some Venus come to earth
> Who thus in flighty mood essayed
> The role of man in masquerade.

In the same tone is the picture of the ball:

> Where headlong in his cab Onegin
> Has dashed already. On past tall
> Dim houses where the horses' feet
> Wake echoes in the sleeping street,
> The carriage lamps, a double row,
> Cast rainbow shadows on the snow.
> Sown all around with firepots
> A great house gleams; across the glass
> Of lighted windows shadows pass,
> Profiles of heads, and groups and knots
> Of ladies with their cavaliers —
> One moment, then each disappears.

In contrast with the life of this "child of luxury and pleasure," who comes home at dawn to sleep, is the picture of St. Petersburg waking up in the morning to the roll of drums. The working city starts its daily round: the cabman drags his horse to the stand, merchants and peddlers prepare to display their wares, an Ochta milk girl hurries by over the crunching snow with her pail, shutters open, blue smoke curls from chimneys, and through the window the German baker in his paper cap has already passed out their morning loaves to many customers.

Such passages certainly lay themselves open to the criticism of being merely genre pictures, charming scenes, but definitely minor poetry, bits to add to the history of manners. Tatyana's letter, which has often been called the high point of the poem, would probably not be very moving, and might sound distinctly sentimental, out of context.

It was there that the "out of context" gave me the answer and explanation I wanted. For *Eugene Onegin* is a narrative, a novel in verse; and its essential value lies in the creation in brief space, heightened by poetry, of two memorable figures, the hero and heroine, moving against a lively background of other characters. There is Lenski, Olga's young lover, the product of the German idealistic education of the day. He was

> A poet and a devotee
> Of Kant. From misty Germany
> He brought complete enlightenment:
> High dreams of freedom democratic,
> A spirit ardent if erratic,
> A tongue forever eloquent.
> A handsome youth, with fire and grace
> And black curls falling round his face.

Lenski

> — thought somewhere, some kindred spirit
> Was born for union with his own,
> Some maiden waiting for him hourly,
> And longing to be his alone.
> He thought the men he loved would spend
> Their lives in prison to defend
> His honor, and would not demur
> To crush his venomous slanderer.
> He thought there were some men appointed
> By fate, whose lot it was to be
> A sort of friendly hierarchy,
> A deathless band of the anointed,
> Whose light would pierce our dark abyss
> Some day and lead the world to bliss.

On his return to his native Russia he piously visits the grave of his old friend, Olga's father, and remembers how as a child he used to play

> With his Ochakov decoration.
> He gave me Olga, and he'd say:
> "Shall I be here to see the day?"
> And thereupon, his inspiration
> Wakened by grief, Vladimir penned
> An elegy upon his friend.

When Onegin flirts with Olga, Lenski in a lover's frenzy decides that

> Two pistols, nothing else, must be
> His arbiters of destiny.
>
> . . . .
>
> He reasons, "I will come between
> And save her from that libertine,
> Who with his sighs and flattery
> Would tempt her heart away from me.
> Shall the vile, venomous worm be let
> To gnaw the lily's stem and kill
> The blossom of two mornings, still
> A bud and not all opened yet?"
> Which means, dear readers, in the end:
> "I'll fight this duel with my friend."

After Lenski's untimely death, the author meditates realistically on him: he might have come to fame and written undying poetry; on the other hand, he might have suffered the fate of the Decembrists; or he might have settled down early in the country and there finally died an inglorious, dull death. The portrait is of a romanticist, but it is written by a realist in fairly modern vein.

With Olga, Pushkin deals less kindly:

> Olga was always good and modest,
> Gay as the morning sun above,
> As simple-hearted as the poet,
> Sweet as the kiss of one's true love.
> Her smile, her flaxen curls, her eyes
> As blue as are the summer skies —
> Her voice, her slimness, and her quick
> And graceful movements — all. — But pick
> Up any novel — you will see
> Her portrait — it is charming, too,
> And once it thrilled me through and through,
> But now it bores me utterly.

Onegin's dictum on her is:

> "There is no life in Olga's face;
> Like a Madonna of Van Dyck,
> Expressionless and round and red
> As the dull moon above your head
> In that dull sky I so dislike."

In the morning her sister's door

> Bursts open. Olga, pinker than
> Aurora's rosy caravan,
> Light as a swallow, stands before
> Her sister, asking, all delight,
> "Whom did you dream about last night?"

Then after her lover's death we are told:

> Poor Lenski! No, she did not weep you
> For very long nor waste away;
> Your youthful bride was not too faithful,
> Her sorrow did not come to stay.
> For even now another fills
> Her mind, another now instils
> Into her soul a lover's balm.
> It is an uhlan thus could calm
> Her heart and whom she loves again;
> And now before the altar she
> Is standing, bending bashfully
> Her downcast head, and even then
> Her eyes are lit with fire while
> Her lips are parted in a smile.

Pushkin was often a realist, but he did like his heroines to have some of the virtues of romance.

Hardly more space is given to old Madame Larina, Tatyana's and Olga's mother, but she is very clear: once devoted to the heroes of sentimental stories, she is now the hospitable, economical housewife, very anxious to marry off her daughters properly. In her youth she had worshiped Richardson and been in love with a sergeant of the Guards, but, married against her will,

> She learned the trick of how to rule
> Her husband like an autocrat,
> And all went smoothly after that.
> She watched the field work under way,
> She salted mushrooms for the next
> Long winter, beat her maids when vexed,
> And took the baths on Saturday,
> Kept books, sent off the new recruits —
> All without marital disputes.

She had been wont to write in albums
Of girlish friends in blood, and call
Praskovya her Pauline, and lengthen
Each sentence to a genteel drawl.
She laced her corsets very tight,
And said her Russian *n's* in quite
The best French manner, through her nose.

But by degrees she dropped her pose:
Corsets and album and Pauline,
The notebook full of tender rhyme —
All were forgotten, and in time
Akulka had replaced Celine;
Till finally she went about
In cap and wrapper wadded out.

Onegin calls her charming, but adds that her huckleberry juice is going to disagree with him.

We have her husband, good Dmitri Larin, "God's servant and a brigadier," who never interfered with his wife, nor with his daughter's novel-reading, since he thought books a vanity but no harm:

And when a man has never read,
The books his daughter takes to bed
With her will cause him no alarm.

Then there is Zaretski, the old gambler and duelist and trouble-maker, now reformed and

Sheltered at last from storms, a sage
Who planted cabbages and praised
The chickens and the geese he raised,
Like Horace in another age.
And there beneath his locust trees
He taught his young their A B C's.

Onegin "could not esteem his heart," yet that did not keep him from enjoying his clever conversation. He was

. . . of a classic pedantry
In duels, he would not depart
From rule. To stretch a man out you
Must do it all according to
The strictest canons of the art
In all the old traditional ways.

We have also the country guests at Tatyana's name-day party and her old peasant nurse who had been married through the offices of the village match-maker when she was thirteen, and the Moscow cousins with their gossip and their new styles of hairdressing, and kind old Princess Aline in the fourth year of a consumption, and the dandies of the city ballrooms — described by a stanza or a few lines or an epithet, but a long list to be contained in a poem of some five thousand lines. And it would be too bad to leave out Onegin's uncle, who for forty years kept his accounts in the country, caught flies, and quarreled and played cards with his housekeeper.

The principal figures, of course, are Eugene and Tatyana. Eugene is Pushkin's fullest portrait of the hero who appears in so many of his poems — the glittering, jaded youth of the city, whose false sophistication ruins his chances for happiness with the simpler and stronger nature of the girl who loves him. Here he is at eighteen:

Behold our hero! Not a flaw,
Modelled on fashion's latest law,
A London dandy, combed and curled,
Prepared at last to see the world.
His French was perfect; he could write
And speak without a foreign taint;
His bow was free of all constraint,
His step in the mazurka light.
The verdict was no more than truth:
A charming, cultivated youth.

We all achieve a little learning
Somehow, somewhere, with the result
That dazzling by one's erudition
With us is never difficult.
And so Eugene, by those who grudged
Their praises often, was adjudged
Well-read — almost to pedantry.
He could discourse most happily
Like an inspired amateur
On anything in Christendom,

And when the talk grew grave, become
The wise and silent connoisseur,
Then suddenly let fly a shaft
Of wit till all the ladies laughed.

Latin of late is out of fashion,
And so our scholar, if I am
To tell the truth, could muster barely
Enough to read an epigram,
To mention Juvenal, and better,
To add a *Vale* to his letter,
Or quote from Virgil without break
Two lines, though not without mistake.
He had no love for history's pages
Nor any antiquarian lust
For digging into ancient dust,
But anecdotes of other ages
From Romulus to us he'd find
And store away within his mind.

.   .   .   .

All of the things Eugene had studied
I could not possibly impart,
But that wherein he was a genius,
Which was his own peculiar art,
That which from youth had been his pleasure,
The toil and torment of his leisure,
Which filled his days of idleness
With melancholy, vague distress —
That was the art which Ovid sung,
The art of love...

"Was he happy in this life of pleasure?" his author asks, and
answers "No." He had lost his freshness and had tired of society.
Beauties and belles caused him no passion stronger than ennui.
Intrigues, friendships, rare foods, even dueling, had palled on him.
Eugene is bored and useless, but still the picture is not a very ugly
one. He behaves in an honorable if pedantic fashion to Tatyana —
not large enough to accept her love but a little touched by it. So
also in his relations with Lenski. He

> Listened with a smile to Lenski —
> His bright and ardent conversation,
> His unripe reasoning, and always
> The poet's glance of inspiration.
> All this was novel to Eugene.
> He struggled not to intervene
> And chill such youthful ecstasy.

Always,

> Though alien to his intellect
> He treated feeling with respect.

He kills his friend in a duel, but at least he is horrified. Too late, he is capable of love for Tatyana. The stanza towards the end of the poem, where he reviews his life, is not the picture of a wretch, but of a sensitive man:

> And gradually thoughts and feelings
> Slipped further and still further back;
> Before him his imagination
> Dealt out its colored faro pack.
> He saw upon the thawing snow
> A boy lie motionless as though
> Asleep at night, but then instead
> A voice came echoing, "He is dead!"
> And then he saw old enemies
> And cowards, wretched slanderers,
> And friends contemptible as curs
> And sweethearts full of treacheries —
> Then, gazing out in revery
> On quiet meadows, always she!

We may smile on realizing that the man looking back on a life now past and gone is still in his twenties, but it is a smile we can be sure Pushkin shared. Eugene is famous as a Russian type of the gifted, ineffectual man, but he is also famous as an individual portrait which the long line of literary likenesses which followed him never surpassed.

Last of all we come to Tatyana, one of the supremely popular heroines in Russian fiction, who has been admired and copied, but

who has never grown banal; Tatyana, who was a "friend to medi-
tation," who wandered in the woods and fields, who was

> Somber and silent and withdrawn,
> As timid as a woodland fawn,

who

> — loved to stand before the sunrise
> Upon the balcony and watch
> The galaxy of stars departing
> From the pale sky and the first blotch
> Of faintest light where earth met sky,
> And feel the little winds that sigh
> In greeting to the risen dawn.

Tatyana

> — took to novel reading early,
> And all her days became a glow
> Of rapturous love for the creations
> Of Richardson and of Rousseau.

She was

> Herself the heroine in fancy
> Of all her favorite authors' tales:

Tatyana, the superstitious, quiet country girl "with a heart all
Russian," who "had discovered the hidden joy in horror," and
yet of whom it is so easy to believe that she did really become the
great lady of Moscow while still retaining her strength and her
simplicity of feeling: Tatyana who falls in love with Eugene and
confesses her love to him and suffers for it, whom her author
loves and laughs at and writes of with an honorable directness
equal to her own:

> But O Tatyana, dear Tatyana!
> The tears are gathering in my eyes;
> Already to a modern despot
> You've given yourself as sacrifice.
> You will be lost, my dear, but first
> You'll call up in a dazzling burst
> Of hope this unknown happiness,
> And taste the joy life may possess.

Here it is worth noting that Pushkin's model for Tatyana was the Princess Volkonskaya, who, the Polish critic Lednicki has shown, was the author's one passionate love. There is little point in tracing literary derivations here, but because the Princess Volkonskaya is one of the most fascinating figures in Russian history, with her young, heroic devotion to her husband, hers is a pleasant name to dwell on. She was one of the wives of the Decembrists who voluntarily followed their husbands into exile in Siberia in spite of all the dissuasions and difficulties that were put in their way. That Pushkin never forgot his love for her gives us, if nothing more, an added confidence in his taste.

To say that the greatest gift Pushkin displays in *Eugene Onegin* is his power of creating characters is not at all to deny the significance of his other qualities as a writer. It merely allows them to fall into their own places where we can value them still. So we may speak of the gracefulness and ease of his verse and the elegiac calm of his stanzas with admiration. Today in our country we have outgrown a taste which esteemed diamonds only when they were in the rough, and we recognize urbanity as less apt to be a sign of weakness than of self-control. Polish, indeed, presupposes a hard and enduring surface to work on. Pushkin did not have to fear meeting with the misfortune of the zealous Dutch housewife who polished the noses off her children's faces: the features of his poem are still firm and pronounced. Nor is his story of a girl of eighteen in Russia too simple to hold our attention. The story of young love in Verona is a simple one too, but still interesting, as it is one of Hollywood's latest triumphs to have shown.

We can also talk of Pushkin's sharpness and wit and romanticism that are like Byron's, and his irony that is like Heine's; and if Byron has a more sonorous utterance and Heine a more tragic passion, yet Pushkin has a health and a breadth of interest and an affection for the country and the people and the customs he describes which neither of the other poets possessed. He, the cynic of a sophisticated world, did not, like his hero, become unable to use his own powers. Onegin and Lenski were as different as "prose and poetry, cold ice and flame, firm rock and sea" but, as the critics have pointed out, Pushkin was both Lenski and Onegin, a man with the understanding and the hearts of both, a man aloof and yet with a social consciousness and a real interest in humanity.

Again, we can speak of the variety in the panorama this one poem unrolls. The kaleidoscope of pictures shifts from city streets and ballrooms to country houses and country fields, from the urban rustling of a crowded theatre to a courtyard full of guests departing from a funeral wake, and to a fairy-tale hut in a snowy forest and back again to Moscow drawing-rooms, through spring and summer and winter landscapes, all affectionately dwelt on.

In this love for the country Pushkin is again peculiarly individual. He loves lonely scenes, but not with the somewhat non-agrarian love of the pure romanticist. He likes to be lonely not too far from home. The woodland path ends at a manor house, the virgin snow is furrowed by the peasant's horse; there is a solitary stream and tree, but a shepherd weaving his bast shoes beside them. Even along the shores of his desolate midnight ocean, a Russian Lenore gallops. Yet neither is his country too trim. His gardens are great neglected gardens haunted by dryads, and one fancies that the alley bordered with lilacs down which Tatyana fled from Eugene was not too closely clipped.

But perhaps to protest at all is always to protest too much, and to list the scenes in *Eugene Onegin* is not a very good way to convince anyone of their importance. It is better to quote Pushkin himself, and if one is obliged to choose bits out of what is essentially a whole, as good a choice as any is the description of a Russian winter and Tatyana's dream in Chapter V, so full of the naïve and even uncouth imagery of folklore, but so rich and brilliant.

> That year the autumn weather lasted
> Well on through Christmas time, while all
> Of nature waited for the winter,

And still the first snow did not fall
Till January third. That night
It came: Tatyana, waking bright
And early, looked outdoors and found
Roofs, fences, flower-beds and ground
All hidden. There the magpies, gay
And cheerful, strutted. Through the glass,
Now lightly traced in frost, a mass
Of silver hid the trees and lay,
A gentle carpet, on the hill,
And all was white and clear and still.

Winter! The peasant in its honor
Marks out the roadway with his sleigh;
His poor horse ploughing through the furrows
Goes jogging, stumbling, on its way;
While piling powdery ridges high,
A swift *kibitka* dashes by,
The coachman in his sheepskin pelt
Upon the box, with scarlet belt.
A little peasant boy runs past;
His dog is riding in his sled
And he is harnessed there instead.
One finger's nipped — he's not downcast,
Though at the window he can see
His mother gesture warningly.

.   .   .   .

That night Tatyana dreamed of marvels.
She thought she was surrounded by
A gloomy mist where she was walking
Upon a meadow-land piled high
With snowdrifts; and that on before
She heard a river foam and roar,
Its dark and whirling waters still
Ice-free in all the winter chill.
Two planks cemented by the ice
Were laid across the foaming stream,
A narrow bridge that well might seem
A risky span for that abyss.
So caught up by a sudden spasm
Of doubt she stopped before the chasm.

Tatyana fretted as if seeing
Some trifling check that might deter
Her progress, for she saw nobody
Beyond to reach a hand to her.
Then suddenly a snowdrift moved,
And out from underneath it shoved
A huge and shaggy bear before
Her eyes. She gasped. He gave a roar,
And offered her his sharp-clawed paw,
And trembling, almost fainting, she
Stretched out her hand reluctantly,
And falteringly let him draw
Her on across the stream. Once there
She kept on, followed by the bear.

Not daring once to turn she hurries,
But close behind her comes that shape;
Her tousled footman still attends her,
She cannot manage to escape.
The hateful bear with groans and signs
Advances. Now a forest lies
Before them; stern and motionless
The pine trees stand, a heavy dress
Of snow upon their branches. Through
The barren tops of aspens, birches,
And lindens shine the night's bright torches
But not a path or shrub in view —
The storm has buried all below
The heaped-up piles of mounded snow.

.   .   .   .

Tatyana races on till she comes to a lighted hut in the forest:

Tatyana breathes and looks around her.
She's on a porch — no bear at all.
Within are shouts and clinking glasses
As at some great man's funeral.
Just what it means she cannot think.
Then looking softly through a chink
She sees a table; circling it
All shapes and kinds of monsters sit:
One has a rooster's head, and one
The muzzle of a dog and horns;
She sees a goat's beard that adorns

A witch; a haughty skeleton,
A short-tailed dwarf, and something that
Is half a crane and half a cat.

It grows more strange and still more dreadful:
A crawfish strides a spider's back;
A skull in scarlet cape is whirling
Around upon a goose's neck.
A windmill dances Cossack-wise
With rattling wings; all over rise
Songs, laughter, horses' stamping — each
Gives vent to barks or human speech.
But what in heaven could it mean
When in that crew Tatyana saw
The one she loved and held in awe,
The hero of our verse, Eugene!
He sat at table with his glance
Directed towards the door, askance.

.   .   .   .

Once more Tatyana is in terror
And tries to run; she cannot seem
To move, and though in wild impatience
She cannot fly, she cannot scream.
And now Eugene has pushed the door
And there Tatyana stands before
The eyes of all those fiends from hell.
She hears their crazy laughter swell
And burst, and every animal
With hoofs and tusks and tufted tails,
Warped trunks and bloody tongues and nails,
Feelers and horns and fingers, all
Are pointing with a dreadful sign
And shrieking out "She's mine, she's mine!"

"Mine!" cried Eugene with threatening gesture,
And suddenly the crowd was gone;
There in the frosty dusk Tatyana
And he were in the room alone.
Onegin seats her silently
Upon a shaky bench and he,
Sitting beside her, lays his head
Upon her shoulder, quieted.
Then Olga suddenly appears

With Lenski. Next a flash of light —
And now Onegin has his right
Arm lifted wildly as he jeers
His unasked guests, and then lets loose
A feverish torrent of abuse.

Half-swooning, Tanya hears the quarrel
Grow louder, sees Onegin lift
A dagger and sees Lenski prostrate.
Then dreadful shadows gathering swift
Blot out the light. The cottage shakes
And Tanya in her terror wakes — —

A sickness, for whose cure and treatment
We ought to find the formula,
The thing they call the spleen in England,
Our Russian hypochondria,
Had mastered him by slow degrees;
And though, praise God, it did not please
The youth to blow his brains out, still
Life was a desert, dark and chill.
So, like Childe Harold, steeped in gloom,
Oblivious to the allure
Of gossip, Boston, sighs demure,
He would pass through a drawing-room,
Observing nothing that was there,
Nor altering his cheerless air.

BERKELEY, CALIFORNIA

PUSHKIN IN WORLD LITERATURE

By GEORGE RAPALL NOYES

Every nation is the best judge of its own literature. The Russian nation has pronounced Pushkin its greatest poet, and it is right beyond question, if by poet one means — as is generally the case — a writer of verse. But one may question whether Pushkin is also a world poet, whether he is a man of the stature of Homer, of Dante, Shakespeare, Milton, Molière, Goethe. Is he a man who has appealed in the past, or who will appeal in the future, to generations of men in other lands than Russia, to men of average cultivation as well as to special students of literature, even as he appeals now, one hundred years after his death, to his fellow-countrymen of all classes, despite the profound changes in the political, social, and economic ideals of the Russian people during that hundred years?

As to the past the answer is easy. In 1840, three years after the death of Pushkin, Carlyle wrote in his lecture on *The Hero as Poet*:

"The Czar of all the Russias, he is strong, with so many bayonets, Cossacks and cannons; and does a great feat in keeping such a tract of Earth politically together; but he cannot yet speak. Something great in him, but it is a dumb greatness. He has had no voice of genius, to be heard of all men and times. He must learn to speak. He is a great dumb monster hitherto."

As far as Pushkin is concerned, Carlyle's contemptuous words remain essentially true in 1937. Pushkin's name, to be sure, has become known in Western Europe, but his poetry, whether in Russian or in translations, has had no great body of readers outside his own country, and it has exerted practically no influence on the development of literature in England or France, Germany or Italy. Russia has gained voices since Carlyle wrote those scornful lines, but they have been the voices of writers of prose. Tolstoi, to mention only one of those writers, has been read by millions of men and women outside his own land; he has affected profoundly the work of western novelists, and he has been a force of some moment in religious and social discussion, even in social action. Are the Russians right in now forgetting or ignoring him, and in thinking that Pushkin is the greatest man of letters whom their country has produced? Only an Olympian could answer that question with assurance; one not a prophet can merely hazard an opinion and give some reasons for it.

Pushkin's failure to win hitherto the triumph that the Russians say he deserves is not due solely to the fact that he is a poet, and that therefore he cannot be adequately translated. Of the great poets of the past many have influenced humanity even more in translations than in the languages in which they wrote. One may divide poetry — or rather great poetry, for poor poetry has only an historical interest, and deserves translation only in the same sense as does the Code of Hammurabi — into the sort that can make an effective appeal in translation, and the sort that in translation loses all its savor. Homer and Horace come readily to mind as illustrations. The *Iliad* has appealed constantly ever since the seventeenth century, to thousands of English men and women, boys and girls, in translations as diverse as those of Chapman; of Pope; of Lang, Leaf, and Myers. Those translations may fall far short of Homer; they may misrepresent him and even distort him; but the charm that readers find in them was put there by Homer, not by his translators. Achilles' boyish, hot-tempered valor, Helen's beauty, the pathos of Hector's farewell to Andromache and of his death, lie at the center of the poem and make it eternal: only a version that violates all our sense of fitness in English style can disguise them. With Horace the case is different. His substance is commonplace; his greatness lies in his *curiosa felicitas,* the "felicity gained by care," with which he expresses commonplaces. Statesmen and divines, lawyers and bankers have made him their constant companion from boyhood to old age, have carried him on vacation strolls through the woods, and have committed his odes to memory; but their pleasure in him has always come from the Latin text, with its easy grace, its concision and its precision. Translation of his odes into verse has been a favorite indoor sport for generations of more or less gifted students, but no generations of readers have found any great delight in the results of their labors. The prose translations have been only cribs for school boys, or reference books for the ignorant. Horace had the luck to write in a language that for centuries remained the common property of all men who received a literary education. Had he written in Persian, perhaps even if he had written in Greek, he would today have only historical importance; his odes would be known only to special students of literature: his fate would have been that of Hafiz or of Pindar.

In order to be a truly universal poet a man must be more than an artist in verse. He must deal in great themes. He must create men and women with whom we feel a vital kinship. Or he must treat fundamental emotions with a high seriousness and be filled with a certain prophetic spirit, even though he prophesy of things temporal and passing. Virgil's absorption in the grandeur of Rome, a real grandeur even though it was transient, makes his poetry permanent; the dignity of his *Aeneid* survives in a translation. So the devotion of Mickiewicz to his shattered country, his picture of what was fair and lovely in Polish life, his ardent faith in Poland's future, may yet gain him a place among the great classics of the world. The Psalms are lyric poetry written in Hebrew, a tongue now understood by few. But they have been known and loved in many languages, from Greek to Church Slavic and English. Their expression of man's awe of the Deity and of his trust in Him has a perennial appeal independent of language and of historical circumstances. In Russia of the nineteenth century, the Bible as a whole was no necessary part of a general education, but the Gospels and the Psalms were still honored. And one may doubt whether even under the Soviet regime the most convinced atheist, if he possess any literary sensitiveness, can read them without emotion. They appeal to the religious instinct of humanity, an instinct that cannot be obliterated by any amount of intellectual scepticism.

One could multiply illustrations indefinitely. Goethe's *Faust*, in translation as well as in the original, appeals to thoughtful men the world over, but his lyric poetry speaks only to persons who can read German. Shakespeare's dramas, or some of them, have traveled into all lands; but, so far as I know, his sonnets have made no impression when translated. As a matter of fact, the translated dramas are said to reach popular audiences in foreign countries better than do the original plays in England and America, where the Elizabethan diction is a barrier between the actor and the common folk in the gallery. Byron's rampant individuality, his powerful expression of certain moods, made his poetry a force all over Europe, and his influence was due in large part to translations of his poems. Even today his fame is greater abroad than at home, where his particular brand of cussedness has gone out of fashion. Keats, on the other hand, has had little success in translation. A prose version of Milton's *Paradise Lost* was better known to the humbler folk of Russia in the nineteenth century than was the original to the same sort of people in England. The moral dignity and vigor of the English Puritan spoke powerfully even to untrained readers who knew nothing of his humanistic cultivation and who would have been baffled by his elaborate poetic style.

Now Pushkin is in almost all his work a poet of the type of Horace, not of the type of Homer. He is the great master of technique in Russian verse, and his technique can be fully appreciated only by readers who know Russian extremely well. His style develops from one period of his life to another; more than that, it varies greatly in poems written at almost the same time, but on different subjects and in different moods. But at its best, and that means almost constantly in all the important poems, it has the *curiosa felicitas* of Horace. And, like Horace's odes, most of Pushkin's work becomes commonplace in translation. His love songs, rendered into English, are as dead as those of Burns would be in Russian. His ballads and his popular tales are stirring or charming in the original, but the glow of the expression vanishes in a foreign tongue; at the very best the beautiful woman becomes a wax figure. One may remark that Pushkin himself was one of the few masters of translation; his versions of Mickiewicz are perhaps even better than the originals.

Here I must interpose a personal confession. Russian verse is very different from English verse, though it is built on the same principle of accent and though its meters are fundamentally the same. It is far more regular; its iambic rhythm is not broken by inversions, and is varied merely by the changing position of the caesura. I know Russian tolerably well; but, since my ear for verse was trained on Wordsworth, Byron, Tennyson, and their comrades, with their perpetually varying rhythms, continually broken by inversions, Russian verse, even the verse of Pushkin, is apt to impress me as a monotonous sing-song; I cannot read it for long stretches without becoming bored. Conversely, Russian friends, who know English better than I know Russian, tell me that for them the verse of Byron, for instance, verges on rimed prose, not giving them the same pleasure that they find in the more regular Russian rhythms; they find in Pope a poet who writes verse that is more like the poetry of Pushkin. I suppose that they are impressed by Byron and Tennyson as I am by English "free verse." It would be stupid to argue that Russian verse is less artistic than English — or the reverse. Each reader must bow to the sense for rhythmic beauty that has slowly grown up within him. I merely point out the difficulty that any student who has learned a foreign language in somewhat mature years necessarily encounters when he tries to judge accurately of poetry in that language. An Englishman or an American must needs become as a little child, divesting himself of acquired, almost inherited associations, before he can appreciate all the charm that Pushkin has for the Russians. And that feat I cannot fully accomplish.

Aside from its technique, Pushkin's poetry of course reflects his temperament and the conditions of his life. Born in 1799 of a family famous in Russian history, he was educated at an aristocratic school, where he at once became a leader in a group of friends devoted to literature: poetry was in the air in the Russia of that period. He was dissipated and licentious; wine, cards, and above all women played a great part in his existence. The most serious interest in his life was his devotion to his calling as a poet. He learned how to express himself before he had anything important to express. As a lad of sixteen he was already a master of poetic style, inferior to no Russian poet of his own time or of an earlier time. His intellect was quick and active; he read widely, but he did not become a scholar in the technical sense of the word until much later in life. His temperament was sensual and turbulent rather than passionate; he seemed incapable — though this is disputed — of steadfast enthusiasm for ideas; he was certainly incapable of lasting hatreds: he was no Shelley or Byron. Though in his youth he wrote an *Ode to Freedom* and a poem in which he expressed abhorrence of serfdom, he was not of the stuff whereof revolutionary heroes are made. Exiled in 1820 to the south of Russia, he had glimpses of life in the Caucasus and in the Crimea; from 1824 to 1826 he was confined by the government to his own estate at Mikhailovskoe, in the province of Pskov. This exile prevented him from being implicated in the Decembrist conspiracy of 1825, with several leaders of which he was on intimate terms. In 1826 he made his peace with Nicholas I, and he seems for several years to have cherished gratitude and personal affection for that ruler. He passed the rest of his life in close dependence on the court, sometimes chafing at his semi-servitude, at others showing his loyalty to Russia by patriotic poems. Whether during his last years he really laid aside his aversion for autocracy or whether he merely concealed it is a point on which scholars differ. In 1837 he was killed in a sordid duel.

Pushkin is a writer of the most various moods. He has no pervading high seriousness such as, in different forms, is found in Wordsworth and in Virgil; he has no constant force of passion such as animates Byron. He is sensitive, responsive, alert both emotionally and intellectually. But the efforts of Russian critics to find depth of thought in him have been futile; he is a poet of "art for art's sake." He has no philosophy, unless one include under philosophy that cheery, optimistic, friendly outlook on the world which has made Russians commend him as an author to be studied in schools, as a wholesome guide for youth. His animality is never morbid; the general temper of his work is bright and sunny. Only in his latest years does a gloomy strain in his work become prominent, and even then he shows none of the brooding pessimism that is characteristic of many of the later Russian authors. In his youth he was an atheist and scoffed at all religion; later he at least showed respect for religious feeling in others, though he never acquired much of it himself. In his almost total indifference to religion, and in his quick reaction to all other emotions, Pushkin has a certain kinship with Shakespeare; he partially deserves the title of "the all-man" bestowed on him by Dostoevski. He wrote beastly epigrams worthy of the Earl of Rochester, and love lyrics delicate as those of Shelley. In *Tsar Nikita* he descends to the most astounding smut; in *Eugene Onegin* he rises to tender sympathy with womanly devotion.

Pushkin defies classification under any school. He was nurtured on the French satiric, sceptical, and erotic poetry of the eighteenth century; Voltaire and Parny were among his chief teachers. And to the end of his life he never completely departed from the French classic tradition. He has none of the exuberant diction, the mysticism, the vague aspiration of the English romantic poets; his work is intellectually clear and simple. His development may best be traced in his narrative and dramatic verse. His first long poem is *Ruslan and Liudmila* (1820: about 3000 lines), in which he treats a theme derived from Russian folklore in a tone of mischievous, mocking banter that reminds one of Ariosto. In 1821 he wrote his *Gavriliada*, a blasphemous parody of the story of the Annunciation, full of Voltairian scoffing. Meanwhile, in the first years of his exile, he came under the influence of Byron and, prompted both by Byron and his own environment, wrote tales with a half-savage or Oriental background; he became a romantic poet, or at least a poet who treated romantic themes with sympathy. The first two of these tales, *The Prisoner of the Caucasus* (1821) and *The Bakhchisarai Fountain* (1822) approach most nearly the tone of the English master, but they lack his rebellious force. Pushkin's heroes seem very mild-mannered persons when compared to the Corsair and the Giaour of Byron. Later poems, *The Gypsies* (1824), *Poltava* (1828), and *The Bronze Horseman* (1833), retain the rapid, semi-lyrical narrative style characteristic of Byron, but depart entirely from his spirit of revolt. In *The Gypsies* there is a sweet kindliness, a Tolstoian all-forgiving charity. In *Poltava* and *The Bronze Horseman* Pushkin became a patriotic poet, paying tribute to the genius of Peter the Great. His patriotism in those poems, and in his nationalistic lyrics, is not of the sort that infects a foreigner. The famous description of Peter at the battle of Poltava, however poetically suggestive the words may be to a Russian, impresses me as in substance crude bombast: "From his tent, surrounded by a throng of his favorites, Peter comes forth. His eyes glitter. His countenance is awe-inspiring. His movements are swift. He is beautiful; he is through and through like the wrath of God." No re-creation of the character of Peter lies behind these sounding phrases. *The Bronze Horseman*, on the other hand, has true symbolic power. A poor clerk loses his ladylove in the great inundation of St. Petersburg. He is a victim of the city built by Peter, and he is driven mad when he sees before him the bronze statue of the great tsar, furiously galloping forward. His petty happiness has been sacrificed to the glory of the Russian empire. But Pushkin has no lofty ideal of his country's place among the nations. In his patriotic poetry his level of thought is on the whole lower even than that of Kipling, not to speak of Virgil; he does not attain the conception, whether true or false, of a great people that has been chosen to accomplish a great mission in the world.

In 1831-1834, Pushkin came back to folklore themes, and composed in verse a series of fairy tales that are free from his former tone of mockery. He is now reverentially true to the spirit of Russian popular literature. *Tsar Saltan* in particular, or, to give the poem its full title, *The Story of Tsar Saltan, of his Son, the Glorious and Mighty Prince Gvidon Saltanovich, and of the Fair Princess Lebed,* is the most beautiful fairy tale ever written. Pushkin here enters into the realm of childhood fancies, not making sport of them, but accepting them for their own sake. All literary sophistication disappears; daintiness, grace, and perfect harmony characterize the poem. But without the glory of Pushkin's style even *Tsar Saltan* would be merely a folk tale like many others.

At Mikhailovskoe Pushkin fell under the sway of Shakespeare, and in *Boris Godunov* (1825) produced a tragedy modeled on Shakespeare's chronicle histories. The piece, though many of the scenes in it are vivid and striking, has no true dramatic unity; it won success on the stage only in the operatic form given to it by Musorgski. What is a still more serious defect, both Tsar Boris and his opponent Dmitri the Pretender lack vitality; they are wooden and mechanical figures: Pushkin was not at home in the old Muscovy of his ancestors. In a later series of short "dramatic scenes" he did far finer work. For example, in *Mozart and Salieri* (1830: 235 lines) he versified the legend that Salieri poisoned Mozart owing to jealousy of his superior talent. In a few deft, swift strokes Pushkin gives convincing, realistic portraits of the craftsman Salieri, who by hard toil has won mechanical skill, and of the generous, boyish Mozart (in some degree a self-portrait of Pushkin), who has received his genius by the gift of God.

Pushkin's prose tales I need not discuss. They were the best in Russian literature up to his time, but they would not have been thought remarkable in France or England. They have attracted scant attention in translations, and have been thrown completely into the background by the work of later Russians. One may suspect, despite the admiration expressed for them by Russian critics, that they would not be so highly regarded in their own country were it not for the fame of their author as a poet.

In Pushkin one can find traits characteristic of almost all later Russian literary schools. But his general development, to express it in a crude, mechanical formula, is, as we have seen, from eighteenth-century classicism, marked by light, satirical banter, through romanticism of a more or less Byronic type, to realism. That whole development may be traced in his masterpiece, *Eugene Onegin*, a novel in verse of somewhat over five thousand lines, on which he labored from 1823 to 1831. The plot of the long poem is extremely simple. A society dandy, Eugene Onegin, bored by his own idle and dissolute life in St. Petersburg, retires to a country estate that he inherits from an uncle. There he meets a fiery young romantic poet, Vladimir Lenski, who becomes his firm friend. A neighboring family, the Larins, have two daughters, Tatyana, a dreamy girl nurtured on sentimental novels, and Olga, a pretty, light-headed, commonplace young person. Lenski is betrothed to Olga, and introduces Onegin to the Larin family. Onegin divines the superior charm of Tatyana, and reproaches his friend for his poor taste. On her side Tatyana sees in the melancholy, disenchanted Onegin, with his elegant ennui, the Prince Charming of whom she has dreamed. She straightway writes him a letter and tells him frankly of her love for him. Onegin meets her one evening in the garden, discourses to her of his weariness of life, of his own futility, and bids her seek a worthier companion for the years that lie before her. After this Onegin for a time avoids the Larin family; then, at a party in their home, he thought-lessly flirts with Olga and arouses Lenski's jealousy. Lenski challenges Onegin to a duel and Onegin foolishly accepts his challenge. In this duel Onegin kills Lenski — whereupon he leaves the country. More than two years pass by. Olga soon recovers from her grief and marries an uhlan. Tatyana, visiting Onegin's house in his absence, looks over his books and comes to understand the artificial nature of her idol. "Is he not a mere imitation," she queries, "a parody of Byron and his Childe Harold?" Though her affection for him remains steadfast, she yields to the insistence of her family, marries an elderly general, and becomes a society queen in St. Petersburg. Onegin, returning from his wanderings, meets at a fashionable reception the former country girl. This time he falls sincerely in love with her and pours out his affection in a series of letters to which she makes no reply. He penetrates to her room and finds her reading one of his letters and shedding tears over it. Now it is Tatyana's turn to speak. She rejects Onegin; although she still loves him, she will be true to her husband. She leaves the room and her husband, the general, appears. Here the poem closes, save for some half-playful, half-serious comments by the author. The reader is left to guess the future of Onegin and Tatyana.

In *Eugene Onegin,* more than in any other of his works, possibly more than in all of them put together, Pushkin shows a truly creative imagination. Despite all the multitude of men and women portrayed by the novelists of the generations that followed Pushkin, Onegin and Tatyana remain the most famous, perhaps the greatest character studies in Russian literature. Pushkin draws them with abundant detail, but at the same time with a fine power of suggestion. His method is first to give a detailed description of his hero or heroine, apparently telling the whole truth, but at the same time forcing the reader to guess at much that he leaves unsaid. Then, what requires still finer art, he makes his character speak a few decisive words and act in some decisive fashion. The work resembles a French classic tragedy in that the hero and the heroine are tested almost solely by their love for each other; their behavior in the supreme crisis of their lives shows their inmost natures.

Onegin comes on the scene as an idle, futile rake, but Pushkin makes us divine a hidden distinction of character behind his frivolous exterior; he can at least be discontented with his own futility. This inward fineness shows in his treatment of Tatyana's advances to him; he respects her confidence and speaks to her with frankness, though he does not guess that he is casting aside his one chance for happiness in life. (In *The Prisoner of the Caucasus* Pushkin had made his hero repulse with somewhat similar language the advances of a Circassian maid, but in that poem the hero is meant to show the Byronic greatness of his soul!). Then Onegin's spark of nobility is quenched by the conditions of his existence; he is left without hope, never achieving any inward or outward triumph.

On the other hand, Tatyana's simplicity and purity, together with the fundamental common sense hidden beneath her sentimental musings, become more and more apparent as the poem advances. The parting scene between Onegin and Tatyana is among the greatest in all literature. Tatyana does not reject Onegin merely because she must act according to conventional morality; she does not say: "I am now Lady Booby, and must henceforth cut only respectable capers." Her motive is not even a religious concept of duty. Rather she has divined the true nature of the man; though she still loves him she knows that his love can bring her no real happiness. She attains triumph of a sort, though her life also has failed of its true fulfillment.

Pushkin began *Eugene Onegin* under the influence of Byron. Onegin himself, with his pose as a gloomy, disenchanted individual, superior to the common herd, though he does nothing to prove his superiority, is a reflection of the fashionable Byronism of the period. The narrative, in stanza form, with continual comments and reflections by the author, is in somewhat the manner of *Don Juan*, though the influence of Sterne may also have counted for something. But the satire in *Eugene Onegin*, as Pushkin points out in one of his letters, is not at all of the Byronic type. That satire, prominent only in the first chapter, which describes the role played by Onegin in St. Petersburg society, is in the playful vein characteristic of the eighteenth century. A genial smile replaces Byron's sneering grin.

Much might be said of the other elements in Pushkin's masterpiece. The central chapters of the poem are full of simple country life among the Russian gentlefolk, a life later repeatedly described with great detail by Turgenev, Goncharov, and Tolstoi, but rendered by Pushkin with a few apparently simple strokes, distinct and suggestive as the lines in a Japanese print. A folklore motif is introduced into the work in the charming song sung by the peasant girls in the garden on the evening when Tatyana meets Onegin. Grotesque features of popular belief come into the dream of Tatyana in which she sees her fate united with that of Onegin, and which foreshadows the duel in which Lenski perishes. The minor characters are as distinct in their minor way as are Onegin and Tatyana. Tatyana's nurse may be a portrait of Pushkin's own peasant nurse, Arina. Lenski is a young poet, full of fiery inspiration and full also of stupidity; Pushkin characteristically leaves us in doubt what fate would have been his had not his life been cut short.

Eugene Onegin is the first realistic novel of any importance in the history of Russian literature, so that with Pushkin there begins the wonderful development of Russian fiction in the nineteenth century. Turgenev in particular was a direct disciple of Pushkin, constructing his plots in much the same fashion, and creating a whole series of heroes and heroines who are variations on the types of Onegin and Tatyana. Like Pushkin, Turgenev copied his men and women from Russian reality, but without Pushkin as a model he would not have done his work so well. No book has been of more crucial importance than *Eugene Onegin* in the development of a national literature.

Here then is a novel in verse such as has been produced in no other country of the world. And in what verse! The stanza form of *Eugene Onegin* is even more elaborate than that of *The Fairy Queen*, but Pushkin manages it with an ease that banishes any sense of artificiality. The line on Tatyana's father: "He was a simple, kindly squire,..." is typical of the diction throughout the poem. This is as unadorned as Wordsworth's: "And never lifted up a single stone...." And indeed the whole narrative is in a style as natural as Wordsworth's at its best, however much Pushkin's grace, whether flippant or tender, may differ from Wordsworth's solemnity, in *Michael* and elsewhere.

Beginning in a tone of genial mockery, in *Eugene Onegin* Pushkin passes to tender sweetness, and finally rises to the high seriousness that is characteristic of truly great art. The poem closes on the note, *Sunt lacrimae rerum et mentem mortalia tangunt.*

Eugene Onegin constitutes Pushkin's best, perhaps his only claim to rank as a world poet, a poet who has written a message that even in translation will speak powerfully to men of other lands and of other times. Yet, as always, a prose translation could render only the main action of the poem; it could give an idea of the characters of the book and of their fates — but the perfume of the poetry would be lost. And a verse translation must at least be entirely free from a sense of effort. The two English versions so far published (by Spalding: London, 1881; and by Babette Deutsch: New York, 1936) sacrifice much by their desperate adherence to the external form of Pushkin's stanza, with its peculiar alternation of masculine and feminine rimes, a form incongenial to the English language. The *Iliad*, whatever Matthew Arnold may say to the contrary, could not be successfully rendered into English hexameters; no more could the *Aeneid*. One can only hope that soon — one hundred years after Pushkin's death — his masterpiece may become accessible to English readers in a form that will give them some conception of the *curiosa felicitas* of the original.

Finally the question recurs: Is Pushkin the greatest writer, as well as the greatest writer of verse, whom Russia has produced? I think not. Pushkin had perfection of form, and he expressed a wide range of emotions, "from grave to gay, from lively to severe." But vigor of thought, poetic imagination in the creation of characters, moral insight into human problems, came to him only by fits and starts. Of religious feeling and of moral fervor he had only glimpses. Behind his work there is no great personality. Such are the reasons that make me think him not the equal of Tolstoi.

THE UNIVERSITY OF CALIFORNIA

PUSHKIN AS AN HISTORIAN

By Michael Karpovich

I

In Russia, as elsewhere in Europe, the 'twenties and the 'thirties of the last century were a time when interest in historical studies was very keen and widespread. "History," wrote the young Ivan Kireevski in 1830, "is today the center of all knowledge, the science of sciences, the only indispensable condition of every progress: the historical approach embraces *all*." An older contemporary, Chaadaev, expressed the same idea in slightly different terms: "The present tendency of the human mind forces it to give an historical form to every branch of knowledge.... It is as if the mind felt itself at home only in the sphere of history." The number of similar quotations could be easily increased. One might say that for a while the outstanding intellectuals of the country all became historically-minded.

Perhaps such an attitude would be sufficient to account for the strength of the historical element in Pushkin's work. The greatest literary figure of his day, closely connected with all that was of importance in the cultural life of Russia, he could hardly have resisted this general trend of contemporary thought. But in addition he seems to have been endowed with an unusually strong "sense of history." Throughout Pushkin's life interest in historical subjects remained one of the chief preoccupations of his mind. To it we are indebted for some of his most important literary productions. If the early *Ruslan and Liudmila* (1820) belongs rather to the field of historical folklore, we enter into the field of history with *Boris Godunov* (1825), *Poltava* (1828), *The Bronze Horseman* (1833) and *The Captain's Daughter* (1836). "The whole history of a nation belongs to the poet," [1] — and acting upon this principle, which he himself had formulated, Pushkin appropriated for his own poetical usage three of the most decisive periods in Russian history.

With some of those historical events he felt intimately connected through family traditions. In *Boris Godunov* a Pushkin acts as one of the Pretender's principal agents in Moscow. Other members of the family took part in the election of the first Romanov to the throne of Moscow. In 1825, writing to a friend from his exile in Mikhailovskoe, Pushkin half-jokingly accused the reigning Russian dynasty of black ingratitude: "Oh, the ungrateful ones! Six Pushkins affixed their signatures to the electoral charter, and two more, being illiterate, put some signs to it. And I, their literate descendant, what am I, and where am I?"[2] It is well known that through the exotic person of his maternal great-grandfather, the Ethiopian Hannibal, Pushkin was connected with the epoch of Peter the Great, while another Hannibal, the son of the former, distinguished himself in the days of Catherine II. The poet liked to dwell on various facts of his family history, and he took a great pride in his ancestry. To him it was not a question of personal vanity, but the recognition of one's intimate connection with the past. On many occasions he discoursed on the importance, both for the individual and the nation, of a reverent attitude toward their historical inheritance. "An educated Frenchman or Englishman cherishes every line of an old chronicle in which the name of his ancestors is mentioned. But the Kalmucks have neither nobility, nor history. Only barbarism, villainy and ignorance do not respect the past, cringing before the present alone."[3] And he boldly identified the history of one's family with the history of one's country.

One of Pushkin's characteristic traits was the great interest he took in memoir literature. Not only was he an assiduous reader of memoirs, but he also translated and published some. Moreover, he encouraged others, and attempted himself to write memoirs.[4] Here to his preoccupation with the past was added his interest in "current history." It was his fate to live in a period of decisive historical events. Born only a decade after the outbreak of the French Revolution, he was a boy of thirteen at the time of the Napoleonic invasion of Russia. In the years that followed he witnessed the downfall of Napoleon, the "greatness and decline" of Alexander I, the South European revolutions in the West and the Decembrist uprising at home, the establishment of the July Monarchy, and the first Polish insurrection. All of these left some traces either in his poetry or in the numerous fragmentary notes of autobiographical nature.[5]

II

Pushkin had not received any special historical training. Whatever historical background he possessed was acquired as part of his general literary education. Brought up on the French literature of the Age of Enlightenment, he knew and appreciated the historical works of Voltaire. In particular, both the *Histoire de Charles XII* and the *Histoire de l'empire de Russie sous Pierre le Grand* served him as historical sources when he was working on *Poltava*. He had a high opinion of Voltaire's importance in European historiography: "Voltaire was the first to follow the new road, and to bring the lamp of philosophy into the dark archives of history."[6] From the point of view of priority, Pushkin gave Voltaire preference over the great English historians of the eighteenth century, Gibbon, Hume and Robertson, with whose works he apparently was well acquainted.[7] No literary education based on the eighteenth-century French culture could avoid the classics, and we know that Pushkin was a diligent and attentive reader of Tacitus and some other ancient historians.[8]

At the same time Pushkin tried to follow the new developments in European historical literature, and we find in his library works of Niebuhr and Hallam (both in French translations) as well as those of Barante, Guizot, Thierry, Thiers, Mignet and Michelet. With a perspicacity which does credit to his critical sense, he noticed the indebtedness of the "new school of French historians" to Walter Scott. The Scotch novelist had shown to the historians "entirely new sources which had hitherto remained undetected, even after the creation of the historical drama by Shakespeare and Goethe." [9] One can doubt, however, the thoroughness of Pushkin's acquaintance with this new historical literature, and it is certain that he was not influenced by the main theoretical tenets of the school.

Pushkin's lukewarmness toward the "new history" became apparent during that lively Karamzin-Polevoi controversy which stirred Russia's academic and literary circles in the early eighteen-thirties.[10] The famous "historiographer" himself died in 1826, but in the battle his side was taken by devoted friends and admirers. Among them was Pushkin. It is hardly necessary to dwell upon the poet's admiration for Karamzin, to which he repeatedly gave such eloquent expression both in his published work and in private correspondence. In spite of occasional differences of opinion, Pushkin retained this admiration intact. The *History of the Russian State* was to him a literary masterpiece, an "immortal work," and a great patriotic feat. To the memory of Karamzin, "sacred to the Russians," he dedicated his *Boris Godunov*, which, according to his own statement, was essentially based on the last two volumes of Karamzin's history. One should not exaggerate, however, the extent of Karamzin's influence on Pushkin. As has been shown by I. N. Zhdanov, in his study of Boris Godunov,[11] the poet was far from following his historical guide in a spirit of unquestioning credulity. For some parts of his tragedy he went to other sources, including the contemporary chronicles, and on some important points he did not accept Karamzin's interpretation.[12] In general, Pushkin was aware of the presence in Karamzin's work of some definitely old-fashioned elements: "Karamzin is our first historian and our last annalist. In his criticism he belongs to (the world of) history, in his simple-mindedness and in his apophthegms, to that of the chronicles." [13] What Pushkin valued in Karamzin above everything else was that he discovered for the Russians a living image of their own past. In this sense he was to Pushkin "the Columbus of Russian history." At the same time Pushkin insisted on Karamzin's intellectual honesty, and he saw in the numerous notes to the *History of the Russian State* an indisputable evidence of the historian's extensive scholarship.

One should not wonder, therefore, at Pushkin's unfavorable reaction to the publication in 1829 of the first volume of Polevoi's *History of the Russian People*. This work, the very title of which was significant (history of the *people*, not of the *state*) was planned by its author as a refutation of Karamzin. It contained a direct attack on the latter's approach to history, and it flatly questioned the validity of his scholarship. At the same time, Polevoi pretended to begin a new chapter in Russian historiography by bringing it in line with the contemporary developments in Western Europe. His work was dedicated to Niebuhr, and he openly allied himself with Guizot and Thierry, whose ideas he tried to combine with those of Schelling. Here was "new history" arrayed against the old. The polemics that followed had not history alone for their battleground. The conflicting interests of various literary coteries became involved, as well as personal rivalries. To the clash of ideas was added that of literary styles. Recently an interesting attempt has been made to interpret the whole episode in Marxian terms as a class struggle between the "landed aristocracy" and the "rising bourgeoisie." [14]

It seems to me, however, that in Pushkin's case it was not so much a matter of class antagonism as an instinctive opposition to an intellectual current fundamentally alien to his mind and culture. By education and natural inclinations alike, Pushkin in many respects belongs more to the eighteenth than to the nineteenth century. Unlike so many of his contemporaries, he remained totally unaffected by German idealistic philosophy and allied tendencies in European romanticism. Even when he spoke of philosophy in history, what he meant was "philosophy" in the sense of Voltaire, not of Schelling. Hence his suspicious attitude toward every attempt at wide generalizations of the nature of "universal history." "The properties of his mind," says Vyazemski, an intimate friend, "were clarity, precision, and soberness. He shunned all artificially constructed general systems; moreover, he felt hostile toward them." In addition, Pushkin suspected, and with due reason, that Polevoi's ambitious attempt was built on a very flimsy foundation,[16] while his undistinguished style, in striking contrast with Karamzin's magnificent prose, offended Pushkin's artistic sensibility.

During the same years which witnessed the outburst of the Karamzin-Polevoi controversy, seeds were sown for another, and much more important, conflict of ideas, that of the Slavophiles and the Westerners. Characteristically, Pushkin stayed out of this incipient quarrel. In 1830, Ivan Kireevski published in a literary almanach his *Review of Russian Literature in 1829,* concluding it with what might be considered one of the earliest statements of the Slavophile doctrine:[17] all leading western nations had "fulfilled their destiny" and were in a state of "stagnation," and now it was the turn of Russia to say a new word in the world's history. Pushkin commented on Kireevski's article in a fairly long review published by him in the *Literaturnaya Gazeta* (1830), but he concentrated entirely on Kireevski's literary judgments, neglecting even to mention the latter's "philosophy of history." He could not do likewise, however, in the case of Chaadaev, who sent the poet the manuscript of his *Lettres philosophiques,* long before their ill-fated publication in 1838. Unfortunately, in Pushkin's letters we have only passing references to Chaadaev's manuscript, one of which is significant: "Votre manière de concevoir l'histoire m'étant tout à fait nouvelle, je ne puis toujours être de votre avis."[18] Chaadaev's "manière de concevoir l'histoire" was another of these "universal history" conceptions with which, as we know, Pushkin felt so little in common. Proceeding from a philosophical and religious basis, Chaadaev saw the unifying principle of historical development in Christianity in its Roman Catholic form. Because Russia remained apart from the Western Christian community she was outside of history. On her side there was nothing but barbarism, ignorance, and slavery. She had no cultural traditions, no national heroes, no inspiring historical memories. The publication of the first *Philosophical Letter* in the *Telescope* provoked a storm of indignation in the nationalist circles of Russian society, and it brought upon the head of the author official repression. Pushkin, who was bound to Chaadaev by ties of mutual respect and affection, apparently felt that he must define his attitude toward this bold denial of Russia's national history. He did it in an extremely interesting letter which, for one reason or another, he never sent to Chaadaev.[19] True to himself, he again left without discussion the fundamental philosophical premises of Chaadaev's conception. All his objections were directed against the more definite parts of Chaadaev's statement, concerning Russia's "historical nullity." How was it possible to say that Russia had nothing outstanding to remember in her past when, as a matter of fact, this past was full of dramatic interest? He reminded Chaadaev of the campaigns of Oleg and Svyatoslav, of the struggle against the Tatars, of Russia's national unification, of the two Ivans and the Times of Trouble, of Peter the Great ("qui à lui seul est une histoire universelle"), of Catherine and Alexander. And was there not in the contemporary position of Russia with regard to the outside world "something that was bound to strike the future historian"? "Croyez-vous qu'il nous mettra hors l'Europe?" Moreover, even if in the earlier period of her history Russia had been isolated from the West, she had had her own European mission to perform: by absorbing the shock of the Tatar invasion Russia had saved Christian civilization. Pushkin concluded by assuring Chaadaev that he, for one, was satisfied with Russian history, "telle que Dieu nous l'a donnée." At any rate, it was a fascinating subject for study, more particularly in its later phases. "What a field is this modern Russian history! And to think only that it still remains unexplored, and that save ourselves, the Russians, nobody can even attempt the task!" [20]

III

Pushkin's own historiographical plans were quite ambitious. In his application for permission to use the state archives (1831) he spoke of his "old desire to write the history of Peter the Great and his successors down to the Emperor Peter III." [21] There is some evidence, however, that he thought of extending his history to Paul I, in which case it would have covered the whole eighteenth century.[22] The most important part of the scheme was, of course, the one dealing with Peter the Great. The poet was fascinated with the dynamic personality of the reforming tsar, and he had a clear appreciation of his significance in Russian history. In an unfinished note written in 1834, Pushkin has left us something like a general summary of his views on Russia's historical development. For a long time Russia remained separated from Western Europe because of peculiar historical circumstances. Converted by Constantinople, she could not participate either in the political or in the intellectual life of the medieval Roman Catholic world. She had known no chivalry,[23] and she did not feel the "beneficial shock" of the Crusades. Neither had she experienced the influence of the Renaissance. Under the Tatars, for more than two centuries the clergy alone kept unextinguished "the feeble sparks of Byzantine scholarship." But the intellectual life of the people scarcely developed at all. Unlike the Arabs, the Tatars did not bring with them "either algebra or Aristotle." In the next period likewise conditions "did not favor free development or enlightenment." But in times of crises both the tsar and the boyars usually agreed on one point: the necessity of establishing closer contact with Western Europe. "Finally came Peter," and by his "beneficial and fruitful wars" he solved the problem: "The success of the national reform was the direct result of Poltava, and European education landed on the shores of the conquered Neva." [24] In this way the reign of Peter was for Pushkin the central point of Russian history, and in his attitude toward the reform he differed sharply from the Slavophile doctrine.[25] But he was by no means blind to the existence of a darker side in his hero's nature and activity. He wondered at the striking difference between Peter's permanent establishment and temporary measures. The former showed great wisdom and foresight, while the latter often were arbitrary and cruel, "as if written by the knout." [26]

It is difficult to be very positive in answering the question as to how far Pushkin actually advanced in his study of Peter's reign. The foundations for his closer acquaintance with the period were laid in 1828 when he was working on *Poltava*, but it was not until July of 1831 that he decided to ask the emperor for permission to use state documents for his proposed historical work. After that date we find in Pushkin's correspondence repeated references to his intention of "burying himself in the archives." We know that in February of 1832 he received permission to use the library of Voltaire which, since the days of Catherine, had been housed in the Hermitage.[27] We know also of his attempt to enlist the professional coöperation of the historian Pogodin. But there is no evidence of progress really achieved. In June 1834, Pushkin wrote to his wife that there was a possibility of the first volume being published before winter, but that could have been a mere expression of hope or good intentions. In a recent study devoted to this question, the author has arrived at the conclusion that Pushkin actually worked on Peter's reign during the last year of his life only, and that this work still was in the very preliminary stage.[28] Whether or not this is an exaggeration, the fact remains that of Pushkin's history of Peter the Great we do not possess anything but a few fragmentary notes and outlines.[29]

IV

It seems that some other subjects were attracting Pushkin's attention at various moments of his life as a possible field for historical exploration,[30] but his only completed historical work remains the *History of the Pugachev Rebellion*.[31] It is on the basis of this performance that he must be judged as an historian. We do not know exactly how and when the idea of writing this history originated in Pushkin's mind. Some of Pushkin's earlier editors and commentators advanced the theory that his original intention was to write a biography of Suvorov. It was in the process of working on that project that the poet was brought to occupy himself with the Pugachev Rebellion in the suppression of which Suvorov had taken some part. Recently this theory of the "accidental" origin of the *History* has been subjected to a thorough, and in my opinion, quite effective criticism.[32] But I am not convinced of the soundness of the hypothesis which the critic himself substitutes for the one he has rejected. In his eagerness to find "class motivation" for Pushkin's historical undertaking, Mr. Oksman connects it with the impression produced upon Pushkin by the revolt of the "military colonists" in the summer of 1831. Scared by the specter of peasant revolution, so runs the argument, the poet naturally turned his attention to the last large-scale peasant movement in the past. This sounds plausible, but, as a matter of fact, there is good reason to believe that Pushkin's interest in Pugachev goes several years back of 1831. In a letter to his brother, written by Pushkin from Mikhailovskoe in November of 1824, we find a request for a life of Pugachev, significantly followed a few days later by another request for a "factual historical notice" on Razin, Pugachev's famous predecessor. Two years later, in 1826, Pushkin composed three songs on Razin (in imitation of folksongs on the same subject), and his interest in the Cossack chieftain was still alive in 1834 when he discussed him at length with Count Grabbe.[33] A similar interest in Razin was known to be displayed by N. Raevski, an intimate friend of Pushkin in the earlier period of his life. All this evidence lends considerable strength to the late L. Maikov's suggestion that Pushkin's interest in the Cossack movements originated in 1820, when the poet, together with Raevski, traveled in the Cossack regions of southeastern Russia. Probably it was there that Pushkin became acquainted with the Razin folklore, and apparently it struck his imagination. From Razin to Pugachev there was but one step. If the former, according to Pushkin, was "the only poetical figure in Russian history;" there also was enough of the picturesque in the latter. And for an historical study Pugachev presented obvious advantages. He belonged to an epoch which was much more familiar to Pushkin than the middle of the seventeenth century, and of which he knew personally some of the survivors.

As far as we can judge, Pushkin began to work on the *History of the Pugachev Rebellion* early in 1833.[34] By September of that year, he completed his study of published and manuscript material, which he decided to supplement with a personal investigation on the spot. His journey took him to Kazan, Simbirsk, Orenburg, the village of Berdy (where Pugachev for a while had had his headquarters), and Uralsk. Altogether Pushkin spent in that region about three weeks, and he succeeded in obtaining some valuable information from the surviving eye-witnesses. The next month was taken up with writing, and by November the text of the *History* was ready for publication.

In his work, which was done with obvious haste, Pushkin had to face rather serious handicaps. Literature on the Pugachev Rebellion was practically non-existent,[35] and the few published accounts that were available, whether Russian or foreign, could give Pushkin but little help. He was able to use a considerable amount of unpublished material, but he failed to gain access to some of the most important documents, which were still considered "secret," including the files of the investigating committee with

Pugachev's own deposition. Pushkin himself felt these limitations acutely. In the preface to the *History* he modestly called it a "fragment," and he left it to a future historian to correct and supplement it on the basis of wider evidence.[36] For his own "imperfect but conscientious" attempt he claimed very little: its primary purpose was to give the military history of the struggle between the rebels and the government forces. Even that limited task had required a good deal of investigation, the evidence of which could be seen in the fairly extensive notes to the *History* and in the appendix, consisting of a whole volume of hitherto unpublished documents.[37]

In making these statements Pushkin anticipated, as it were, some of the modern criticism directed against his work. Foremost among these modern critics was Professor N. Firsov, who, in his editorial notes to the *History of the Pugachev Rebellion*, in the "Academy" edition of Pushkin's works, passed a rather severe judgment on Pushkin's historical method and scholarship. Some of Mr. Firsov's detailed remarks are of a decidedly "pin-pricking" variety, while in others the critic ignores all the handicaps under which Pushkin was forced to work. More interesting are Mr. Firsov's general observations on Pushkin's approach to his subject.[38] In the eyes of his critic, the poet's chief fault was that he clung to an antiquated historical theory, which he borrowed from Karamzin, and that he failed to appreciate the significance of the new historiographical school as represented by Polevoi in Russia and the contemporary French historians in the West. The idea that one had to study the history of popular masses and not of outstanding personalities, and to seek in the historical development for regularity rather than for accidents, remained entirely alien to Pushkin's mind. No wonder therefore that he approached the Pugachev Rebellion as an "unhappy accident," and that in his *History* he concentrated his attention on the leaders of the movement, practically ignoring the popular masses.

Let us see, however, to what extent a somewhat closer analysis of Pushkin's *History* bears out such a criticism. The *History of the Pugachev Rebellion* opens with an introductory chapter, the purpose of which is to summarize the previous history of the Yaik Cossacks, and to give a picture of the state of affairs on the eve of the Rebellion. Reasons for discontent are duly noted, both in the case of the Cossacks themselves and of the neighboring alien tribes, and the general conclusion of the historian is given in the following words: "All foreshadowed a new revolt. Only a leader was lacking. He did not fail to appear." [39] It is obvious that Pushkin did not see in the uprising a mere "accident." On the contrary, he had a clear realization of its inevitability. What was "accidental" was precisely the personality of Pugachev, to which, we are told, Pushkin has attributed an unduly great importance. On this point again the author of the *History* is quite explicit. He emphasizes the fact that Pugachev was "created" by the Cossacks on whom he was wholly dependent. He says of the leader of the Rebellion that "he had no other merits but a certain amount of military experience and extraordinary daring." He qualifies as "remarkable" the following words of Bibikov written at the time of the Rebellion: "Not Pugachev, but general discontent is of importance." [40] To show to what extent the personality of Pugachev was of little consequence, Pushkin points out the growth of the Rebellion at the very time when the leader himself was in flight: "Never was his success more formidable, never did the rebellion rage with a greater force. It passed from one village to another, from one province to the neighboring one.... Everywhere bands of rebels were formed, and *each had its own Pugachev*." [41]

In fact, the wide popular character of the movement is emphasized by Pushkin from the beginning to the end. Among the discontented who joined the Cossacks in the Rebellion he mentions the various alien tribes of the region, the peasants, the workers of the Ural factions, and the religious dissenters. To this comprehensive list modern scholarship has not added a single element. There can be no doubt that the class character of the struggle was clearly understood by Pushkin. He saw that from a Cossack uprising the movement rapidly developed into a peasant revolution. On several occasions he points out that the chief aim of the rebels was to wipe out the landowning gentry, and he speaks of the popularity of Pugachev with the serfs even in Moscow where his arrival was expected "with obvious impatience." In the uncensored note prepared for the emperor Pushkin summed up his views on the social nature of the Rebellion with complete frankness: "The popular masses as a whole (*"ves cherny narod"*) were for Pugachev.... The gentry (*"dvoryanstvo"*) alone openly sided with the government." [42]

Certainly, this does not sound like ignoring the popular character and the social significance of the uprising. One is struck, on the contrary, with the keenness of Pushkin's penetration into the social aspect of his subject. In 1929, Professor Firsov published his own account of the Pugachev Rebellion,[43] and I must confess that I find no substantial difference between his presentation and that of Pushkin. His characterization of Pugachev and the part he played in the movement comes very close to what Pushkin has said on the subject. So does his enumeration of the various elements of discontent which made the Rebellion possible. And finally his general scheme of its development, with one single exception,[44] is essentially the same as the one underlying Pushkin's *History*: Chapters II-V of the latter correspond to Professor Firsov's Orenburg or Cossack-Nomad phase of the Rebellion, Chapters VI-VII to the Bashkir-Ural phase, and Chapter VII to the Volga or Peasant-Revolution phase. Of course, there is a difference in emphasis, as is clearly shown by the very distribution of material in Pushkin's work. Pushkin devoted more than one half of his narrative to the first phase, and only one chapter to the last. This does not prove, however, that he considered the Cossacks as being so much more important than the peasants. The disproportion in his *History* can be easily explained: he had more material for the first period of the Rebellion than for its later stages, and he could not dwell on the peasant side of it because of censorship.[45]

I am no more strongly impressed with the arguments advanced by another of Pushkin's modern critics, the late M. N. Pokrovski. In his introduction to the collection of documents on the Pugachev Rebellion,[46] the noted Marxian scholar attempts to destroy the "legend" created, according to him, by the "gentry historian," of the Cossack-peasant uprising. Instead of a "Russian revolt, senseless and merciless" (Pushkin's words), Pokrovski sees in the movement a class-conscious and well organized attempt to destroy the existing social order. "Merciless it certainly was, but only with regard to one class — that of the gentry. As to its being senseless, it could appear as such to the gentry only, who of course could not see any particular sense in the destruction of their own domination." To prove his point, Pokrovski brings forward the following arguments:

(1) Pugachev had a well developed propaganda department, and a regular chancery out of which issued a considerable number of written documents.

(2) His army was only "slightly worse than that of Catherine" both with regard to equipment and tactical skill.

(3) He made an attempt to organize the conquered territory and, in particular, to protect the life and property of the peasants.

Was Pushkin totally ignorant of this evidence or did he try to suppress it? I turn to the *History of the Pugachev Rebellion* and I find there several references to Pugachev's written proclamations, and to his "secretaries," with a frank acknowledgment of the superiority of his propaganda over that of the governmental authorities. I find there also an equally frank acknowledgment of the comparative military strength of the rebels, only without Pokrovski's exaggeration: while the latter apparently extends his judgment to the whole of Catherine's army (the bulk of which at the time was engaged in a fairly successful war with Turkey), Pushkin limits himself to saying that few of the local governmental commanders were able to cope with Pugachev and his associates. And finally, the "gentry historian" noted also that very attempt to protect the property of the peasants, and in general to maintain order and discipline, in which his critic sees a discovery of Marxian scholarship. As to the incriminating sentence about "the Russian revolt, senseless and merciless," one would look for it in vain in the *History of the Pugachev Rebellion*. It is in *The Captain's Daughter* where it is put by the author into the mouth of his hero. Even if Pushkin the man shared the feeling, it is significant that Pushkin the historian omitted its expression from his historical work. On the contrary, in the same unpublished notes to the *History*, which have been mentioned before, we find the following unqualified statement: "In considering the measures employed by Pugachev and his associates, one must admit that the rebels had chosen means most certain to serve their purpose effectively." [47]

So much for Pushkin's *understanding* of the origins, the aims, and the character of the Rebellion. How about his *attitude* toward it? Both Firsov and Pokrovski speak of Pushkin's "class hostility" toward the rebels, a hostility that supposedly marred his judgment. It goes without saying that Pushkin was thoroughly out of sympathy with the aims of Pugachev and his followers. It would be strange if it were otherwise. Pushkin was firmly convinced of the futility of revolutions, and the repeatedly condemned violence.[48] He was particularly afraid of a revolutionary upheaval in Russia in view of the low cultural standard prevailing within the country. And finally, he regarded the landed gentry as an important constructive element in the national life of Russia, and consequently he could not wish for its destruction. All this is undoubtedly true. But to admit these indisputable facts does not mean to subscribe to an opinion which tends to represent Pushkin the historian as a helpless victim of his uncontrolled class prejudices. On the contrary, one is impressed with the degree of detachment and objectivity he was able to preserve in dealing with his subject. By its aims as well as by its spirit the Pugachev Rebellion should have offended every one of Pushkin's deep-seated convictions and natural tendencies, and yet we do not find in his *History* any signs of vindictiveness or any outbursts of indignation. The narrative, remarkable for its clarity and simplicity, has a certain epic quality to it, and on the whole the author's restraint does not abandon him from beginning to end. In the *History*, Pugachev is not pictured as a villain, while in *The Captain's Daughter* he is even somewhat idealized.[49]

The *History of the Pugachev Rebellion* is not one of Pushkin's greatest works, and it is not an historical "classic." But neither is it a mere "fragment," as the author himself styled it, and it certainly gives more than a narrative of military events. In fact, it is the first Russian monograph in social history. The pioneer character of Pushkin's undertaking should not be lost sight of. Even Firsov admits that with Pushkin virtually begins the literature on the Pugachev Rebellion. He was the first to study that important historical event, and the first to publish a considerable body of documentary evidence bearing on it. Half a century had to pass before another history of the Rebellion was published by N. Dubrovin.[50] Based on a much more extensive use of documentary material (including some documents not accessible to Pushkin), it gave a more complete picture of the movement, but it did not change Pushkin's conception in any essential respect.[51] In the years that followed some valuable monographs have been produced, dealing with various aspects of the Pugachev Rebellion, and more documents have been made available to the students of Russian history, but up to this date no attempt has been made to write a full-sized general history of the movement that would definitely supersede Pushkin's preliminary account.

In his brilliant commemorative address on Pushkin (1880) [52] Kliuchevski said of the poet that "he was an historian where he did not intend to be one," and that there was more history in *The Captain's Daughter* than in the *History of the Pugachev Re-*

bellion, which gave the impression of being "one long explanatory note to the novel." This is one of Kliuchevski's typical witticisms, and I venture to disagree with the famous historian. No doubt Pushkin displayed wonderful historical intuition in *The Captain's Daughter,* as well as in some of his poetical creations. But he was no mean historian even when he "intended to be one." With all its limitations, the *History of the Pugachev Rebellion* occupies a definite and a fairly important place in Russian historiography.

HARVARD UNIVERSITY

NOTES

[1] *Perepiska,* No. 131, I, 182.
[2] *Ibid.,* No. 170, I, 231.
[3] *Opyt otrazheniya nekotorykh neliteraturnykh obvineni* (VI, 75).
[4] For a summary of Pushkin's attempts in this direction see B. L. Modzalevski's introduction to *Dnevnik Pushkina, 1833-1835* (Moscow: 1823).
[5] Cf. B. L. Modzalevski, *Dnevnik Pushkina,* and G. Vernadsky, "Pushkin kak istorik," *Zapiski Russkoi Uchenoi Kollegii v Prage* I² (1924).
[6] *Zametki o frantsuzskikh istorikakh i poetakh* (VI, 15).
[7] Works of Gibbon and Robertson were in Pushkin's library in French translations. For a description of Pushkin's library see B. L. Modzalevski's article in *Pushkin i ego sovremenniki,* IX-X (1910), supplemented by L. B. Modzalevski in *Literaturnoe Nasledstvo,* XVI-XVIII (Moscow: 1934). Cf. B. Modzalevski's description of the Trigorskoe library, which Pushkin used extensively during his exile in Mikhailovskoe (*Pushkin i ego sovremenniki,* I (1903).
[8] All of these he read in French translations. See M. N. Pokrovski, "Pushkin i rimskie istoriki," *Sbornik statei posvyashchennykh V. O. Kliuchevskomu* (1909), and A. Malein's note on Pushkin, Aurelius Victor and Tacitus, *Pushkin v mirovoi literature* (1926).
[9] *Istoriya russkogo naroda* (V, 41).
[10] The story of this polemic has been told by P. Miliukov in his *Glavnyya techeniya russkoi istoricheskoi mysli* (St. Petersburg: 1898), and more recently by V. Orlov in his introduction to *Nikolai Polevoi i materialy po istorii russkoi literatury i zhurnalistiki tridtsatykh godov* (Moscow: 1934).
[11] See his *Sochineniya* (St. Petersburg: 1907), vol. II.
[12] As another evidence of Pushkin's critical attitude towards his historical authorities, one could cite the following note on Tacitus: "The more I read Tacitus, the more I reconcile myself with Tiberius. He was one of the greatest statesmen of antiquity" (*Perepiska,* No. 178, I, 241-242). This statement, written in 1825, is highly interesting as anticipating, perhaps in a somewhat exaggerated fashion, the later revaluation of Tiberius by modern scholarship.
[13] *Istoriya russkogo naroda* (V, 40). There can be no doubt that Pushkin was well acquainted with Russian historical literature both before and after Karamzin.

[14] Cf. V. Orlov, *Nikolai Polevoi*.

[15] P. Vyazemski, *Polnoe sobranie sochineni*, ed. Count S. D. Sheremetev (St. Petersburg: 1878-1887), II, 373-374.

[16] Miliukov in his *Glavnyya techeniya* speaks of Polevoi's insufficient scientific and philosophical preparation.

[17] On the beginning of Slavophilism, see A. Koyré, *La philosophie et le problème national en Russie au début du XIXème siècle* (1929).

[18] *Perepiska*, No. 563, II, 269.

[19] *Ibid.*, No. 1083, III, 387.

[20] *Ibid.*, No. 1079, III, 383.

[21] *Ibid.*, No. 571, II, 279.

[22] Cf. G. Vernadsky, "Pushkin kak istorik."

[23] It is interesting to note that Pushkin disputed Polevoi's assertions concerning a "feudal period" in Russian history. He hesitated, however, between a flat denial and a qualified recognition of the existence of feudalism in Russia. See *Nabroski tretei stati ob "Istorii Russkogo Naroda" N. A. Polevogo* (VI, 92-93).

[24] *O russkoi literature, s ocherkom frantsuzskoi* (VI, 149-151).

[25] It must be said, however, that the early writings of Kireevski contain statements similar to those of Pushkin. The Slavophile opposition to Peter was not developed until later.

[26] *Zametki v neizdannykh tetradyakh* (VI, 246). ̦Pushkin spoke of Peter's dualism in still another sense: to him he was at one and the same time "the Robespierre and the Napoleon" of the Russian cultural revolution, the man who both made the revolution and consolidated its results.

[27] The library contained the material which had been forwarded to Voltaire by the Russian government when he had been working on his *Histoire de l'empire russe sous Pierre le Grand*. See E. Shmurlo, *Voltaire i ego kniga o Petre Velikom* (1929), and D. Yakubovich, "Pushkin v biblioteke Voltaire'a," *Literaturnoe Nasledstvo*, XVI-XVIII, 905.

[28] P. Popov, "Pushkin v rabote nad istoriei Petra I," *Literaturnoe Nasledstvo*, XVI-XVIII, 467.

[29] Of particular interest is the outline of the introduction to the *History of Peter the Great*. It shows on what a large scale Pushkin planned his work. The introduction was to cover both the international position of Russia and her internal conditions on the eve of the reform, the latter under the following headings: taxation, commerce, armed forces, nobility, population, laws, education, "spirit of the times" (*"dukh vremeni"*).

[30] Such as history of Little Russia, Suvorov, discovery and settlement of Kamchatka, conquest of the Caucasus, and outside Russia, the French Revolution.

[31] *Istoriya Pugachevskogo Bunta* (V, 281).

[32] Iu. Oksman, "Pushkin v rabote nad *Istoriei Pugacheva*," *Literaturnoe Nasledstvo*, XVI-XVIII, 443.

[33] Cf. "Zapiski Grafa P. Grabbe," *Russki Arkhiv*, (1873), V, 786.

[34] Simultaneously he was working also on *The Captain's Daughter* in which the same historical events were to be treated in a fictional form.

[35] Out of 181 books and articles listed in the bibliography compiled by N. Dubrovin in 1884, only 13 belong to the period prior to the publication of Pushkin's work.

[36] Pushkin continued to work on the Pugachev Rebellion after the publication of his *History*, looking for new evidence in order to "satisfy his historical conscience," as he himself expressed it.

[37] See Pushkin's answer to Bronevski's criticism of the *History* (*Kritika g. Bronevskogo*, V, 457).

[38] For a summary of Professor Firsov's views, see his article, "Pushkin kak istorik" in vol. VI of the Vengerov edition of Pushkin's works. A defence of Pushkin can be found in V. Briusov's "Pushkin pered sudom uchenago istorika," *Russkaya Mysl*, 1916, II.

[39] *Istoriya Pugachevskogo Bunta* (V, 289).

[40] *Ibid.* (V, 309-310, 333).

[41] *Ibid.* (V, 366). Italics are mine. Cf. the remark of Pushkin that five other persons had assumed the name of Peter III before Pugachev. This remark was not included in the text of the *History*, but together with other "unpublished notes" it was transmitted by Pushkin to Nicholas I for his personal information. The "unpublished notes" are of great importance for the proper appreciation of Pushkin's approach to his subject. For text see *Ibid.* (V, 446-455).

[42] *Ibid.* (V, 453). Pushkin also makes extremely interesting observations on the ambiguous attitude of the clergy and the lower officialdom.

[43] In his *Narodnye dvizheniya v Rossii do XIX veka*.

[44] Professor Firsov thinks that the idea of Pugachev's leadership, and his assuming the name of Peter III, originated with the Old Believers. This interesting suggestion is only an hypothesis.

[45] It is significant that in *The Captain's Daughter* the chapter dealing with the peasant revolt on the Grinev estate was omitted by Pushkin before publication.

[46] *Pugachevshchina*, 3 vols. (Moscow: 1926-1931). I have not been able to see Mr. Pokrovski's article on Pushkin as an historian in the *Krasnaya Niva* edition of Pushkin's works.

[47] *Istoriya Pugachevskogo Bunta* (V, 454).

[48] Even his early "political" poems, *Ode to Freedom* (1817) and *The Dagger* (1821), were directed both against royal despotism and revolutionary terror.

[49] This was noted also by Vyazemski.

[50] *Pugachev i ego soobshchniki*, 3 vols. (St. Petersburg: 1884).

[51] Cf. Firsov's article in the Vengerov edition of Pushkin's works, and Vernadsky, "Pushkin kak istorik."

[52] Reprinted in his *Ocherki i rechi*.

PUSHKIN IN SOVIET CRITICISM

By Samuel H. Cross

While the belief prevails among the uninformed that intellectual life in the Soviet Union is so dominated by materialistic aims as to preclude the development of a sincere interest in the monuments of pre-revolutionary classical literature, there is no other country in which so much zeal is at present devoted to the analysis and interpretation of the national literary heritage. This concerted effort to revaluate the past not only derives from the conviction that the proletariat is the residuary legatee of the best which the previous ruling classes have produced, but is also connected both with the current rapid advance in popular education and with the fresh output of literary research and criticism which the present regime has stimulated. As organs of protest and instruments of propaganda, the major items of classic Russian literature are essential steps in the progress of the Russian revolutionary movement. However modest the aspirations of the early nineteenth-century liberals in comparison with the achievements of revolutionary thought and action in modern times, these aspirations are the precursors of present attainments, and as such are genetically linked with the dominant ideology of today. It is thus logical that native scholars should hark back with enthusiasm to the greatest Russian authors, not merely studying them as models of style and composition, but formulating their biographies and appraising their works as expressions of the intellectual and social progress of the nation.

This enthusiastic research has not been confined to the political poets, the great novelists, and the materialistic critics of the nineteenth century, but has extended likewise to eclectic versifiers like Tiutchev, to Derzhavin, the panegyrist of Catherine II, and to such eighteenth-century pioneers as Lomonosov and Sumarokov. But no author has received attention equal to that now paid to Alexander Pushkin, the centenary of whose death the present volume commemorates. During the last three years the Russian presses have ground out such an amazing grist of new texts, hitherto unknown fragments, biographical studies, and sociological interpretations as almost to create the impression that a regime of literary Stakhanovism has been enforced to demonstrate the vitality of the Pushkin cult in modern Russian life.

In view of the past history of Pushkin criticism in Russia, there is more than a casual interest in present Soviet efforts to define Pushkin's significance for the present generation. In Pushkin's own lifetime, his talent was accurately appraised only by a select few. The essays devoted to him during the 'forties by Vissarion Belinski, the founder of Russian literary criticism, are the basic definition of Pushkin's function as the first Russian author in whom genius and social consciousness fused to create a series of truly national works typified by realism and humaneness, the two chief subsequent characteristics of Russian literary art. Indeed, it is safe to say that present-day acceptance of Pushkin as the greatest Russian poet, apart from the intensity, the restraint, and the spontaneity which are the perennial virtues of his works in both prose and verse, is due more to Belinski's reasoned judgment than to any amount of meticulous investigation by Soviet scholars, many of whom fail to command the historical method which assures the fundamental validity of Belinski's estimate. Even Belinski himself had frankly recognized that Pushkin, as a product of his time and station, could not altogether satisfy a generation determined to impose upon literature a partisan role which Pushkin by his essence was unable to play. Within twenty years after the appearance of Belinski's essays, Dobroliubov went so far as to deny that Pushkin was a truly national poet because he was not imbued with the popular spirit, had not lived the life of the people or stood upon their level, and had been unable to cast aside the prejudices of his class. While the idealistic theorists of the 'fifties again placed Pushkin above empirical limitations of this character, Pisarev ten years later denied the eminence of Pushkin altogether, and disparaged his supreme command of form in comparison with the wealth of ideas which the critic himself discovered in Goethe and Heine. Only at the turn of the present century did the so-called individualistic decadents, and Valeri Briusov in particular, return to an enthusiastic admiration for Pushkin as an artist. Yet in the early days of the October revolution the futurist Mayakovski wrote:

> They have set up guns on the forest's edge,
> Deaf to the White Guard's charm,
> Why is not Pushkin attacked
> And the other classical generals?
> We preserve rubbish under the name of art!

Pushkin is also a poet to whom international recognition has so far been sparingly granted. Rather than a testimony to his lack of universality, this fact is mainly a reflex of the difficulty experienced in translating the lyrics of a master distinguished for concentrated simplicity, and at the same time, a result of the remoteness of the period in which the tragedy of his life was staged. The novelists of the realist school and of the literature of accusation dealt with scenes exemplifying concrete abuses which the democratic West could understand without undue strain on the imagination. Whatever Pushkin's political notions were, his interpretation of the environment, except in his prose works, is often so exclusively personal as not always to convey to the uninitiated a clear conception of the social system with which he was at odds.

In connection with *The Bronze Horseman*, D. S. Mirsky remarks [1] that the combination of circumstances before which Pushkin stood in perplexed reflection are comprehensible to the Russian reader, but not to the foreigner, who thus misses the unifying idea of the poem. On the other hand, Mirsky continues, "Gogol's *Inspector General* and *Dead Souls,* which are practically contemporaneous with Pushkin, suffer from no such national limitations because Gogol, who portrayed the facts of Russian serfdom with more realistic concreteness than his mentor, also described it with wider generalization, selecting from it what was typical on a broad historical scale, and produced simultaneously both a portrayal and a generalizing form of the reality of serfdom, in the struggle with which the Russian revolution evolved." It might with more propriety be asserted that the appeal of Gogol lies rather in his gift for caricature, which speaks a universal language regardless of the subjective reaction of the author to the abuses he attacks or of the restricted local significance of the abuses themselves. For one foreigner who understands the symbolism of *The Bronze Horseman*, a thousand appreciate the corruption of the provincial society typified by Gogol's small-town officials and the inhumanity of the system by which Chichikov hoped to become rich.

But this is not so much a proof of Pushkin's national limitations as of the periodic stamp of his better-known works, and as one of Mirsky's critics asserts, the fact that the West is little acquainted with Pushkin is less the fault of the author himself than of the culture of the foreign readers who fail to do him justice. Obviously, Pushkin's world reputation can hardly stand on his realistic prose works alone. Hence it is to be hoped that the present intensified study of Pushkin will eventually produce a generally acceptable definition of his place in world literature and a concrete statement of the factors which not only make him so far the most eminent figure in Russian lyric and epic poetry, but also determine his popularity in a society so different from that in which he lived.

Soviet Pushkinists distinguish their own work from that of previous investigators by the assertion that they are studying Pushkin from the point of view of the class needs of the proletariat as one of the elements in the secular artistic experience of the past, the critical assimilation of which is an essential factor in the proletarian effort to build up the artistic culture of a classless socialist society. Though bourgeois literary historians are reproached with using their Pushkin studies for class purposes by attributing to him various ideological attributes which he did not possess, it is at the same time currently admitted that some Marxist scholars have committed a corresponding error by creating a new legend regarding Pushkin's political and social views. Certain of the early post-revolutionary Pushkin enthusiasts thus depicted him as a Jacobin, hostile to the autocracy and to feudal land-tenure, endeavoring in this way to rehabilitate him in the eyes of the modern generation. More recent students are convinced that current ideas scarcely need to be consecrated by the authority of great names from the past, so that the portrayal of Pushkin as a forerunner of present day social theories is no longer a matter of vital interest, even if such a portrayal were objectively justifiable.

One ideal of the Soviet Pushkinist is the study of Pushkin as historically interpreted on the basis of his own epoch, and the definition of the motives of class struggle expressed in his works, since without such accurate definition no solution can be found for the problem of integrating his artistic legacy in the development of socialist culture. The study of Pushkin from this point of view has produced two widely divergent opinions of his sociological orientation. He is regarded sometimes as typifying a declining and impoverished aristocracy drifting toward the status of a proletarianized intelligentsia; sometimes as the representative of conservative Decembrist theory, i.e., as a typical member of the minor nobility, which in his day was being forced into capitalistic channels and thus constrained to favor a minimum of liberal reform destined to modify the prevailing feudal system to a point where capitalistic evolution would be accelerated. It is often urged that the liberal tendencies of this group were restricted by their apprehension of a peasant uprising, so that they were reduced to a half-hearted attitude which made them incapable of effective action and compelled them to compromise with the autocracy. These factors are used to explain not only Pushkin's apparent reconciliation with the government after the failure of the Decembrist conspiracy, but the whole sociological tone of his writing after 1825.

The chief proponent of the first view is D. D. Blagoi, whose basic monograph, *The Sociology of Pushkin's Works*,[2] as well as his subsequent articles, has provided abundant material for debate among his colleagues. This scholar remarks: "We have observed this objective process of the transformation of the nobility into bourgeoisie as subjectively experienced in the consciousness of the greatest representative not only of his time but of all Russian culture in general." There is no question that Blagoi knows Pushkin better than most of his critics, and traces of his interpretation occur as far back as Annenkov, who can hardly be reproached with materialism. But one of Blagoi's opponents asserts that the major defect in his construction lies in his credulous and uncritical attitude toward Pushkin's personal characterization of his own sociological views and status,[3] and therefore censures him for failing to appreciate the implications of Marx's statement that, while any shopkeeper could distinguish what a man is from what he says he is, contemporary historiography had not acquired this ability. It is thus argued against Blagoi that, instead of determining to what point historical reality was subjectively modified by Pushkin, he endeavored to reconstruct it solely on the basis of Pushkin's subjective interpretation. Pushkin himself was hardly in a position to give a full and objectively accurate picture of the historical reality which surrounded him. Hence, Pushkin's own works of sociological implication should not be taken at their face value, but checked against contemporary non-literary materials.

Blagoi furthermore attaches considerable importance to the fact that Pushkin, by his own admission, wrote for a living. The Rus-

sian investigator thus views Pushkin's so-called professionalism
as "the specific of penetration into his personal life of that profoundly progressive social-historical process, the transformation
of the reality of Russian feudalism and serfdom into a bourgeois
system." The fact is, however, that while Pushkin frankly confessed, even before 1825, that for him poetry was a trade *pas plus
vil qu'un autre,* he was far from admitting that this attitude
stamped him as middle-class. In 1825, he was still referring with
pride to his "six-hundred-year-old nobility," and this pride of birth
found its most emphatic expression toward the close of his life in
the lyric of August 14, 1836, beginning, "When outside the city re-
flectively I wander," [4] in which he contrasts the ostentatious monuments of the bourgeoisie with the modest tombs of his ancestors
in a remote country churchyard.

Pushkin had no hesitation in making literature his livelihood —
in fact, it was the only gainful occupation for which he was tem-
peramentally qualified — but he could still regret, in 1834, that the
profession of letters, which had once been noble, was then nothing
but a "lousy market." In other words, as A. Aleksandrov has
pointed out,[5] the growth of democratic principles in Pushkin's
work is obvious, but it has no connection with the professionalism
emphasized by Blagoi. As the son of a notoriously improvident
family, and gifted personally with little or no financial ingenuity,
Pushkin literally wrote to keep the wolf from the door. He had
at the same time a sufficiently high conception of his own talents
to feel that they were not debased by mercenary motives as long
as his works were the fruits of his characteristic intellectual honesty. To draw broad sociological conclusions from factors peculiar
to Pushkin's personal life and circumstances thus constitutes a mis-
placed generalization which not even the most extreme materialist critic can successfully justify.

Aleksandrov also cites two passages indicating Pushkin's aversion to the status of bourgeois society both in England and in the
United States, which are not without interest for the Anglo-Saxon

reader. Speaking of the lot of the British laboring classes, Pushkin wrote:

"Read the complaints of British factory workers — your hair will stand
on end. How many abhorrent torments and incomprehensible trials! What
cold barbarity on one hand, and on the other, what awful poverty! You
will think it is a question of building Pharaoh's pyramids, of the Jews
working under the whips of the Egyptians. Not at all; it is a matter of
Mr. Smith's textiles or Mr. Thomson's needles. It appears there is nothing
unhappier in the world than the English workman; what is worse than
his lot? See what happens among us when a new machine is invented
which frees five or ten thousand people from exhausting labor and deprives them of their last means of livelihood."

Derived from de Tocqueville, his comments on America are no
more favorable:

"My confidence in this new people and its constitution, the fruit of the
most modern culture, has been greatly shaken. With astonishment men
have seen democracy in its abhorrent cynicism, in its cruel prejudices, in
its unbearable tyranny. Everything noble and disinterested, everything
that elevates the soul of man, is crushed by inexorable egotism and the
passion for material satisfaction — a majority boldly oppressing society;
negro slavery in the midst of culture and liberty." [6]

These are scarcely the sentiments of an impoverished nobleman
reduced to the ranks of the middle class.

The second current characterization of Pushkin as the representative of the moderate section of the Decembrists forced into
compromise with the established authorities by fear of a peasant
revolution is questioned by many Soviet scholars on the ground
of the difficulty of fixing precisely the point at which the capitula-
tion of the moderate liberals took place. Some controversy has
also developed, indeed, as to how far the Decembrist uprising
can be classed as a specifically bourgeois movement. In any case,
Sergeevski points out:

"The curve of bourgeois liberalism, in connection with intensified reaction in the West and the growth of peasant unrest in Russia itself, falls
appreciably as early as the eve of the 'twenties. The agrarian crisis menacing
the landed aristocracy, in the conditions of which the *corvée* was evaluated

as more profitable than free hired labor, removes from the order of the day the question of liquidating serfdom, and definitively deprives liberal yearnings at the beginning of the century of any nutritive base." [7]

He thus emphasizes that Pushkin's surrender to the regime of serfdom began not only before December 1825, but even previous to his dismissal from St. Petersburg.[8] Sergeevski considers that the basic significance of *Eugene Onegin* lies in Pushkin's open condemnation of the liberal dreams of contemporary youth and in his surrender to the principle of patriarchal proprietorship. Hence, in his view, Pushkin's movement toward reconciliation with conservative principles cannot be regarded as subsequent to the Decembrist catastrophe without running contrary to established fact. Pushkin's own attitude toward serfdom was, indeed, by no means uniform, ranging from approval to the sharpest criticism, and this variation fails to justify classing him either as a convinced aristocrat or as a déclassé nobleman of bourgeois tendency. On the whole, the motives behind the contradictions in Pushkin's social philosophy are, in Sergeevski's opinion, not as yet clarified, and may possibly be related to social and economic history. He thus emphasizes that Lenin's own conception of the Russian historical process was chiefly evolved for application to the post-reform period (after 1861), and that no concrete steps have been taken to prolong this schematization backward toward the beginning of the century and thus provide a more valid definition of the contemporary influences which conditioned the variations of Pushkin's social outlook.

Closely related to these divergent views of Pushkin's sociological status are various modern studies of his aristocratic ideology. Pushkin was inexorably hostile to the new official nobility which hovered around the throne. He held the opinion that patents of nobility by imperial favor were simply a means of surrounding the autocrat with loyal mercenaries and of crushing all opposition and independence. These mercenaries were the official aristocracy whom Lermontov later bitterly characterized as "the descendants of sires whose baseness is their fame, and who crush under their slavish heel the remnants of lines offended by the play of fortune," — "the hangmen of liberty, genius and glory." [9] Pushkin was equally capable of classing the Romanovs as *revolutionnaires et niveleurs,* or of telling a grand duke that men of his own origin were *aussi bons gentilshommes que l'empereur et vous.*[10]

Yet, as Aleksandrov points out, the theme of old nobility with Pushkin was neither reactionary nor conservative. Pushkin held, paradoxically enough, that the hereditary character of the nobility was the best guarantee of its independence, and, as Annenkov indicated eighty years ago, he believed that this independent and hereditary nobility was bound to be the safeguard of the industrious element of the population, and that its role would cease "if the well-being and influence of the nobility are founded independently of, or in contradiction to, the prosperity of the whole nation." [11] He thus thought in national terms, not in terms of a single aggressively selfish caste, nor was he irrevocably attached to the exclusive privileges of the nobility as such. Furthermore, he did not attribute to the Russian bourgeoisie any useful function in the maintenance of national liberty; this role belonged, he felt, to the industrious and enlightened aristocratic intelligentsia which sprang from the impoverished older nobility. It is only fair to observe that this lack of respect for the Russian bourgeoisie was shared by other Russian thinkers of his day (e.g., N. Turgenev), and the commercial element had shown no sympathy whatever with the Decembrist conspirators. Noting these interesting items of Pushkin's political philosophy, Aleksandrov observes that he shared with the aristocratic revolutionaries the class limitations of their principles. He believes that these liberals underestimated the mercantile and industrial bourgeoisie. They also exaggerated the importance of an infinitesimal enlightened minority among the aristocracy, who, as a rule, resembled Gogol's country gentry more than they did Pushkin's unselfish and progressive ideal.

On the other hand, Pushkin assigned no role to the peasantry themselves except as recipients of the benevolence of this public-spirited minority. Pushkin, as Aleksandrov observes, based his ideal of effective aristocratic leadership on the material fact of the impoverishment of the older nobility, but missed the basic factors which, in the course of history, tended to undermine both the aristocracy and the autocracy. His theory looked backward rather than forward, since he stood further right than the Romanovs and regarded their innovations as responsible for the overthrow of his ideal. Aleksandrov thus interprets Pushkin's reconciliation with reality not as surrender, but as the realization that his ideal contradicted historical evolution: "he regarded as rational that which had never been." On the other hand, this surrender was never complete, for the poet repeatedly returned to the ideal which, though essentially erroneous, was nobler than any rationalistic adaptation to the regime of Nicholas I. Hence (according to Aleksandrov), the duality of philosophy noted by Dobroliubov in Pushkin's later career: "regardless of a desire to stifle his doubts, he still could not free himself from the vital impulses of his youth, the proud and independent strivings of earlier years." Indeed, Aleksandrov finds in *The Bronze Horseman* the late fruits of this internal conflict, which he attributes to the crisis besetting the aristocratic revolutionary spirit. The essential contradiction in Pushkin's political attitude could have been overcome, in Aleksandrov's view, only by a break with his class which Pushkin sought to avoid, though by avoiding it he estranged himself from the masses. It was only in the next generation, as Lenin observed, that the closer approach of the revolutionary intelligentsia to the masses began. Yet Pushkin's later prose works, like *The Station Master* and *The History of the Village of Goriukhino*, by their realism and popular orientation, as Aleksandrov admits, unite him in spirit with the generation of Nekrasov, and the essayist concludes with the dictum that Pushkin's art was broader and greater than his theories.

Though the output of similar discussions is so voluminous as to preclude an exhaustive analysis within the compass of a brief study, I have summarized certain salient points in these few recent articles to show in what degree they are useful for a definition of the role of an author as he reflects the historical process and the social background of the epoch in which his lot is cast. In some instances, the conceptions cited may seem excessively doctrinaire. But since scholarship never moves at an even pace, individual items in such a large body of research are bound to suffer from false emphasis or hasty formulation. Nevertheless, this research is productive, and may well contribute to a sounder estimate of the place Pushkin occupies in nineteenth-century literature.

Yet there is a sensible lacuna in this type of investigation. While the negation of aesthetic criticism goes back to Belinski and Chernyshevski, it is inevitably easier to define the social factors which govern the ideology of an author than to characterize those elusive elements which make us accept as great the expression which the author gives it. The materialistic critic is obligated not to beg the question by using such extensible abstracts as beauty, and performs no service by expounding his subjective reasons for admiring a certain author or for believing that a wider public should follow his example. But Pushkin was recognized as great before dialectic materialism was even thought of. Hence his greatness is not solely dependent upon this method for its justification. Even if we grant the necessity of explaining the relation of Pushkin to the revolutionary phases of his day and thus of integrating him in the process of Russian social development, it may be questioned whether this sociological fixation can maintain itself as the most vital element in Pushkin criticism of international scope. No one would deny that it adds to our appreciation of Pushkin as a national figure. Whether it adds to his stature as a poet is a query of grave implication. One may well agree with Dobroliubov that aesthetic criticism is the function of sentimental young ladies. But it would seem that something else beside Blagoi's treatise on

Pushkin's sociology (and the related polemics), or Vinogradov's able monograph on Pushkin's language, is needed to make it apparent why men derive more momentary or permanent satisfaction from reading Pushkin than from the perusal, say, of Herzen and Mikhailovski, or even of Nekrasov. It is thus doubtful whether aesthetic considerations san be properly omitted from the analysis of a poet whose typical and celebrated lyrics (e.g., *The Prophet*) frequently have, if I mistake not, no sociological connotation whatever, unless a forced interpretation is wished upon them, and yet are no less respected on that account.

On the whole, therefore, current Russian research which deals with Pushkin's biography, with the publication and annotation of hitherto unpublished fragments, and with problems of comparative literature suggested by his works, undoubtedly represents a body of investigation intrinsically more engrossing for the foreign reader. The largest recent complex of such materials was gathered in the special Pushkin volume of the annual publication *Literary Heritage*,[12] published in 1934, which includes not only general discussions of the significance of Pushkin for Soviet culture, but also a suggestive essay by the late A. V. Lunacharski on "Pushkin the Critic," an analysis of Pushkin's evolution toward realism by Ivan Vinogradov ("Pushkin's Road to Realism"), and an article "On Pushkin's Style" (of doubtful value) by Victor Vinogradov. The same volume embodies, *inter alia,* the results of an investigation, by I. N. Tynyanov, of Pushkin's relations with his school friend Kiukhelbeker ("Pushkin and Kiukhelbeker"), an important survey, by B. V. Tomashevski, of the whole problem of the tenth chapter of *Eugene Onegin,* burned by Pushkin in 1830 and later partially rewritten by him in a tolerably difficult cipher, S. M. Bondi's article on "Pushkin's Essays in Literary History," studies by Iu. G. Oksman and P. Popov, respectively, on Pushkin's historical researches on Peter I and the Pugachev Rebellion, and a discussion by T. G. Zenger of "Nicholas I as an Editor of Pushkin." [13] Though I doubt, on the whole, whether there is any one of these articles which does not suffer to some extent from the haste with which the collection was apparently organized, they provide, nevertheless, a large body of useful information. The Pushkin volume likewise includes several unpublished letters written to the poet by various contemporaries, and numerous documents relating to Pushkin from the archives of M. P. Pogodin and S. A. Sobolevski. These letters and documents count among their editors such distinguished contemporary Pushkinists as M. A. Tsyavlovski and L. B. Modzalevski. Modzalevski also contributed a treatment of a hitherto unknown poem of Pushkin's lyceum days, "The Shade of Fonvizin."[14] Of exceptional value to foreign readers is the discussion "On the Iconography of Pushkin," by a group of authors who describe the various portraits and sketches of the poet; most of the important items of this character are reproduced throughout the volume, the 1180 pages of which are profusely illustrated.

Another recent and important collection of Pushkiniana is *By Pushkin's Hand*,[15] edited by M. A. Tsyavlovski, L. B. Modzalevski, and T. G. Zenger, whose studies contributed so generously to the quality of the Pushkin volume of the *Literary Heritage*. The book was intended as a collection, in convenient form, of all the texts of Pushkin which are not strictly literary, and yet are closely connected with his life and writings: e.g., materials from Pushkin's personal files, frequently of an intimate character, or texts of more or less public nature in various official archives. The resulting collection is based upon a meticulous examination of literally all Pushkin manuscripts. From a biographical standpoint, among its most significant items are those related to Pushkin's financial affairs, which exemplify only too well his constant pecuniary embarrassment from 1819 to the day of his death.

The Institute of Literature of the Academy of Sciences of the Soviet Union has also begun the publication of a series entitled *Pushkin Annals*,[16] of which the first volume appeared during the past summer. The bibliographical summaries of this publication are of special interest to foreign students, since they list the significant Pushkiniana in Russian periodical literature which might otherwise be lost sight of. Beside the first printed text of "The Shade of Fonvizin" (already referred to), this volume contains a discussion of "The *Adolphe* of Benjamin Constant in Pushkin's Writing," by A. A. Akhmatova, as well as B. V. Tomashevski's highly stimulating treatment of "Pushkin's *Little Tragedies* and Molière," which casts considerable light on the diversity of the influences exercised upon Pushkin by Shakespeare and by the master of French classic comedy, a valuable essay by M. K. Azadovski on "The Sources of Pushkin's *Skazki,*" and V. F. Pereverzev's "Pushkin in Conflict with the Picaresque Novel," with interesting references to Bulwer-Lytton's *Pelham*. Among the biographical contributions to this volume, the two most significant are Iu. G. Oksman's note "On The History of Pushkin's Expulsion from St. Petersburg in 1820," with the text of a hitherto unknown letter from Pushkin's father to Zhukovski, notable for a grateful reference to Miloradovich, the governor-general of the St. Petersburg district, and B. V. Kazanski's "New Materials on the Duel and Death of Pushkin." This second article includes excerpts from the diary of Aleksandra Durnovo, the highly intelligent daughter of Prince P. M. Volkonski (minister of the imperial court) and herself a distant acquaintance of Pushkin, as well as a lengthy letter from Madame Durnovo to her mother written on February 11, 1837, the day after Pushkin's death, and describing the antecedent events in some detail. These items are accompanied by a "Relation sur le Duel de Pouschkine" in the hand of Princess A. M. Gorchakova. Whether or not her own composition, it contains information supplied by intimate friends of Pushkin in the Vyazemski family.

Such a volume would not be Russian if it failed to include a certain amount of polemics. One such discussion relates to D. S. Mirsky's article "The Problem of Pushkin," which has provoked so far no less than eight critical retorts. Mirsky is of course well known in this country as a former professor at the University of London and as the author of two excellent handbooks on Russian literature and of the only competent English biography of Pushkin prior to the work of Dr. E. J. Simmons, which is to appear contemporaneously with the present volume of essays. In his own article Mirsky had taken up the cudgels against the sociological interpretation of Blagoi,[17] but characterized Pushkin's outward reconciliation with reality as "cringing servility" (*lakeistvo*), and attributed his catastrophe to "excessive social snobism," qualifying Pushkin's internal struggle as that between "the already stinking noble" (*sic*) with the great poet of bourgeois liberation. V. V. Hippius objects to the lack of unity in this conception, to Mirsky's estimate of Pushkin's status on an international scale, and to his assertion that Pushkin reveals "the absence of a coherent view on Russian reality" — an assertion which Mirsky based on a forced interpretation of *Eugene Onegin*. Another polemical article in the same volume of the *Pushkin Annals* is a similar critique of D. P. Yakubovich's analysis of Pushkin's diaries by B. V. Kazanski, who emphasizes their personal and non-political character, despite the irritation frequently expressed by the poet at the tricks of officialdom in the days of Nicholas I.

These three publications are representative of the intense scholarly activity inspired by the Pushkin centenary, and (apart from the reservations already made as to the doctrinaire quality of certain sociological interpretations) are, for the most part, worthy of the better traditions of Russian scholarship. They have been accompanied by various detailed studies of individual works of Pushkin, of which one, the collective work of B. P. Gorodetski, A. L. Slonimski, M. P. Alekseev, G. O. Vinokur, and A. N. Glumov, may be cited as an example. This volume (*Pushkin's Boris Godunov*) [18] was recently issued under the auspices of the State Academic Theater of the Drama in Leningrad, and is connected with the new mounting of the play undertaken by that theater in 1934. It is intended "to initiate the reader into the sphere of the basic questions related to the study and the literary-historical appreciation of Pushkin's tragedy." While Gorodetski thus characterizes the relation of the drama to the complex of Pushkin's literary work, A. L. Slonimski concerns himself with its position in the dramatic literature of the 'twenties, and M. P. Alekseev reviews the foreign treatments of Boris Godunov and the False Dmitri from Lope de Vega's *El gran Duque di Moscovia* in the early seventeenth century to Henry von Heiseler's *Die Kinder Godunovs*, first played at Regensburg in 1930. Among other items, Alekseev considers it impossible that Pushkin should have been acquainted with Schiller's *Demetrius* fragment, on the grounds that the poet's knowledge of German was slight and Zhukovski's proposed translation was never more than barely begun. The volume ends with two philological essays, one by G. O. Vinokur on "The Language of *Boris Godunov*," the other by A. N. Glumov on "The Pronunciation of the Verse of *Boris Godunov*." Vinokur concludes that Pushkin replaced the conventional declamatory style of the Russian pseudo-classic drama (e.g., Ozerov, Katenin) with the poetic language of the 'twenties, which he himself had largely been instrumental in creating. Glumov's article is intimately related to Stanislavsky's theories on stage pronunciation, and provides valuable directions for the appropriate oral handling of Pushkin's majestic iambics.

Such items of linguistic and rhetorical interest represent a phase of modern Pushkin-study even better typified by V. V. Vinogradov's *The Language of Pushkin*.[19] This monograph deals extensively with the Church Slavic and the French elements in Pushkin's language, defining the influence exerted upon Pushkin by the so-called bourgeois literary dialect of the period and his relation to the current vernacular, and also analyzing Pushkin's position in the controversy on the literary language which characterized the early decades of the nineteenth century. Vinogradov is without doubt the greatest living authority on the Russian literary language, and his analysis rests on a profound study of the modern tongue from its origins in the early eighteenth century to its present status. The book has been criticized for its disregard of the problem of Pushkin's style as connected with his linguistic usage. But if one may judge from the same author's article on this topic in the *Literary Heritage*, which is marred by undue schematization and by the use of a basic terminology so subjective as to be well-nigh meaningless without extensive glosses, the present monograph rather gains in effectiveness by the author's neglect of this particular aspect of the subject. Vinogradov himself states that considerations of length forced him to omit certain data on syntax and morphology which would obviously have possessed additional value. His observations concerning the French influences in Pushkin's language are thus excellent as far as they go, but they might with profit have been expanded to cover sentence structure. The influence of French prose on all exposition in the major European languages was tremendous during the eighteenth century, just as the French influence on poetic convention was strong from the Pléiade forward. Much of the phraseology cited by Vinogradov in this connection could thus be paralleled without difficulty in either English or German, and the transmission of romantic clichés through Zhukovski's translations is another subdivision of the general subject which also deserves attentive examination. On the whole, then, Vinogradov's monograph is rather a starting-point for further research and formulation than a definitive solution of the problem, which can hardly be attacked with assurance until a satisfactory concordance or lexicon of Pushkin is available.

This lack was noted in a recent article by G. O. Vinokur,[20] whose acute remarks on the present direction of Pushkin scholarship awaken sympathetic chords in the foreign reader who has been professionally obliged at least to follow this material — for its very volume makes its integral assimilation almost impossible. Vinokur justly protests against the excessive use of the word Pushkinist, since after all the study of Pushkin is not a self-contained branch of research, but the synthesis of numerous related disciplines harmonized and unified by a basic philosophy. With the enormous present expansion of the information available on Pushkin, it is obvious that some specialists must concentrate upon it, but (according to Vinokur) it is their task to treat the raw materials on which an accurate knowledge of Pushkin is based, while it is the function of the critic to evaluate the significance of Pushkin for contemporary society.

Yet, as Vinokur remarks, apart from a few inconclusive articles by the late A. V. Lunacharski, Soviet criticism has been regrettably silent on this subject. Even in the field of comparative literature and literary history, as Vinokur emphasizes, little more than a modest beginning has been made in the genetic study of Pushkin's individual works. Interest in Pushkin's biography has been limited to aspects which illuminate and illustrate his political and sociological views. Vinokur quotes one Soviet writer (Elizaveta Polonskaya) as even saying that Pushkin's biography and personality are of little interest to her, because it is tactless to interfere with even a dead writer's personal life. He also observes that the current Soviet distaste for biography rises, in the case of Pushkin, from the low level of individual biographical studies which come to the attention of the outsider unacquainted with the general movement of Pushkin scholarship. In this connection Vinokur makes the telling point that no cultured reader of Pushkin is likely to be edified by texts in which genuine biographical investigation is replaced by detective work on the poet's love affairs or on his restaurant and bar checks. The reference here is of course to certain "gynecological excursuses" (the term is Vinokur's) on Pushkin's relations with a pretty serf-seamstress who caught his friend Pushchin's eye at Mikhailovskoe, and for whose support in her subsequent maternity Pushkin was obliged to make special arrangements — a topic discussed with superfluous detail in P. E. Shchegolev's generally valuable monograph on *Pushkin and the Peasants*.

Vinokur also criticizes severely recent editors of Pushkin texts.

It is a fact that, prior to the revolution, the texts not only of Push-kin, but of practically all the earlier poets, were published by well-intentioned amateurs with no technical training and therefore scant appreciation of the scientific problems involved. In this respect, Soviet text-specialists have registered significant progress, especially in manuscript studies, though in many of the texts published so far there are manifest signs of a lack of literary and philological preparation among the younger specialists concerned. Hence, both Vinokur and D. D. Blagoi have pointed to serious divergencies in concurrently published texts of the same work, at least some of which rise from insufficient acquaintance with Push-kin's sources (e.g., the scene of the German mercenaries in *Boris Godunov*). Vinokur is doubtless right in thinking that there can never be an absolutely definitive text of Pushkin, but textual specialists are obligated to do their best on the basis of available materials, and also to see that the text which they establish makes its way through the press with a minimum of distortion and typo-graphical error. The most glaring example of precisely the oppo-site state of affairs was the edition of the six-volume collection of Pushkin published in 1934 by the State Publishing House for Artistic Literature, which was characterized not only by an ex-cessive ratio of misprints, but even by the occasional omission of whole stanzas. This happens to be so far the most convenient text for use with foreign students, and while corrected editions have since been issued, it should not be necessary to apologize for the text placed in the students' hands.

Vinokur also addresses a few pointed admonitions to Soviet literary critics. They exhibit, he asserts, a regrettable tendency to confine their efforts to polemical discussions of contemporary works, rather than sharpening their wits and perfecting their tech-nique by the analysis of the great works of world literature. I am only echoing Vinokur's sentiments in inquiring whether there is one Soviet critic now writing who, using the dialectic method, could sum up the past evolution and accomplishments of Russian literature in a binding interpretation comparable with Belinski's *Literary Reflections*. The Russians are entitled to evaluate their literature in the light of any ideology they see fit to adopt, and foreign specialists in the field will listen to them with respect and understanding. Certainly no author is better calculated to stimulate such a critical synthesis than Pushkin, yet in running through current articles relating to his works one distinguishes much too little disposition to undertake this fundamental duty of literary research and criticism.

It was Belinski who remarked in the 'forties that "the notion of some pure isolated art living in its own sphere, having nothing in common with other aspects of life, is an abstract, visionary idea"; and Chernyshevski subsequently added, "art for art's sake is an idea as strange in our day as wealth for wealth's sake, or science for science's sake." Since their time, indeed, no major item of Russian literature has been insulated from the national life. Yet, there are two distinct subjective elements in artistic creation: first, the personal satisfaction derived by the artist from the projection of his ideas, perceptions, opinions, or emotions in a form commensurate with his aesthetic taste, and second, the attempt to perform an altruistic service by the transmission of these phases of his intellectual and physical experience to others. Certainly no author, however mercenary, writes without deriving some personal satisfaction from self-expression, and many are as concerned with the influence exercised by their self-expression as with the process itself. Neither of these factors is eliminated by the materialist theory that the author reflects his social and political environment. It is thus fallacious to argue that either Tiutchev or A. K. Tolstoi, who were poets of pure art in that both were primarily concerned with self-expression and fathered no ideas which they particularly wished to publicize, were totally unaffected by their milieu. Tiutchev's letters and A. K. Tolstoi's resentment of the barbarity of Russian mediaevalism prove precisely the contrary. Yet, in Nekrasov's poetry "of vengeance and of sorrow" the second factor dominated, making his verse the poetic phase of the literature of accusation. Though in Pushkin the two factors fuse harmoniously, there were also moments of his creative career when personal moods and emotions possessed infinitely more subjective importance for him than any thought of generalizing either his experience or his protest against the system in which he was enmeshed. Nor are these moments any less characteristic or artistically less impressive than those in which his political and social consciousness was more vocal.

It is natural that Pushkin's works in the latter spirit are more interesting to a generation engrossed in a new social philosophy, and seeking its own likeness or intellectual ancestry in the social conflicts of the past. But the criteria of purely sociological criticism are neither exclusive nor universal, nor does the new philological analysis of Pushkin's works reveal the essence of his power. However valuable and brilliant the contributions so far made by Soviet scholars to our knowledge of isolated phases of Pushkin's career and writings, it must be admitted with regret that there is as yet no tendency toward a synthesis which would combine sound factual knowledge with a materialistic interpretation capable of offering more than a one-sided picture of the artist and the man. None of the previous results of research is in any sense a debit. But the primary desideratum is so far unrealized, and Pushkin deserves better of his compatriots.

HARVARD UNIVERSITY

NOTES

[1] "Problema Pushkina," *Literaturnoe Nasledstvo* (Moscow: 1934), XVI-XVIII, 104.

[2] *Sotsiologiya tvorchestva Pushkina* (2nd ed. Moscow: 1931).

[3] I. Sergeevski, "O nekotorykh voprosach izucheniya Pushkina," *Literaturnoe Nasledstvo*, XVI-XVIII, 118-119. I am indebted to this author's suggestive summary for other material in these paragraphs.

[4] "Kogda za gorodom, zadumchiv, ya brozhu" (II, 189).

[5] "Shestisotletnee Dvoryanstvo," *Literaturny Kritik* (1936), No. 7, pp. 13-40.

[6] *Ibid.*, pp. 18-19.

[7] "O nekotorykh voprosach izucheniya Pushkina," p. 120.

[8] In a later article ("O Pushkine," *Literaturny Kritik*, No. 2, 1936, p. 153), Blagoi expresses the conviction that Pushkin abandoned his liberal ideas and turned to the right only in 1823, but argues that there is no question of Pushkin's abandoning the Decembrists at the decisive moment, since he had drifted away from them considerably earlier. It is a fact, however, that in later years Pushkin identified himself unreservedly with the element from which the Decembrists sprang.

[9] Lermontov, *Smert Pushkina,*

[10] Cf. the references in A. Aleksandrov, "Shestisotletnee Dvoryanstvo," pp. 25-26.

[11] Cited, *ibid.,* p. 30-31.

[12] *Literaturnoe Nasledstvo.*

[13] In the same connection reference should also be made to G. O. Vinokur, "Who Was the Censor of Boris Godunov?" *Pushkin-Vremennik* (Moscow: 1936), I, 203-214.

[14] Text and notes by the same editor in *Pushkin-Vremennik,* I, 1-25.

[15] *Rukoiu Pushkina* (Academia, Moscow: 1935).

[16] *Pushkin-Vremennik.*

[17] Cf. above, p. 7.

[18] *Boris Godunov A. S. Pushkina* (Leningrad: 1936).

[19] *Yazyk Pushkina* (Academia, Moscow: 1935).

[20] "Ob izuchenii Pushkina," *Literaturny Kritik* (1936), No. 3, pp. 66-82.

LERMONTOV

The Death of Pushkin

Now is the poet dead. Let honour claim
Her votary, though slander smirched his name.
Hot for revenge he met the unworthy foe;
Now is the proud heart pierced, the proud head low.
Too long a poet's soul endured the sting
Of shameful rumour and vain gossiping.
The false conventions of society
Roused him alone, and roused him but to die.
Slain! How shall sorrow speak now he is slain,
When shouts of praise and sobs alike are vain?
Perhaps it was his destiny that willed;
But you, through whom her edict was fulfilled,
Who persecuted him, who kindled flame
Of genius merely to betray his name,
Your foul amusement is the epitaph
Of genius extinguished for a laugh.
The murderer's empty heart still sends the flow
Of cold blood through the hand that dealt the blow.
The pistol never trembled in that hand,
Nor could the sneering spirit understand
The tongue and customs of a foreign land.

Now he is dead, the prey of jealousy,
He and the songs he would have written die
To please the slanderers whose only joy
Is to deceive with gifts whom they destroy.
Their crown was laurel, but too clearly now
We see the hidden thorns that tore his brow.
Deceived and unavenged he lies at rest,
His songs in silence sleeping in his breast.

And you, degenerate descendants bred
In living evil from the evil dead,
Beslaverers of fortune, hearts of stone,
Greedy servility about the throne;
Hangmen of genius, liberty, and fame,
Who hide behind the law's corrupted name, —

The court and justice may condone your crime
But God's tribunal stands beyond all time.
The dread Judge waits, and on his lips, behold
No smile responds to clink of bribing gold.
Wash off the poet's righteous blood? In vain!
Your own eternal vileness spreads the stain.

Translated by ROBERT HILLYER